Visible | Invisible

NO SMOKING

Visible | Invisible

Landscape Works of Reed Hilderbrand

Douglas Reed and Gary Hilderbrand
Texts by Peter Walker, Robert Pogue Harrison, Gary Hilderbrand, Suzanne Turner, Niall Kirkwood, and William S. Saunders
Edited by Eric Kramer
Published by Metropolis Books

Contents

Peter Walker

Preface

To successfully build a fine work of landscape architecture is one of the most difficult tasks in the world of design. To master the challenges of climate, site, soils, drainage, plant selection, and the craft of construction, not to mention the challenges of financial, political, and aesthetic concerns, is arduous. Success is therefore rare. As the great teacher Stanley White put it long ago, "All planting is good, but some is so much better than others." It is, then, with great pleasure and a real sense of pride that I introduce Reed Hilderbrand's new monograph.

The firm, founded in 1993, is part of the third wave of postwar landscape design, which is to say that the work embodies a confident awareness of history and ecological concerns while consistently expanding the parameters of what I call classical modernism. These gardens, parks, plazas, and campuses have been conceived and constructed at the highest level of landscape work being produced today. They are also tremendous achievements in today's commercially driven design environment. In this monograph, the works, beautifully explained in image, text, and plan, show a deep sense of complex imagery, always avoiding the melodramatic flourish in favor of the gesture determined by a careful understanding of specific place and time.

The monograph is a wonderfully real and mature contribution to the art of landscape architecture. Project after project, from a variety of programmatic, cultural, and climatic situations, is presented in the loving detail achieved by only the finest of documentary publications. Here one will find not only many new landscape works, but several familiar ones respectfully revisited.

Of course, many contemporary works delight when we see them published, only to disappoint when we visit them in person. This is not the case with the work of Reed Hilderbrand. One can walk through these spaces again and again and be taken each time by some new and delightful intellectual or aesthetic surprise. In this way the works included here, like the book itself, keep our anticipation high for the next encounter, and for other landscapes yet to come. Keep looking. You will be rewarded.

Introduction

Our approach to producing this monograph emerged over a long conversation. All of our colleagues at Reed Hilderbrand participated in some way. We heard strong voices and enjoyed many lengthy debates. We'd known for some time that we wanted a book driven as much by ideas as by projects, and that our collective voice should be heard in it, along with commentary by others. Beyond that, we committed to demonstrating *how we think about the work*, by talking about the preoccupations, influences, consistent themes, and repeated challenges we engage as we work with diverse commissions and clients. We settled, finally, on a reflective, expository book that would speak of the values and convictions we carry from the work of the present to the circumstances of the future. We hope that we have at least partly achieved that here.

We've asked ourselves this question over the years: How can we produce coherence and continuity throughout a body of work, given that the nature and scale of our commissions varies enormously? Coherence is something rooted in logic, and rationality, and legibility, no matter the scale or time frame. We like it when the world coheres. We've become confident that the basics of our approach are scalable, smaller to larger, shorter to longer, whether we are working for a single owner or for an agency or institution. We've insisted on fine craftsmanship, precise grading of the land, and clarity in material assembly. We know that we have developed an identifiable sensibility—a measure of congruity in the spatial, experiential realms of our work, whether we are building in rural New England, in Dallas or Boston, or in downtown Baton Rouge. We've figured out that the only approach to overcoming all that might stand in the way of achieving beauty

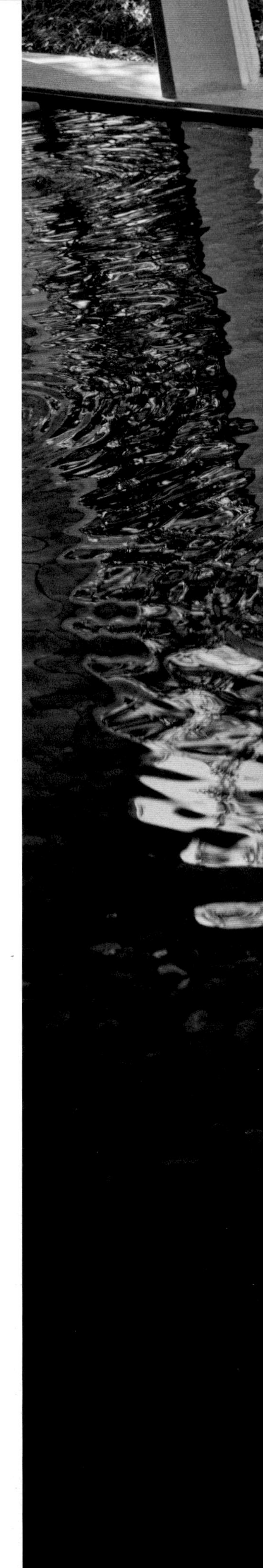

or cultural relevance is developing conviction on an idea and staying with it—through persuasiveness, authority, willingness to take risks, flexibility, an allowance for occasional bouts of insecurity, and sometimes sheer force of will in the face of daunting circumstances. Beauty and coherence rarely happen otherwise.

We've known since we met over thirty years ago that we share passions for landscapes and cities, a love of Abstract Expressionism and contemporary sculpture, and an appetite for modernism in all its dimensions. We have other things in common, as well as complementary traits—not least an obsessive need for order and calm in dealing with whatever is in front of us at the moment. For one of us this need is rooted in confidence and clarity of outlook, everything fitting into place; for the other it may come from recurring self-doubt and a tendency to reason out two sides of nearly any issue, looking for a sane and serene place to land. It doesn't matter which you associate with whom; we exhibit these traits regularly and interchangeably.

We also encountered some eminent teachers in our time as graduate students at Harvard—Peter Walker, Ian Tyndall, Carl Steinitz, Laurie Olin, Michael Van Valkenburgh, and the historians Albert Fein and John Stilgoe, among others. Over the course of several early conversations on the prospect of working together, in the mid-1990s, it became clear that we had a strong common interest in the traditions that shaped our field and in the forces that could motivate expression in landscapes, wherever they came from. We devised a manifesto that would guide our responses to the kinds of investigations and queries that came with each commission. We built our words on values that seemed important to us then and that have held up well to this day:

Robert Motherwell, *Elegy to the Spanish Republic No. 110*, Easter Day, 1971, acrylic with graphite and charcoal on canvas, 82 x 114 inches, Solomon R. Guggenheim Museum, New York, gift of Agnes Gund. Art © Dedalus Foundation, Inc. / Licensed by VAGA, New York

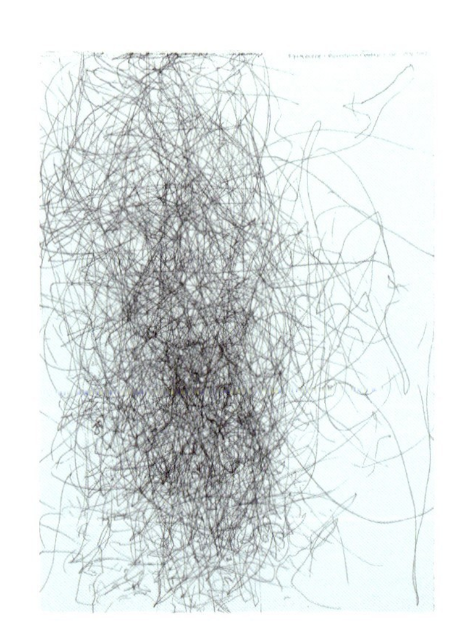

Pat Pickett, *Sycamore–Equestrian Center–1 hr–May 2002*. © Pat Pickett, courtesy of The Drawing Room, East Hampton, New York

Among many influences, we are attracted to works that pursue essential issues of shape and form, gesture, line, density, figure and field, repetition, and contrast—from Abstract Expressionists including Robert Motherwell (top) to contemporary artists like Pat Pickett, who suspends an ink stylus from tree branches, using the wind to translate energy into line and tone.

the freedom of a contemporary aesthetic; an interest in economy of means and a studied distillation of sources and ideas; traditions of responsible care for the land; and a passion for nature's spatial and ecological characteristics. We were attracted then—and today we remain compelled—by the productive tensions we find in juxtaposing analytical, rational thought against the more common emotive responses people bring to the landscapes we work in.

The path from the firm's beginnings to the practice that we share with our colleagues today must be told here in outline form. After a partnership with Susan Child, which produced significant works including South Cove in New York's Battery Park City and a widely praised plan for Stan Hywet Hall in Akron, Ohio, Doug Reed opened his firm in 1993. The early days of Doug's venture were propelled by a few key commissions brought to him through Salvatore LaRosa and Ron Bentley of B Five Studio in New York. Recognition came quickly with the Children's Therapeutic Garden at the Institute for Child and Adolescent Development in Wellesley, Massachusetts—a work that generated broad interest from designers, writers, and social scientists, and still prompts research or reference calls to our office, nearly twenty years later.

After several years of practice and some immersion in the history of the discipline as a research assistant at Harvard, Gary Hilderbrand assumed a consulting position supporting the scholar Cynthia Zaitzevsky in the analysis of Frederick Law Olmsted's Boston Park System and alterations over its first one hundred years. In 1990 he began teaching in Harvard's design studios and technology courses; he has continued to teach there since, and has published two books and over twenty essays on design

Gertrude Jekyll, photograph from Album 5, #1546, "Cistus by the Wood Path," Gertrude Jekyll Collection, Environmental Design Archives, University of California, Berkeley

Garden precedents constantly inform our work; this one, Gertrude Jekyll's "wide wood walk," aided in conceptualizing the project for new interment sites at Mount Auburn Cemetery.

Battery Park City's South Cove, a formative project for Doug Reed as a young designer, completed in 1986.

practice. Throughout these pursuits he has embraced the complications and rewards that derive from overlaps among teaching, writing, and professional practice.

We merged our individual firms after together producing the winning design in an invited competition for a new shrub and vine collection at the Arnold Arboretum of Harvard University, in 1997. With this and other commissions that followed—for the renowned Mount Auburn Cemetery in Cambridge, Massachusetts, the Hobart Urban Nature Preserve in Ohio, and several adaptive projects on Boston's Christian Science Plaza—we gained experience in making precise and sensitive interventions within publicly accessible places where design heritage mattered. The local institutional successes built on our prior individual experiences working alongside some great practitioners: Jon Emerson and Wayne Womack, Suzanne Turner, Susan Child, Duncan Alford, Morgan Wheelock, Keith LeBlanc, M. Perry Chapman, Kenneth Bassett, Stuart Dawson, Alan Ward, Tom Ryan, Richard Burck, and others. Varied nuggets of professional outlook and habits of mind from all these individuals found their way into our early collaboration and helped form our ethos. They endure.

Landscape architecture practice evolved significantly in the 1990s, and our young firm felt the force of its shifts. Newly fertile pursuits of landscape research and scholarship emerged around us. We addressed rigors of practice in describing and protecting significant landscapes, while developing for ourselves an outlook on history as a form of knowledge that helps position well-argued strategies for stewardship and for change. We witnessed the struggles and successes of advocacy—and some potent examples of enterprising leadership—that revived some of the most time-ravaged heritage sites in America, chief among them New York's Central Park and Brooklyn's Prospect Park. During this time, specialists working

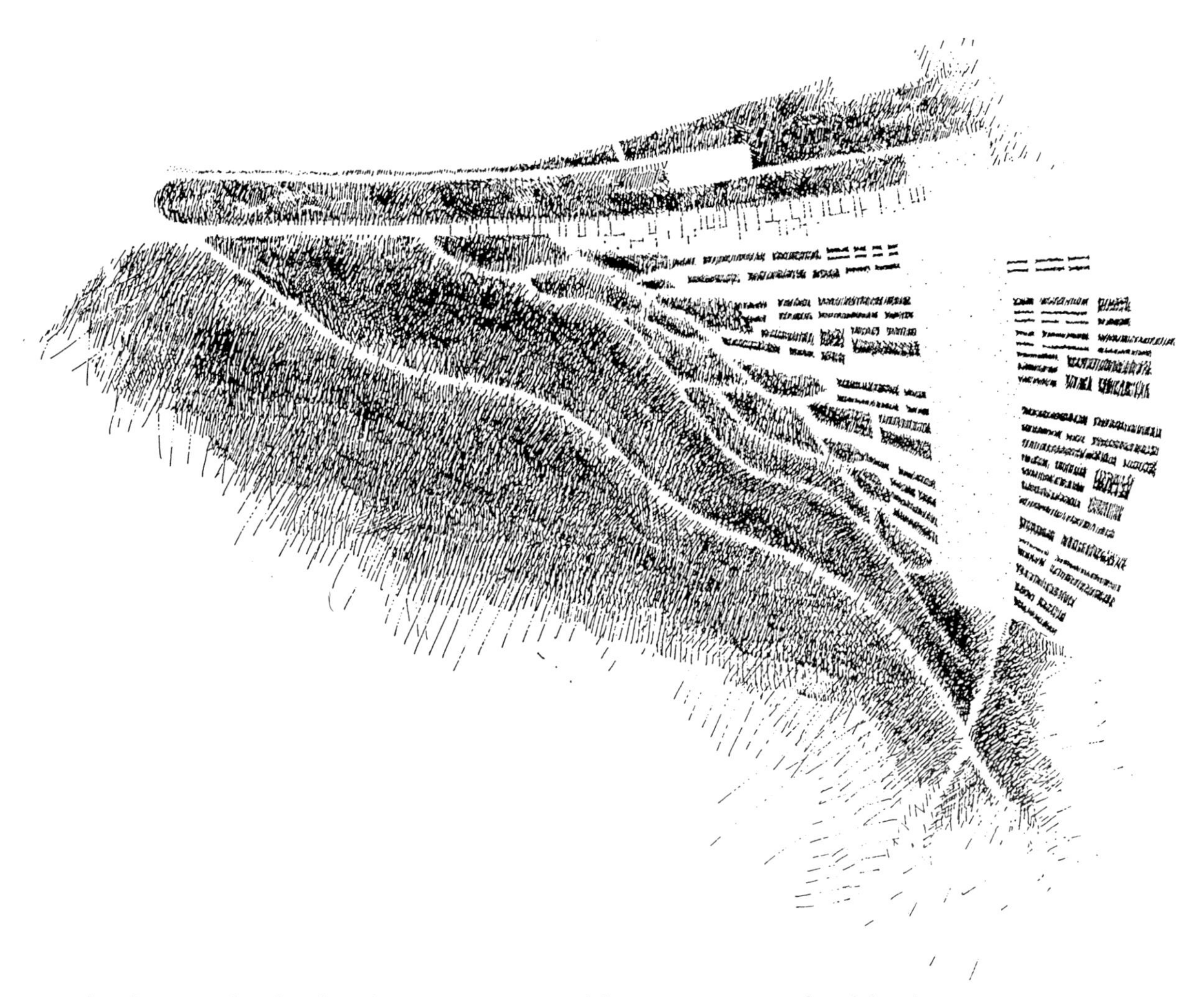

Hand sketch of the "organic parterre" from the design competition entry for the shrub and vine collection at the Arnold Arboretum of Harvard University.

in the ecological sciences were taking account of critical components of disturbed sites and human-occupied landscapes. Ecologists began to work regularly during these years *with* designers instead of in opposition to them. Scientists and landscape architects together learned that our shared task on denatured sites was not simply restoring natural conditions or earlier period circumstances, but rather recovering at least some measure of ecological function and system health and actively shaping the development of ecosystems. Finally, we saw, and perhaps helped in our own ways to catalyze, the emergence of a generation of work that joined ecological resilience with the formal and phenomenological investigations pursued by artists working with a medium we knew to be our own. Those investigations now reside squarely within the practice of landscape architecture and have improved its discourse profoundly for two decades.

During the growth economy of the late 1990s and the resurgent boom years of post-9/11 America, we engaged the kind of increasingly challenging commissions that enabled the firm to broaden its portfolio and its capacities. Work outside the New England/New York region grew from single projects in Ohio, Pennsylvania, and Virginia to more complex and overlapping relationships in Texas, Arizona, Louisiana, the Carolinas, and beyond. Complexity became the norm: campus projects with telescoping scales and long durations, urban parks on postindustrial sites, and larger urban revitalization and infrastructure schemes conceived for implementation over many years, or even decades.

Today, Reed Hilderbrand's leadership has broadened and its structure has evolved—deliberately but organically, we like to say. We've emphasized an open and collaborative studio atmosphere, and like many practices we aim to be a teaching office, with lectures and seminars, regular infusions of energetic young interns, and a commitment to shared responsibility for those things essential to completing the work durably and sustainably. We must be quick to acknowledge that the works illustrated in these pages are truly collective efforts. The coherence they embody is due in great measure to talented, committed professionals whose names do not appear on the cover of this book or on the sign on our door.

How do the operations of the practice contribute to consistency and continuity in the work? In conventional business models, owners apportion responsibilities to achieve efficiency and strength. We have allowed no division of interests or obligations between us as owners: We remain equal producers and worriers. Mostly, we share

The Evelyn Marshall Field residence, Long Island, New York, designed by Richard Webel, anticipates modernist garden space, as posited in *Making a Landscape of Continuity: The Practice of Innocenti & Webel*, Gary R. Hilderbrand, ed. Samuel Gottscho photograph, ca 1933

Doug Reed, left, and Gary Hilderbrand in the studio.

responsibility with a group of principals and colleagues who have grown with us, and who, complementing our generalist instincts, divide accountability for operations in ways tuned to individual strengths. Each of them has helped us build the firm, but has also helped us to refine our design language. They bear responsibility—and deserve credit—for both. Moreover, they have collectively developed the means of ensuring great performance and productive collaboration with consultants, growers, contractors, gardeners, city officials, owners, and, once in a while, problem clients or bad actors. They've devised the look and feel of the office's worldly presence and curated the record of thought that lies behind our landscapes.

There is one other thing worth mentioning about the pursuit of coherence and consistency that has to do with how we document our projects. Here we return to the issue of making a book. How do we convey to the world, through a two-dimensional medium, what we see and experience in living, dynamic works of landscape architecture? We have chosen in this volume to favor effects over processes, and outcomes over operations. We've done this by emphasizing what a few very special artists and friends—Alan Ward, Millicent Harvey, Andrea Jones, and Charles Mayer—have captured for us in pictures. Their work reveals many of the qualities we love about our work. There is nothing like the experience of the wind or the salt air or the maturing growth of trees or the rattle and bustle of city streets to make you feel that a landscape work is really performing as you had hoped it would. But the photographs in this book are the next best thing, and we are grateful for them. As a collection, they cohere, and they convey something about how we see our work. And how we think about it.

—Douglas Reed and Gary Hilderbrand

Like designers making choices about which characteristics to bring forward in a landscape, photographers define for themselves what stance they will take and which format they will use to show the world what they see. In recent years, Reed Hilderbrand has worked with Millicent Harvey to produce a singular body of photographs on sites where we have worked. We've thought of this enterprise as an artist's commission, and it has proceeded without much steering from us. Millicent's interpretations, made primarily with black and white film, capture things we already treasured and things we had not seen in our landscapes. She surprises us by unearthing spatial conditions we may not have studied. She happily embraces the impacts of the weather and always emphasizes the fall of light and shadow; these allow the viewer to detect specific material qualities in the work and perhaps to imagine the tectonic decisions behind them. And in the tradition of photographers who have viewed life in the street as a provocative rendering of time and place, she picks up on everyday uses and activities on sites that designers sometimes overlook. We have come to think that this body of work, which is Millicent's own project, is most suitably presented as a collection. Her work has made our landscapes—places we thought we knew exceedingly well—ever more visible.

Millicent Harvey: A Photographer's View

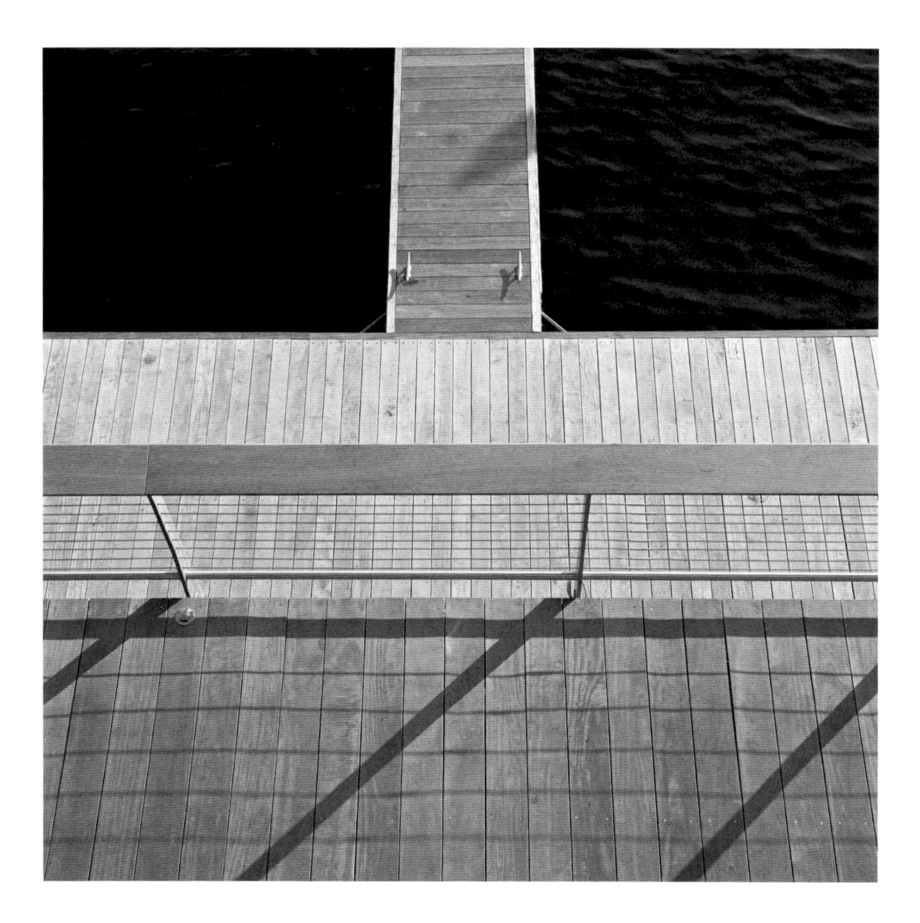

CC
County

ESPECIALLY
FOR YOU.

Essays

Robert Pogue Harrison

Toward a More Thoughtful, More Hopeful Modernity

An Italian architect once declared that, in addition to being the greatest poet of his age, Dante was one of its greatest architects. Certainly the architectonics of the *Divine Comedy* are as sublime as anything that has come down to us in wood or stone from that era. Yet I would add that Dante was also one of the visionary *landscape* architects of his time. As we follow his Pilgrim into Hell, we enter a realm of moral disfigurement filled with broken bridges, smoky swamps, dark and gnarled thickets, somber cemeteries, scorched wastelands, and polluted rivers. Continuing up the Mountain of Purgatory we experience auroral shorelines, semicircular valleys, terraces contoured with bas-reliefs, and finally Eden, with its sheltering shade and clear-flowing streams. Landscape in the *Divine Comedy* is the visible correlate of what the Italians call *lo stato d'animo*, or state of mind. The aesthetic integrity of the shores of the Mountain of Purgatory is the first sign of the Pilgrim's deliverance from Hell.

Dante's *Inferno* seems more familiar to modern readers than does his *Purgatorio*, not only because the immoralities it depicts remain as virulent now as in his time but also because our modern habitat has a great deal more in common with the blaring, claustrophobic, and scrofulous landscapes of his Hell than with the serene, soothing scenery of the *Divine Comedy*'s second canticle. The political, social, and environmental devastations of the twentieth century make it one of the most hellish in human history; it remains to be seen whether the twenty-first century will outdo it, or whether we will find a way to get beyond its self-consuming, self-perpetuating frenzy and neurasthenia. Many of us have become so wearied by the contemporary habitat that we hardly take notice of it anymore. That is one reason why the work of Reed Hilderbrand—in its quiet and even joyful sanity—produces the paradoxical effect of a shock. It is jolting to be shown (and not merely told) that Hell is not our only alternative; that there is a way of being modern other than the fiendish and demoralizing one we have tended to pursue in our efforts at "modernization." Modernity promised a new world, yet many of the overwhelming forces it unleashed—technology, cupidity, and an unrestrained will to power—have instead brought about a systematic unworlding of the world. The work of

Reed Hilderbrand offers a countermovement to this unworlding that takes the form of restoring the promise that has been lost in the process.

The landscapes of Reed Hilderbrand strike me as purgatorial in essence, not in the religious or doctrinal sense but because once you are in them you have a feeling of having escaped from a pathological realm that threatened to trap you within its abyss. Such is Dante's apprehension when he first emerges from Hell onto the shores of Purgatory. His sense of enormous relief joins a deep inner need of consolation and regeneration. Likewise, in a Reed Hilderbrand landscape, one has a sense of having narrowly escaped a mortal danger. Escape must be understood here not as evasion but as *rescue*. What one has been rescued from does not disappear in these landscapes; it remains (like Dante's Hell throughout the rest of his journey) conspicuously present, as something that has been overcome. It is not often that overcoming takes the form of self-gathered serenity. It requires a special genius—or what I would call historical maturity—to infuse a landscape with the kind of tension one finds in the work of Reed Hilderbrand.

One difference between Dante's Purgatory and Reed Hilderbrand's landscapes is that the former remains topographically separate from Hell, while the latter must create pockets of rescue *within* the more or less degraded habitats of the modern Inferno. These landscapes evoke for me the last words Marco Polo utters to the emperor Kublai Khan in Italo Calvino's *Invisible Cities*: "There are two ways to escape suffering from the inferno where we live every day, that we form by being together," he says. The first is "to accept the inferno and become such a part of it that you can no longer see it." The second "is risky and demands constant vigilance and apprehension: seek and learn to recognize who and what, in the midst of the inferno, are not inferno, then make them endure, give them space." Reed Hilderbrand has embraced that second alternative. The firm seeks, studies, learns, and constantly spies out the world-affirming potential of the sites they transform. In so doing they make room for—give space to—the redemptive possibilities in the midst of our habitats.

If Hell is the impossibility of reason, as some have said, it is also the impossibility of hearing. What I have called the unworlding of the world produces a great deal of noise—of rage, misery, and uprootedness; of vendors, vatics, and propagandists; of self-assertion or self-mutilation—and this noise overwhelms us in a Babel of accents. Noise militates against thinking, which at bottom is a form of listening. Reed Hilderbrand makes it one of their highest priorities to create landscapes that mute the din of our world so that a certain kind of thinking—or a certain kind of listening—can take place. Indeed, the overwhelming impression I get from their work is of thoughtful reticence. Here one finds a deliberate withholding of declaration in favor of heeding.

Reed Hilderbrand heeds in various ways. Certainly as designers they pay close attention to, and deliberately ponder, both the natural and historical character of the sites they work with—responding, through calibrated design and discriminating use of materials, to what these sites discreetly reveal of their hidden, charismatic potential. This kind of attention listens to, not only looks at, the historicized nature of the sites in question. In that respect it becomes a form of invocation, insofar as these designs seem to *call forth* latent, site-specific energies, allowing them to permeate their landscapes like invisible currents of grace. Reed Hilderbrand has an extraordinary ability to liberate these local currents in which the forces of life are gathered and stored.

This power of summoning no doubt arises from the design's being attuned to what I would call the site's *phenomenon*. There is more to a phenomenon than what meets the physical, or even theoretical, eye. In manifesting itself the phenomenon reveals the presence of something that is not in itself apparent but without which the phenomenon would have no density, no depth, and no dynamism. Every site, properly speaking, is a phenomenon of this sort. Every site has its recessive penumbra and protective shadows within which the depths of natural and historical time are gathered and stored. It would be easy to overlook this reserve of natural and historical time in the phenomenon. When I say that Reed Hilderbrand's work listens more than declares, heeds more than asserts, I mean, among other things, that the firm pays attention to what makes the site a phenomenon, rather than a mere location or layout.

In that respect their landscapes provide more than mere context for a given building. They give a recessive depth to both building and context: better, they make room for what I would call, in both a literal and figurative sense, the photophobic dimensions of the phenomenon. The Leventritt Garden at the Arnold Arboretum of Harvard University is a wondrous example of this kind of accommodation. Every path, wall, or terrace, in its relation to a delimiting edge, seems to open rather closely around the contours of the design. What appears to the eye emerges from, and withdraws into, the hidden depths of the phenomenon. Reed Hilderbrand's designers are consummate phenomenologists, in the most concrete sense of the term.

This is perhaps one of the reasons why the firm is so committed to shade. In addition to gratifying desires that run deep in most human beings, the generous presence of trees in their landscapes creates an abundance of shade. What would civilization be without shade? It would not be at all. Shade is the condition, if not source, of all that makes us human, which is why the rehumanization of the habitat that this firm achieves in its landscape art begins and ends with shade—that is, with trees. In their attunement to both latent and manifest recesses of the phenomenon,

Reed Hilderbrand creates shaded spaces where thinking can become thoughtful again. It is in such depths that we hear the muffled voices of the dead, of inchoate thoughts and vagrant reveries, of half-conscious memories or metaphysical abstractions—in sum, the voices of what we used to know as spirit. This kind of thinking, which is neither practical nor calculating but reflective, needs places to take place in: not mental places but embodied places where mind and phenomenon may recover their original kinship. The most explicit example of such recovery was once experienced at the Institute for Child and Adolescent Development, in Wellesley, Massachusetts, where psychologists used the evocative narrative of the garden to diagnose and treat children who had experienced trauma. This project, which has since been demolished, offered the clearest example of the pervasive therapeutic effects of the firm's work.

The therapeutic presence of water in many Reed Hilderbrand landscapes joins with the sheltering presence of shade to offer asylum for such thoughtful reflection. Beyond the ingenious ways in which their long troughs, for example, double as irrigation ditches, they also invite, in their ponds, a reflective baptism, as it were. To put it more formulaically, through their heeding Reed Hilderbrand creates places where thought is free to reawaken, or where it may at the very least "escape," if only momentarily, the aversion to thinking that afflicts modes of being in today's world. Again, thinking needs place to take place in.

What the ancients used to call the *genius loci*, or presiding spirit of a place, personifies whatever enables the mind to permeate the place and the place to permeate the mind. The highest calling of landscape architecture, in my view, is to enable such interpenetration. In *The Garden*, Andrew Marvell evokes "a green thought in a green shade," reminding us that the quality, if not *nature*, of a thought depends in part on where it arises. And what applies to thoughts applies to human dispositions in general. If the wasteland grows without, in the external world, it will also grow within, in what used to be called the soul. The landscape architecture of the *Divine Comedy* reminds us that soul and habitat are more than simply analogous. Hell within creates Hell without, and vice versa. At times—and we are living in one of those times—things get to a point where it is only by reforming the habitat that one can reform corrosive habits. That is why the work of landscape architects like Reed Hilderbrand has such urgency now. When we look at their work we see that a more thoughtful, less disinherited modernity than the one we have embraced so far is still open to us. Reed Hilderbrand does what it takes to make room for it. One cannot ask of landscape architects more than that.

Gary Hilderbrand

On Seeing: Visible | Invisible

In the early morning light of a photograph taken by Alan Ward in the summer of 2010, a canopy of cedar elms hovers over a pavilion, a swimming pool, and gently graded lawn terraces. The image was made on the bank of Upper Bachman Creek in Dallas, Texas, on a 6-acre property where Philip Johnson designed a house in 1964 for Henry S. and Patricia Beck. When Doug Reed and I first visited this site in 2003, the spatial power of these trees was barely visible. Fully engulfed in a tangle of two species of *Ligustrum*—one shrublike, growing up to 12 feet in height, the other with 3-inch trunks reaching nearly 20 feet—the land was virtually impenetrable. For perhaps two decades, an aging Mrs. Beck had neglected portions of her property east of the creek and benignly allowed nature to run its course. More than a hundred volunteer cedar elms and a handful of other trees, including several Texas live oaks and a single giant cottonwood, had formed a canopy that merged with comparably overgrown woodlands on either side of the parcel. We saw a degraded, illegible landscape.

Beck House, looking east through cedar elms toward a pool pavilion by architects Bodron + Fruit.

(left) Grove of cedar elms with concrete risers; in the distance, *Your Space Eruption*, Olafur Eliasson, 2009, set in the trees.

(top) Philip Johnson's Beck House, south façade, before renovations. © Hester + Hardaway

(bottom) Upper Bachman Creek, Johnson's original bridge, and volunteer cedar elm forest cover, before rehabilitative work.

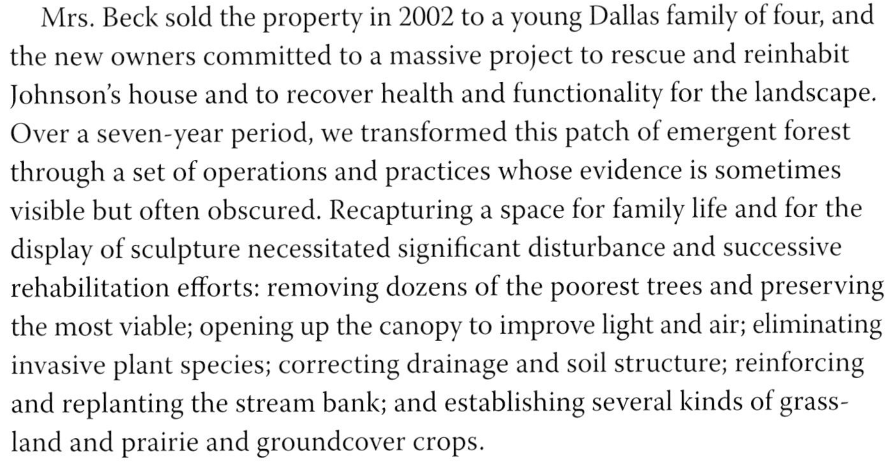

Mrs. Beck sold the property in 2002 to a young Dallas family of four, and the new owners committed to a massive project to rescue and reinhabit Johnson's house and to recover health and functionality for the landscape. Over a seven-year period, we transformed this patch of emergent forest through a set of operations and practices whose evidence is sometimes visible but often obscured. Recapturing a space for family life and for the display of sculpture necessitated significant disturbance and successive rehabilitation efforts: removing dozens of the poorest trees and preserving the most viable; opening up the canopy to improve light and air; eliminating invasive plant species; correcting drainage and soil structure; reinforcing and replanting the stream bank; and establishing several kinds of grassland and prairie and groundcover crops.

Today the tree canopy delimits a restful space—an extended shady grove—populated by the dispersed and irregular gray trunks of the preserved cedar elms. Most of these trees would be poor specimens on their own; they are a unified crop of survivors, managed back to good health and collectively shaping a newly found space of extensive horizontal and vertical reach. *Ulmus crassifolia*, the cedar elm, is a tough and adaptable plant that thrives in the soils of creek banks and upland slopes. The tree

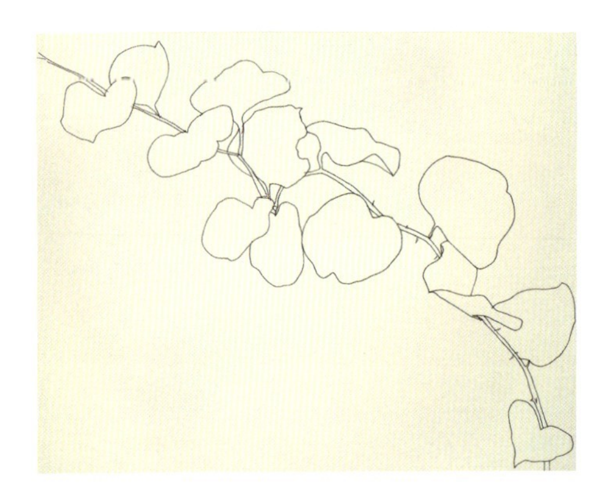

Ellsworth Kelly, *Briar*, 1961, black ink on wove paper, 22 1/2 x 28 1/2 inches, gift of Samuel Wagstaff in memory of Elva McCormick, Wadsworth Atheneum Museum of Art, Hartford, CT / Art Resource, New York

Ellsworth Kelly's plant drawings, produced over an entire career, capture the particular form and habit of plant anatomy.

propagates readily from seed distributed by birds; its roots easily adapt to irregular terrain or obstacles, and in unmanaged conditions, as in Mrs. Beck's floodplain and uplands, individuals can coexist only a few feet apart. Over time, canopies merge with each other in a battle for light and space; through competition, the trees adventitiously twist and swirl in shape, and this results in a calligraphic silhouette of thrusting, pointing branches.

The space beneath the canopy already existed here, though it wasn't easy to see; in simple terms, we unleashed it from an uninhabitable thicket. Inserting a system of concrete risers made it possible to preserve the cedar elms while also creating level spaces for family activities and sculpture platforms. We installed nearly 4,000 feet of these linear grade breaks; they range from single curbs to aggregated sets spread broadly or stacked vertically as steps. The concrete piles that support them keep the riser elevations stable against the swelling and shrinking of the soil; the concrete occasionally bridges over masses of elm root at differential elevations, so as not to disturb critical anchoring or feeding functions.

Behind these precisely accentuated stepping grades lies a complex unseen project to devise a topographic system that would be complementary to Johnson's house but expressive of other design motivations. This work involved balancing existing and proposed grades with real precision; testing and prototyping several configurations of concrete beams and piers; excavating the soils by machine, hand, and pressurized air; forming, curing, and finishing concrete; and rebuilding a landscape surface. This system structures and supports an equally obscured yet vital living dynamic below grade: rooting networks, moisture retention and drainage, and an organically induced soil ecology that promotes nutrient cycling for sustaining growth and maturation. The space beneath the canopy is deceptively simple yet resolutely complex; the means to recover and sustain it are partly evident, mostly unseen.

Visible

> Vision is the art of seeing things invisible.
> —Jonathan Swift, "Thoughts on Various Subjects," from *Miscellanies*, 1711

Observers have said, generally by way of praise, that our firm's work looks somehow inevitable—that qualities one may see in a project seem to reflect a distilled, resonant fit with particular conditions of a site. As if there were no other plausible answer—or, that we just make it look easy. It's not.

At the Beck House, reserved and understated qualities in our work are undeniable and fully intended. We usually aim for that: an edited, essential spatial order, which emphasizes characteristics—obvious or latent—a site may already possess, or which allows for the more palpable experience of selected and specific qualities that derive from the site's geography, microclimate, orientation, or configuration. We pursue this result from a belief in the power of design to turn ordinary characteristics into extraordinary experiences. We also seek it through an unapologetic attachment to the observable phenomena of nature—light, shade, color, scent, moisture, warmth and energy, growth and decay, seasonal change, maturation, senescence—coupled with a drive to make those phenomena apparent by allowing certain characters to come forward.

I know I speak for my colleagues in the firm when I say that a good measure of our approach to design comes in response to the commotion and disarray of everyday built landscape—out of an explicit desire to bring order and clarity to the experience of the complex and vibrant world out there. Too often, we see a cluttered and chaotic landscape. For whatever reasons, many landscapes—whether shaped by property owners, managers, gardeners, architects, or landscape architects—seem to us overwrought, not adequately studied, and undisciplined. They often feel complicated or overdesigned, with too much stuff filling the space or troubling the view. Against this tendency toward either design absence or design excess, we strive for assiduously studied, unambiguous, and precisely framed intentions—clarity—when we give shape to a slope or plant trees on a street.

While much of what we do in landscape architecture is inherently abstract—our maps and drawings and digital technologies of course employ many levels of abstraction—in our practice we seek another, deeper kind of reduction in our plans for altering landscapes. We aim to conceptualize. We look for logics. We never decorate. Here it is useful to invoke Robert Motherwell's reference to Abstract Expressionism as "an art stripped bare" whereby a "reduction of means brings emphasis" to spatial relationships and allows the intensification of selective characteristics to emerge.[1] We try to narrow parameters and to find a reduced and particular essence in each project. This always involves a joining of reason and intuition: to understand what's there, decide what should remain, imagine what can or must be made anew, and invest deliberately and with full force in a few—not many—aspects of appearance and function in the landscape. Though most of what we face in design commissions rises from complicated circumstances, we try to boil things down. We put great stock in Constantin Brancusi's explicit modernist axiom: "Simplicity is complexity resolved."[2]

Constantin Brancusi, *Newborn* [I], 1915, white marble, 5 3/4 x 8 1/4 x 5 7/8 inches, The Louise and Walter Arensberg Collection, Philadelphia Museum of Art / Art Resource, New York

Constantin Brancusi's *Newborn* reduces complex formal and material characteristics to an abstracted and refined expression.

1. Robert Motherwell. "What Abstract Art Means to Me: George L. K. Morris, Willem De Kooning, Alexander Calder, Fritz Glarner, Robert Motherwell and Stuart Davis." *The Bulletin of the Museum of Modern Art*, Vol. 18, No. 3, (Spring, 1951), 2–15.
2. Constantin Brancusi. Quoted by Carmen Giménez in "Endless Brancusi," in Carmen Giménez and Matthew Gale, *Constantin Brancusi: The Essence of Things*. London: Tate Publishing, 2004, 19.

In the normal course of conceptualizing and developing projects of all kinds, we organize the obvious things—movement systems and corridors, building sites, earthworks, drainageways, plantations—with practical deliberateness. Sometimes, we purposefully differentiate the work through contrast against areas where we exert no control. Other times, our work more fully integrates with its context, to the degree that its limits or edges intentionally obscure distinctions and emphasize continuities with existing surroundings. Often, our intentions about the potentially expressive qualities of a place—whether sober or effusive—may be the focus of the work itself: You may not comprehend exactly what's been done, but it appears as though things have been selectively exaggerated, or reduced to essentials, or refined to the point of economy and clarity. Is it important that you see the intention in the work? Has it moved beyond the visible?

Invisible Field

The inadequacy of prediction brings recurring perplexity to landscape architecture. Some of the more ephemeral characteristics of our medium conflict with the impulse to bring highly ordered experience to an irregular world. We work more or less by rearranging earthen matter and plants and moisture so that they can coexist productively with human occupation. The natural tendency of these media moves them toward entropy; dynamic processes, unmanaged, constantly build and erode matter and structure. The change we bring to a landscape is not a singular event; it's perpetual. The photographs in this book are the only proof you need: The momentary status we capture in pictures establishes a record of great importance to us, but as a static representation the photograph reveals its own inability to capture the phenomena of growth or adaptation that define the medium.[3]

Arguments that the field itself is invisible—and refutations—are plentiful.[4] These and other anxieties have troubled landscape architecture, in part because of nature's reluctance to be managed or controlled by any single (or even concerted) force, and in part because it's not easy to identify dependable boundaries prescribing authority or expertise. This familiar discussion provokes recurring questions about the medium's dynamic (ecological) material existence and the breadth of its expressive potential, the work's unseen technical or tectonic sophistication, and the world of motivations behind the ideas in the work. These days it seems everyone works on the landscape, and enormous and ultimately productive overlaps exist among professionals in urbanism, architecture, environmental planning, infrastructure, ecosystem restoration, garden making, sculptural or

3. I raised this topic in reference to Roland Barthes' *Camera Lucida* (1980) in my introduction to Alan Ward, *American Designed Landscapes: A Photographic Interpretation.* Washington, D.C.: Spacemaker Press, 1998.
4. Peter Walker and Melanie Simo discuss landscape architecture's "invisible" tendencies in *Invisible Gardens: The Search for Modernism in the American Landscape.* Cambridge, Mass.: MIT Press, 1994.

We often operate in venerated and mature landscapes, but we also work on sites that undergo substantial turbulence—for instance, along the shore of the Hudson River (left), the site for Long Dock Beacon—or that have been undervalued or degraded, as in a former factory site (right) in Somerville, Massachusetts, which became Edward Leathers Community Park.

media installation, and other modes of practice. These allied disciplines see the opportunities in landscape with comparable interest and authority, and the territory is there for the taking. Landscape architects may find themselves everywhere and nowhere: plenty of varied and diverse commissions on every conceivable scale, with no consensus about theories of practice or ethical frameworks or values that lend cultural authority or relevance to landscape work. But this may be changing.

Today, we work in an expanded field where the economic and social questions on sustainability—quite familiar for landscape architecture—are inescapable in all corners of life. The kinds of commissions and collaborations we pursue today—recovering a poisoned riverfront wasteland, reconstituting a viable public realm in a changing urban neighborhood, devising methods for improved performance and sustainability of the tree canopy in a city—bring with them familiar kinds of problems amid overlapping professional territories.

In truth, I relish the varied intellectual traditions that shape an evolving if ambiguous space for landscape architecture. In our practice, we see benefits in the lack of clear boundaries. Today's discourse on the importance of ecology and sustainability in remaking our world at every scale amplifies concerns we have held for a long time. This broadening conversation leads to vastly diverse kinds of assignments and programs—gardens and sanctuaries, redevelopment sites, parking and transit facilities, artworks, botanical and agricultural plots, rivers and ditches, boardwalks and busy streets, toxic spoils, healthy forests, waterfronts, homes, schools. Landscape architecture's disciplinary frame has been described as chronically vague and somewhat beyond the view of art historians and cultural critics. And again, it seems up for grabs. For us, that is no burden. Rather, it gives us entrée to the broadest range of commissions and moves us to constantly reconfirm our foundations.

Robert Smithson, *Non-site (Palisades-Edgewater, N.J.)*, 1968, enamel on aluminum with stones, 56 x 26 x 36 inches, and map and description of site, Whitney Museum of American Art, New York, purchased with funds from the Howard and Jean Lipman Foundation, Inc. Art © Estate of Robert Smithson / Licensed by VAGA, New York

Robert Smithson's *Non-site* projects brought nature's evidence into the gallery. Later, Smithson's *Spiral Jetty*, near Rozel Point, Utah, 1970 (right), made the actions of natural phenomena become more completely the subject of a work.

Made Visible

No words cut through the predicament of landscape architecture's invisibility more succinctly than Robert Smithson's contention that the landscape is "already there."[5] Smithson recognized that landscape is commonly, perhaps inescapably, seen as a background condition and a thing already made. His brilliant artistic practice pushed him to think otherwise. Having awakened to the striking reality of the constructed landscape of New York's Central Park, he turned for answers to an historical authority—the park's manager, designer, and vociferous advocate, Frederick Law Olmsted, Sr. Smithson's eventual recognition of the awesome power of the landscape as a medium, and his eloquent paean to Olmsted's record of intentions and struggles, drove him to foreground the landscape in his own work. In this he formulated a kind of postmodern artist's zealous polemic: make content visible.

Olmsted appropriated the rock and soil of Manhattan as his medium—a working material we can describe as encompassing both nature and city. Though he embedded it, perhaps invisibly, in a constructed, sometimes pastoral scenography, he believed the physical landscape of the park to be central to a radically conceived mechanism of urban political and social reform. For Olmsted and a handful of other nineteenth-century reformers, parks became organic infrastructures for improving public health in the face of substandard living conditions. In his view, the scale and the corrective potential of these reforms were limited only by a lack of political will or ambition. He pushed against institutional inertia with all his force. Sometimes he succeeded. No less pointedly, the artist Smithson flailed against an entrenched patronage system that exploited artists and their work by commodifying artistic production and privileging gallery owners and traders over its producers. Smithson determined to take his work to

5. Robert Smithson, quoted in Ron Graziani, *Robert Smithson and the American Landscape*. New York: Cambridge University Press, 2004, p. 40. Smithson describes making a landscape of pictorial effects as "repeating another work—a 'landscape'—that already exists elsewhere." This discourse refers also to Smithson's essay "Frederick Law Olmsted and the Dialectical Landscape," 1973, published in Jack Flam, ed., *Robert Smithson: The Collected Writings*. Berkeley: University of California Press, 1996.

Frederick Law Olmsted's Central Park anticipated dramatic contrasts between the built fabric of the city and the natural forces of the park. Smithson published a photograph of the Central Park steps carved in Manhattan schist in his essay on Olmsted's relevance to his own work. © Smudge Studio

a place curators could not control: the landscape. In doing so he forged an art whose visible, temporal characteristics were inseparable from experience—exactly as he had seen Olmsted's work to be. While these two men were separated by a gulf of one hundred years, we discern shared motives: by working explicitly with landscape, both asked the world to rethink the foundations of nature and art and to make the constructed world more visible.

Like Olmsted, Smithson sought an audience for his larger agenda. He cleverly yoked his exposure machine—art journals and catalogues—to the scholarly rehabilitation of Olmsted's career that was emerging in the 1960s and that gained in prominence during the 1970s. By embedding detailed observations on the landscape of New York's Central Park in a body of descriptions of his own art, and by chronicling adaptations he could see layered on top of the park's original constructions, Smithson broadened his reach and earned the attention of cultural critics, urban theorists, and landscape architects. He opened the door for apprehension once again—landscape architects, it seems, had almost forgotten—of the possibilities of using landscape as a medium of meaningful expression and an instrument of cultural relevance. In doing so, he increased our awareness of the physical and cultural forces that Olmsted had grasped. He demonstrated ever more clearly the forces of geomorphology, hydrology, weather, and decay. Smithson conceptualized the landscape and made concrete its phenomenological possibilities. Landscape architecture would reclaim this territory soon after, and a revitalized discourse would emerge from overlaps between his work and that of others who argued for the landscape's primacy.

If we accept Smithson's assertion that a landscape work, to be meaningful, must be situated in a wider geography (or history, or spatiality, or ecology), the problem becomes how to contextualize it, and whether, or

how, to differentiate it from its background. How can we recognize the work? The answer may differ each time we pose the question. With landscape, and within the landscape discipline, one never lays eyes on a tabula rasa; what we do as designers at every scale is seen against, or potentially absorbed by, something larger, something already under way. Whether one objectifies a living work against its dynamic (even ephemeral) context, as Smithson did with his *Spiral Jetty*, may be a matter of circumstance, but is always a matter of conviction. It inevitably involves choice.

The work of our firm embraces this visible/invisible duality and enlarges upon it. Like Smithson, we formulate a nuanced and particularized reading of a site's circumstance, from among many possible readings, and then make plans to act on what is already there—partly visible, portions not. Our actions range from subtle renovation and editing to more ambitious exaggeration of the living forces or particular characteristics we choose to foreground. Over time, and throughout our work, we are conscious of preoccupations that focus our attention and bring satisfaction and constant challenge. These include a recognizably modernist compulsion toward abstracted, open, and flexible spatial organization; a fascination with grading and the affective range that comes with altering and exaggerating the shape of the ground; a drive for orders, logics, patterns, and occasionally frictions that make our ways of shaping space and experience legible; a love of the plant kingdom and its vast expressive potential; a commitment to the stewardship of cultural patrimony and the conservation of the biophysical resources significant in the landscapes we inherit; and a passion for mining those particular qualities we see and feel in a given site. In this, we've evolved a kind of practice that produces both coherence and invention: constant obsessions, changing circumstances.

The Half-Mile Line boardwalk, in western Massachusetts, objectifies a fixed linear trace against an irregular and fluctuating dendritic drainage pattern.

Indeterminate

The work at the Beck House on Upper Bachman Creek carries on today, long after construction, in the form of stewardship. Several times each year, we review growing conditions and make adjustments to canopy, understory, ground plane, soil, and moisture, as the landscape settles in. Assumptions we made on the acclimation of new plants and the renewed vigor of elms and pecans hold up, for the most part, but challenges abound in a landscape of this scale. Though it is not often acknowledged, all constructed and managed landscapes require adjustment. The evidence of stress is often but not always visible; the work of adjusting and adapting takes place on many levels—including, increasingly, on the hidden level of managing microorganism activity in the soil. A landscape grows, and we continue to shape its development toward something resembling that spatial and ecological outcome we imagined a few years ago. Or close to it.

So we approach our work with a kind of double vision: seeing and seeing beyond. Seeing sites for what they are and for what they might become. Imagining growth and time unfolding ahead of us. Our work in cultivated and urbanizing landscapes brings sharpness to things you can see, uncovers and reveals things you otherwise wouldn't, obscures things we choose to suppress in favor of those we foreground, and refers to things you may know about but could never see from one perspective. What you can see, and by extension what you perceive as lived experience on a site, is the tangible, reduced, edited, straightforward reality we build, a kind of baseline of seeing and knowing. But it's never that easy, despite common observations to the contrary. What you don't see in a landscape relates to a telescoping interest that takes in many realms and scales that conspire to lend meaning to the work. It consists, in varied proportions, of what came before, what's beneath the surface, and what's behind the shapes or patterns, below the horizon, past the view, beyond our capacity to see. It relates to conditions and habits of mind that may be objective, subjective, rational, poetic, or just practical and obvious. And it is subject to adaptations that will unfold in time in a partly managed, partly random future. It extends to and embraces the invisible.

Let me return to the most provoking and potent aspect of the invisible in our work: the indeterminate, the future. I want to see all the work we've completed until now—the situations, processes, alterations, errors, and successes—as a kind of foundation or platform from which to operate that anticipates where we might go and prepares us for new things. Because every landscape intervention creates a kind of disturbance of biological forces and relationships, we take risks in reshaping or restarting landscapes; yet we can only operate from a place where speculation and conjecture evolve from the certainty of conviction. Much about a landscape's future is unknown, and we can only guide so much. Here I'm reminded of what has been described as Paul Cézanne's "anxiety of realization," something that plagued him interminably: the knowledge that the final executed work—for him, the painting—could realize but one possibility, perhaps an unjustifiably privileged one amid countless possible answers and limitless scenarios.[6] *How many ways could I paint this?* The difficulty of settling on a color or shape or a perspective angle in the two-dimensional representation of nature became Cézanne's paralyzing struggle. But this same affliction led to the accumulation of a great treasure for humanity. Ultimately it provoked the early twentieth century's most substantive inquiries into the formal, optical, and phenomenal characteristics of our contemporary world. It provided many of the defining motives for generations of artists

6. Maurice Merleau-Ponty describes the irony of Cézanne's great accomplishment amid personal terror in rendering phenomena visible through painting: "The painter recaptures and converts into visible objects what would, without him, remain walled up in the separate life of each consciousness: the vibration of appearances which is the cradle of things." Maurice Merleau-Ponty, "Cézanne's Doubt." In Galen A. Johnson, ed., *The Merleau-Ponty Aesthetics Reader: Philosophy and Painting*, M. Smith (Trans.). Evanston, Ill.: Northwestern University Press, 1993, 59–75. (Original work published 1945).

who followed Cézanne, perhaps in skeptical admiration, embracing the same probing inquiry and comparably challenging experimental ambition.

I identify with Cézanne's anxiety, to be sure: How to frame the questions, how to pursue the work? How to grab hold of the landscape? Which conditions to foreground, which to suppress? These are the questions we ask ourselves in project reviews in the office or in meetings with collaborators. But I know we can use our techniques and beliefs to turn problems of use or condition or ecological imbalance, or the need for correctives (which is where projects generally originate) into healthy living works that can prosper and endure. Approaching new and more complex sets of problems with familiar obsessions and anxieties—that entails a degree of emotional or professional security, rooted in knowledge, coupled with doubt, unpredictability, and risk. And at times, a dose of Cézanne's personal terror. The landscape is bigger than we are. We alter its substance and its processes, and it grows back at us with force. We can't see exactly how, but we know it will. We come to embrace a certain image. Is it right?

Paul Cézanne, *Still Life (Nature morte)*, 1892–1894, oil on canvas, 24 3/4 x 36 3/8 inches. Image © 2012 The Barnes Foundation, Philadelphia, Pa.

Cézanne's still life paintings and landscapes explored innumerable ways of seeing a subject.

> What is essential is invisible to the eye.
> —Antoine de Saint-Exupéry, *The Little Prince*, 1943

The subjectivity of the landscape, the unseen and unrealized, remains a potent motivation for us. It requires of us, in the formulation of the philosopher John Dewey, that our preparation, our outlook, our habit of mind, be "not something ready-made, but something in continuous formation" through study and iteration, reflection, experimentation, and action. Never static. Never entirely in view. As often as not, invisible.

Suzanne Turner

On Reading: Cultural and Natural Significances

> I admit that I am prejudiced against the current American enthusiasm for historic preservation on the small-town, middle-class scale. I admit that I hold the peculiar belief that the value of history is what it teaches us about the future. But I think that I am on firm ground when I say that most of this landscape history deals with an infinitely small fraction of the landscape.... The reason for this is simple: the origin and history of only a very few spaces, very few structures are on record.... But an infinitely greater number of structures and spaces have no documentation at all.... I believe that with the use of modern archaeological techniques, with the use of aerial photography, above all with the use of more imagination, more speculation we could immensely expand our knowledge of the landscape of the past.[1]
>
> —J. B. Jackson

Reed Hilderbrand's philosophy states that the firm works at "the vital intersection of nature and culture." Since natural and cultural systems are the forces that interact to create landscape, this may seem obvious. And yet landscape design in the last half century has shown that practitioners often understand nature but fail to see the cultural underpinnings of the landscapes they shape. Reed Hilderbrand is an exception to this trend.

1. J. B. Jackson, *Discovering the Vernacular Landscape*. New Haven, Conn: Yale University Press, 1984, xi.

Too often, cultural matters are thought to be the purview of historic preservationists. As J. B. Jackson suggests, more often than not it is only those sites with documented pasts whose history plays a part in planning for their futures. But what landscape has not been touched by human intervention? It is precisely these human responses to natural conditions, often subtle or nearly invisible, sometimes embedded beneath the site's surface, that serve as the catalyst for this firm's nuanced approach to complex landscapes.

Reed Hilderbrand often engages in work in significant historic sites, like Mount Auburn Cemetery in Cambridge, Massachusetts, and the Arnold Arboretum in Jamaica Plain, Massachusetts. Important modernist sites have included Philip Johnson's 1964 Beck House and a 1981 Edward Larrabee Barnes house, both in Dallas, Texas, and I. M. Pei and Sasaki Dawson DeMay's Christian Science Plaza in Boston, Massachusetts. Gary Hilderbrand and Doug Reed have, through advocacy, scholarly works, and completed projects, contributed to the larger successes of a movement to understand, interpret, steward, adapt, and preserve cultural landscapes. Yet they do not specialize in historic landscapes; this is an approach they employ for each landscape project they undertake. They see all landscapes as having meaningful cultural and ecological content.

Using research tools employed in history, geography, archaeology, and other humanistic disciplines, the firm first identifies a landscape's essential character, which is necessarily shaped by former uses. That discovery often becomes a starting point in developing a plan for the future, as it did, for example, at Louisiana's Baton Rouge International School, where Reed Hilderbrand, with Trahan Architects, mapped drainage patterns in suburban Baton Rouge to find that the property's stormwater, which originates as a pond left from previous farming operations, follows a course through city drainage channels, local bayous, rivers, and ultimately to

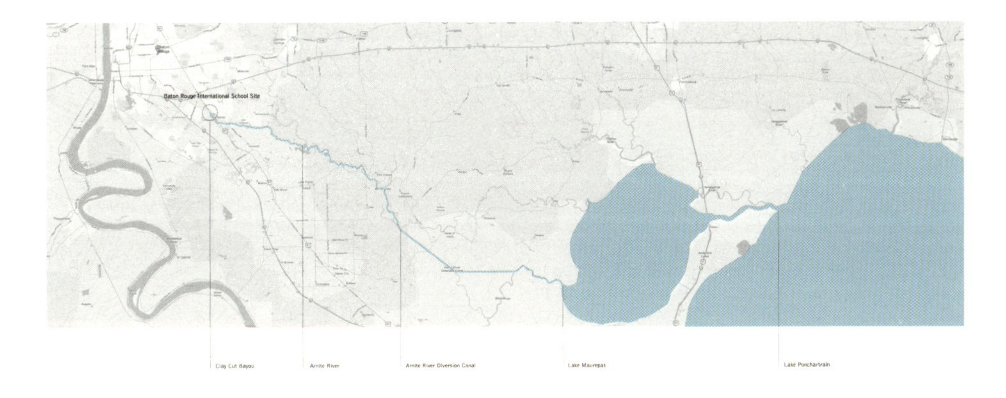

(facing page) Greenlee House, in Dallas, Texas, designed by Edward Larabee Barnes and completed in 1981. Walls, terraces, and planting were developed by Reed Hilderbrand in 2010.

(left) Baton Rouge International School contextual drainage diagram, by Trahan Architects and Reed Hilderbrand.

Lake Pontchartrain before finally reaching the Gulf of Mexico. The school's leaders, struck by the revelation of this larger connected drainage system, saw it as a metaphor for their approach to early and middle-school education, which posits language as a primary vehicle students can use to develop a sense of belonging to and understanding their place in a larger natural and cultural order. The plan organizes buildings, circulation, and play around the flow of water on the site as a potent narrative for the campus design—it has given physical expression to the school's innovative approach to education.

Central to the firm's approach is the idea that all places are the result of a process akin to geologic deposition, with each successive group of inhabitants or users of the land marking or shaping the site in some way, visible or not. Over time, the remnants of occupation build up on a landscape, and one can, using a process somewhat like that of an archaeologist, translate the marks, or artifacts, to understand the various human and natural forces that have created it. In searching to read the landscape, Reed Hilderbrand documents these marks before engaging in an evaluative process to determine the genesis and potential meanings of each imprint, with the goal of prioritizing those meanings that hold the most significance. The designers then develop a logic for the integration of new forms and uses within the context of the natural and cultural systems that have defined a site's character. It is a strategy for opening a dialogue with what came before. This method encompasses an intensive, analytical investigation of the place under consideration, a process that reflects the close ties to academia of the firm's partners. It is a form of in-depth reading that cultural landscapes demand, and which Reed Hilderbrand pursues with vigilance.

One might argue that this kind of careful site study would not distinguish the work of Reed Hilderbrand from that of other landscape architectural firms; mapping, inventory, and analysis are parts of conventional practice, and all landscape architects perform these tasks routinely. But it is the mind-set, the filters, and the list of questions with which the firm approaches the steps of the investigative process that determines the utility and quality of the findings. This is, I believe, key to what distinguishes the Reed Hilderbrand approach, and in turn, the firm's work.

Nature / Culture Divide

May Theilgaard Watts introduced the concept of the landscape as an ecologically intelligible document in her landmark *Reading the Landscape: An Adventure in Ecology* (1957), illustrating concepts like how plant succession occurs and how cemeteries become the last refuge for native

plants. “The land,” Watts later wrote, “offers us good reading, outdoors, from a lively, unfinished manuscript.”[2] In her chapter on prairies, Watts had reported asking where she could find some real prairie, since the fencerows were almost gone. Having been directed to an abandoned cemetery, she found

> It became a pleasure to visit that cemetery, to observe the stages in the confrontation between natives and foreigners. The old marble tombstones were still fairly intact. The grave plantings of old roses, peonies, lilac bushes, six-inch-high purple irises, lilies of the valley, love-in-a-bathtub, still bloomed on schedule. Springtime was especially interesting. Then natives, like yellow stargrass, shooting star, and prairie phlox, wove their way among irises and old red peonies; and the prairie pungencies mingled with the nostalgic fragrances of lily of the valley and lilac. The tensions, the advances and retreats of the two elements of the vegetation, were worth watching even though the natives were sure to win out.[3]

Around the same time, the field of cultural landscape studies emerged, catalyzed by the British geographer W. G. Hoskins in his *Making of the English Landscape* (1955) and, most significantly for Americans, by J. B. Jackson, who wouldn’t accept association with any academic discipline. Hoskins proposed that

> The English landscape itself, to those who know how to read it aright, is the richest historical record we possess. There are discoveries to be made in it for which no written documents exist, or have ever existed. To write its history requires a combination of documentary research and of fieldwork, of laborious scrambling on foot wherever the trail may lead.[4]

“Reading the Land and its Symbols at the Prairie Plowing Match,”(left) an illustration in May Theilgaard Watts, *Reading the Landscape*, 1957.

Village settlement patterns in Kimbolton, Huntingdonshire (Cambridgeshire), England, an illustration in William Hoskins, *Making of the English Landscape*, 1955 (photograph from 1988 ed.).

2. May Theilgaard Watts, *Reading the Landscape of America*. New York: Collier, 1975, v.
3. May Theilgaard Watts, *Reading the Landscape: An Adventure in Ecology*. New York: Macmillan, 1957, 129–30.
4. W. G. Hoskins. *The Making of the English Landscape*. Harmondsworth, U. K.: Penguin Books, 1970, 14–15.

Jackson enlightened subscribers to his journal *Landscape* on the lessons to be gleaned from reading American scenes through a cultural lens. He founded *Landscape* in 1951, and it was his very personal journalistic vehicle until his retirement in 1968. Jackson saw landscape as a "rich and beautiful book [that] is always open before us. We have but to learn to read it."[5] Geographer Peirce Lewis, paying homage to Jackson, writes that he "helped teach a generation of neophyte geographers that there was nothing disreputable about going outdoors and asking naïve questions about what one saw."[6] A generation of graduate students at both Berkeley and Harvard were also profoundly affected by Jackson—he taught a course on the American landscape at both institutions, traveling between them on his motorcycle, the better to read the country firsthand. (Reed took Jackson's course while at Harvard.)

The need to consider landscape as natural (the result of the actions of nature) as well as cultural (the result of the actions of people) became critical during the second half of the twentieth century as social and ecological complexities expanded at an alarming rate. Two separate movements, environmental conservation and cultural preservation, took the national stage and propelled alternative ways of operating in the design disciplines. Divisions became pronounced, and narrow ideologies often prevailed. The denizens of each flank held convictions that shaped advocacy and action somewhat narrowly within their own realms, rather than as the result of interactions between the two.

May Watts favored an ecological filter in her investigation, and Hoskins and Jackson privileged cultural readings. What links them is that all three understood the systemic unity of the resources they studied. They believed that the complex beauty of landscape lay in the interaction between people and place, not in these elements viewed in isolation. This is why their strategies for reading the landscape are such valuable lessons in academia and, by extension, as models for practice today.

Convergence

> Past and present should often be commingled, not separated. Every trace we inherit is a testament not only to the spirit of the past but to our present perspectives.... The past belongs to everyone: the need to return home, to recall the view, to refresh a memory, to retrace a heritage, is universal and essential.[7]
> —David Lowenthal

To appreciate Reed Hilderbrand's approach fully, it is useful to consider the context within which it arose.

5. J. B. Jackson, "The Need of Being Versed in Country Things," *Landscape* 1 (Spring 1951), 5.
6. Peirce F. Lewis, "Axioms for Reading the Landscape," in *Material Culture Studies in America*. Thomas J. Schlereth, ed. Nashville, Tenn.: American Association for State and Local History, 1982, 11.
7. David Lowenthal, "Dilemmas of Preservation," in Lowenthal and Marcus Binney, eds., *Our Past Before Us: Why Do We Save It?* London: Temple Smith, 1981, 213–37.

The 1960s and 1970s were times of unprecedented questioning and cultural turmoil for the nation as well as pivotal years for landscape architecture. The passage of the National Environmental Protection Act in 1969 signaled the federal government's commitment to protect the health of the nation's natural resources. With the publication of *Design with Nature* in the same year, Ian McHarg proclaimed an urgent need to incorporate nature in planning at many scales; his booming voice and potent book reached a national audience, even in the highest levels of the federal government. Some would come to use the word *palimpsest* to suggest the layered quality of the cultural landscape; McHarg introduced the notion of separating the natural systems of a site into discrete layers for analysis—a process of "peeling" sites as one might peel an onion.

Mapping vegetation patterns as a tool for planning that is rooted in the region's ecological systems. Potomac River Basin, an illustration in Ian McHarg, *Design with Nature*, 1967.

In Elizabeth Meyer's 2000 essay "The Post-Earth Day Conundrum: Translating Environmental Values into Landscape Design," the author recounts how during the previous three decades environmentalism shifted from a special-interest concern to a "central theme in American cultural consciousness and political discourse."[8] She illustrates how the profession of landscape architecture responded by incorporating ecological sciences into the curricula, and how landscape architects, in turn, planned designs with this new knowledge. It was during this period that Doug Reed and Gary Hilderbrand were pursuing their undergraduate and graduate studies and beginning their professional practice.

Valuing a site's cultural significance: Richard Haag's design of Gasworks Park, Seattle, Washington, 1975, incorporates remnants of the site's former industrial use.

> The practices of several landscape architects bridged the great divide between ecology and design and between science and art that characterized the profession in the 1970s. In constructing this bridge, a body of work has emerged that not only applies ecological values to a design language, but also suggests a strategy for breaking out of the restrictive tenets of modern art that so marginalized the landscape as a medium and subject.[9]

Meyer cites the work of Lawrence Halprin, George Hargreaves, Michael Van Valkenburgh, Susan Child (in whose firm Doug Reed was a principal), Ken Smith, and urban designer William Morrish. She singles out Richard Haag and Laurie Olin, noting that they "looked for material traces in the land's natural and cultural histories to develop a connection between humans and their constructed places."[10]

But what of the profession's response to the emergence of the historic and cultural landscape as a component equal in importance with aesthetic and ecological considerations of a project? We can date the movement for preservation on a national level to the passage of the 1966 National Historic Preservation Act, which protected designated historic and archaeological sites and required federal agencies to evaluate the impact of all federally funded or permitted projects on historic properties

8. Elizabeth K. Meyer, "The Post-Earth Day Conundrum: Translating Environmental Values into Landscape Design," in Michael Conan, ed., *Environmentalism in Landscape Architecture*. Washington, D.C.: Dumbarton Oaks, 2000, 187.
9. Ibid., 187–88.
10. Ibid., 192.

(Section 106 Review). However significant this legislation, though, in the first decade of environmental awakening, historic preservation—the protection of *cultural* resources—was not on the radar of most landscape architecture practitioners or academics. Nor was the belief that landscape architects needed any particular skills or rigorous methodology to evaluate a site with significant history. At the time, the preservation of historic landscapes was primarily the province of the National Park Service and historic-preservation organizations. In university landscape architecture programs, new coursework was responding to the need for natural-resource conservation and natural-systems assessment, but the study of cultural systems was not given parallel emphasis.

Landscape Architecture magazine, responding to the national Bicentennial, first acknowledged the importance of the historic landscape for the profession in the May 1976 issue, titled "The Emerging Science of Garden Preservation," which excerpted presentations from a 1975 Dumbarton Oaks conference cosponsored with the National Trust for Historic Preservation and the American Horticultural Society. These case studies illustrated, for the most part, the more technical aspects of preservation (pollen analysis at Pompeii, historic archaeology at Carter's Grove, Colonial Williamsburg in Virginia, photogrammetry to record Navajo cliff dwellings). But *Landscape Architecture* editor Grady Clay was quick to point out, in his opening editorial—"Whose Time Is This Place?"—that the task of protecting the nation's landscape heritage was not as straightforward as it might seem. He quoted a letter from J. B. Jackson, warning of the sterility of preserved or reconstructed landscapes, writing that "the power which an ancient environment possesses to command our affection and respect derives from its having accepted change of function (and not) from having been isolated and protected."[11] And Clay noted that James Marston Fitch, in his Dumbarton Oaks essay, had challenged Williamsburg as "a frozen, sweet-smelling, touristic scene," one that had "almost certainly generated profound public misconceptions of the American past…."[12]

To be sure, there were a handful of landscape architects working in the arena of historic and cultural landscapes who raised awareness within the profession, through advocacy and through the example of their work, which applied rapidly developing theory, techniques, and approaches. But the subject of a landscape's cultural assets as potentially meaningful design generators continued to be largely ignored; ecologically based design continued to dominate practice.

By January 1981, however, *Landscape Architecture* magazine announced that "Preservation Leaps the Garden Wall," and was publishing articles on a wide range of project types, from parks to vernacular landscapes. When the July/August 1987 issue addressed the theme "Preservation: Defining an Ethic," editor Susan Frey suggested that it would reveal that

11. Grady Clay, "Whose Time Is This Place?," *Landscape Architecture*, May 1976, 218.
12. Ibid.

The Great Lawn, c. 1911–1916, Stan Hywet Hall, Akron, Ohio, designed by Warren Manning.

preservation had "outgrown its specialty status to join the ethical underpinnings of the profession."[13] Included in the issue was an article chronicling the work of Child Associates in developing a comprehensive master plan for the Warren Manning–designed Stan Hywet Hall, an estate in Akron, Ohio. Doug Reed led the documentary and planning effort for this project, which received the highest recognition from the ASLA in their awards program that year.

In that same issue, Catherine Howett challenged preservation practice, arguing that those doing the preserving "are reluctant to acknowledge, much less to underscore within the interpretive programs of restoration projects, two critical realities: the limits of what we know now or are likely ever to know about the original landscape, and the strenuous artifice we use to try and create the illusion that places out of the past can be accessible to us in precisely the same way that they were for those who brought them into being long ago."[14] Howett proposed that instead of creating landscapes that give the illusion of verisimilitude, we design them in a way that is an "honest expression of our need to make the past useful to us—in order to celebrate the values that our society has discovered in certain landscapes and historic moments."[15]

In the early 1990s the National Park Service began the Historic Landscape Initiative, directed by Charles Birnbaum, which developed standards, practices, and preservation briefs for research, analysis, and decision making related to the country's cultural landscapes. Slowly, over the next decades, landscape architects developed more work for historic properties, but typically it was by the same small group of firms. That virtually all firms were in fact working with cultural landscapes, and that the expertise required to do so should be part of every professional's arsenal of skills, was still not widely accepted. Within the profession, this area of practice

13. Susan Frey, "Preservation: Defining an Ethic," *Landscape Architecture*, July/August 1987, 33.
14. Catherine Howett, "Second Thoughts," *Landscape Architecture*, July/August 1987, 55.
15. Ibid.

continued to be viewed as a specialization of the few offices that chose to do scholarly research to develop special preservation treatments.

In December 1998, *Landscape Architecture* reported on a forum titled "Is Historic Preservation Design?" Gary Hilderbrand, one of the participants, responded in this way: "I find more parallels than differences between the intellectual activities of design and preservation. Maybe the question should be rephrased: 'Are good designers facing up to preservation needs?'"[16] Charles Birnbaum answered in the negative, saying that most landscape architects who develop rehabilitation plans for significant sites have "great reverence for historic places" but that their designs are "tepid," "safe," and "second-rate."[17] Hilderbrand closed the discussion on an optimistic note, predicting that debates over balancing flexibility or strictures in the Secretary of the Interior's Guidelines for the Treatment of Cultural Landscapes (1996) would raise the level of inquiry, and hopefully the quality of the work, being done in the field:

> To many designers, standards and guidelines feel like constraints. They do constrain process. But they also make us all more responsible for researching and documenting the artifacts and spatial patterns that we find on every site, designed or not. Eventually, these processes become not constraints but guarantees that we know in great detail what is being changed. We now have a seriousness about approaches to landscape research on sites, and a recognition that history requires diverse methods, diverse points of view, and diverse constituencies. The influence of cultural landscape studies has informed a generation of designers who can read the history in the landscape, and who are passionate about the character of localities.[18]

Hilderbrand's comments suggest that the guidelines should bring about seriousness in the way designers approach cultural landscapes, so that when changes are proposed, they convey a thoughtful and thorough exploration of a site's history and consider the impact of change upon its essential character. In other words, he suggests that the guidelines would help designers "do the right thing," based on an ethic that values a landscape's integrity and the meanings it holds and has held for its users. And perhaps this is the heart of the matter.

I would question whether the standards have generated the diverse approaches and the seriousness Hilderbrand anticipated, and whether these new landscape "readers" have gone on to create the quality of design he had hoped for. Instead, in many cases, the products of research, interpretation, and design have led to predictable, limited treatments with equally limited impacts. In the end, this has frequently limited what the visitor experiences. The deficiency often results from the specialization of the landscape architect involved, and from the attitude that if NPS

16. Gary Hilderbrand, quoted in J. William Thompson, "Is Historic Preservation Design?" *Landscape Architecture*, December 1998, 56.
17. Charles Birnbaum, ibid., 58.
18. Gary Hilderbrand, ibid., 80.

Historical patterns at Bennington College, Bennington, Vermont: Reed Hilderbrand's site analysis documents features from five eras of development.

methodology is followed, the solution will emerge. The work of Reed Hilderbrand illustrates what can be achieved when process and decision making are not circumscribed, and the standards simply help to identify the meaningful content of a place that must undergo change.

What Reed Hilderbrand does in learning about a landscape's cultural and ecological patterns, in reading its content, its context, its materials, its dynamics, its ephemeral qualities, its internal relationships, its discrepancies, and its discontinuities, cannot be prescribed or described. It is a process finely tuned by practice. It requires tenacity, rapt attention, and the ability to see relationships where they might not be obvious. One must dig deeply to find what distinguishes some landscapes.

This ethos is informed by the sensibilities and experiences of the firm's principals, who are no more preservation specialists than they are ecologists. They are careful, exacting generalists who believe in the power of conviction and a strong argument. Doug Reed and Gary Hilderbrand have managed to collect around them a group of kindred spirits. These talented women and men share a set of core values, and work in a studio environment where mentorship assures that the methods of inquiry, of exploration, of testing, and of processing flow from one hand to another within the design team. This kind of esprit is difficult to create, and requires vigilance to sustain. What makes it work for this team is the genuine love of landscape and the understanding that each new site affords the promise that they will discover a compelling reading with unforeseen power and personality as the basis of design.

It is worth exploring how they pursue this approach in four very different settings.

Hilltop Arboretum

Hilltop Arboretum, a 14-acre property along the natural levee of the Mississippi River in the southern reaches of Baton Rouge, serves as an arboretum and outdoor classroom for Louisiana State University (LSU) students of landscape architecture and for the broader community. It was developed by Emory Smith, an esteemed horticulturist and proponent of landscape design, who made his home there in the 1930s and who continued shaping a subtle yet powerful landscape defined by native Louisiana plants until his death in 1984.

Smith was a master plantsman who seized the horticultural opportunity presented by the site's ravines and uplands, and their diverse soils, to cultivate a wide range of plants. In the 1970s he offered the property to LSU's school of landscape architecture for the teaching of plants. It became a beloved destination for students, and several generations of designers have been influenced by Smith's philosophy of a humble life surrounded by native plants, and by his approach to design based on deep knowledge and empathy for the relationship between plant communities and their cultural requirements, which Hilltop embodied long before the ecological movement took flight. In 1981, at the age of ninety, Smith gave the land to LSU so that it would continue as a laboratory for plant classes.

In 2010 the Friends of Hilltop commissioned Reed Hilderbrand to implement several projects including the replanting of the "Cathedral," a high-canopy glade devastated by hurricanes, and to conceptualize the underdeveloped highland that forms nearly half of the site.

The firm began by considering the entire site and its situation within nearby watersheds, even though the commission was primarily focused on discrete portions of the property. Looking into the land's geographical

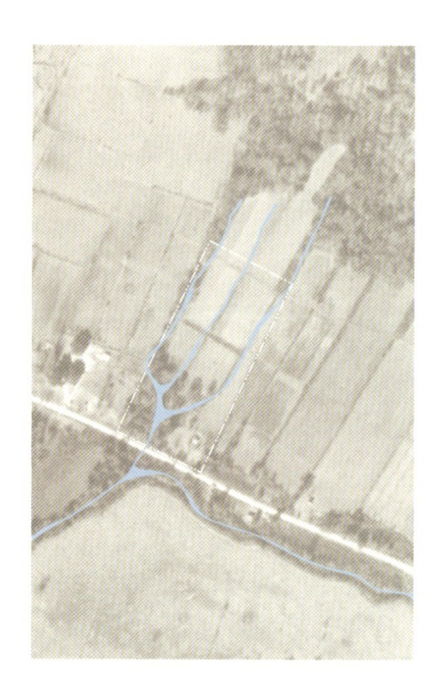

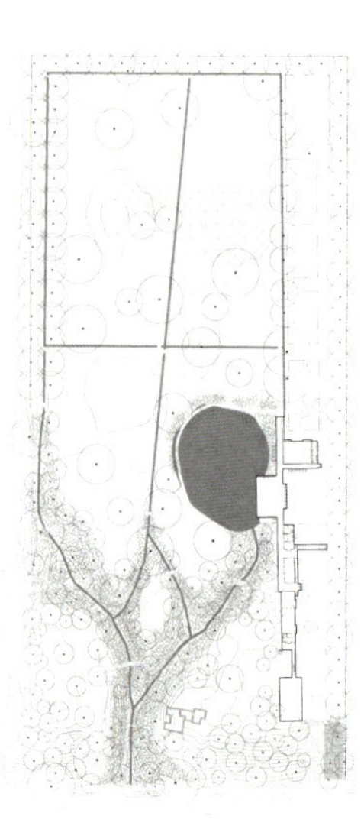

Three illustrations of Hilltop Arboretum, Baton Rouge, La. A typical ravine cutting through upland (left), a hydrology map drawn over an aerial photograph (center), and Reed Hilderbrand's concept plan (right) organized around the site's historic drainage patterns.

context and history, they turned to USGS maps and aerial photographs dating from the 1930s, before Smith's residency. From these, they developed diagrams of the larger drainage patterns that had shaped Hilltop's landscape, primarily channels on the highland that had been added in the twentieth century when the land was still being used for agricultural production. These ditches had fed into—if not created—the ravines, the most dramatic feature of the property.

These patterns formed the skeleton of their plan for the upland plateau, which would include types of meadows endemic to Louisiana, an area of lowland vegetation along the restored and new drainage channels, and new pedestrian paths. Other areas, for horticultural production and teaching display, would lie efficiently along the southern edge of the site, as an extension of other more recent interventions forming the programmatic spine of the arboretum—the entry drive, parking lot, and administrative and educational buildings.

Reed Hilderbrand's plan starts with patterns resembling those that farmers utilize to respond to the natural fall of the land, and with the impulse to drain it efficiently during the heavy south Louisiana rainy seasons. In fact, their design makes drainage the predominant and unifying element in the site, declaring water the progenitor of landforms, particularly of the ravines Smith had exploited for the development of a great variety of plants. The scheme employs very few gestures—ditches, hedgerows, paths, and open spaces—which join with the restored ravines to evoke the agrarian past at the same time that they preserve Smith's spatial and horticultural intentions. This design concept enables a more complete realization of Smith's skills at cultivating native plants according to soil type and moisture content, topographic aspect and orientation, and vegetative communities with like cultural requirements. By expanding Hilltop's horticultural offerings to include a more comprehensive list of plants identified with the state's grasslands and wetlands, it fully aligns with the founder's devotion to Louisiana's native plants and his philosophy of planting design.

River House

River House is no more a historic site than anywhere else in the Commonwealth of Massachusetts—the entire state was settled early, and its landscape has absorbed many layers of habitation and alteration. Upon first study, this 43-acre property appeared straightforward: a broad expanse of meadow and lowland woods along the Westport River, where the client intended to build a weekend home. But closer scrutiny revealed strange anomalies, suggesting that the site had been meddled with in

Head of Westport looking west from just above the Wolf Pit School across the river to the Bell School. Courtesy Westport Historical Society, Westport, Mass.

Remnant fieldstone walls and hedgerows uncovered at River House in Westport, Mass. (right), descend from nineteenth-century agricultural patterns in nearby Head of Westport (left).

some important ways. There were landforms in the woodlands that didn't make sense as results of natural processes like glaciation. And there were large stands of eastern white pine in sections of the property—which in this particular area of the state's south coast indicate disturbance, specifically by sand and gravel mining: the tree is the only one that can establish itself in the depleted condition in which mining leaves the land.

Over the course of several years of site reconnaissance, land management, and inquiry into the history of the place, Reed Hilderbrand discovered that the gently rolling, low-lying features had in fact been shaped by mining operations in the mid-twentieth century, during which some thirty feet of elevation had been removed, leaving spoils of stone and bedrock outcroppings across the property. After the mining had ceased, a resident farmer had restored 19 acres along the river, making a field for crops by rebuilding the soils. This had left a landscape of lowland woods covering hummocks of spoils, with streams and pockets of wetlands, and a field defined by vegetation that had been allowed to grow unchecked for decades. In fact, the vegetation communities reflected the varying moisture levels and soil profiles left by mining and farming, creating an uneven matrix across the site.

The work that most revealed the site's potential, and disclosed the story of its evolution, involved managing this vegetation over three years, well before beginning the design of the house. While the field offered a great expanse of open space that allowed long views of sky and meadow, its edges were choked with wild rose, bittersweet, catbrier, and poison ivy. Aggressively removing this invasive and undesirable vegetation, and hauling out years' worth of dead trees and broken limbs, made remnants of stone walls and cherry hedgerows indicating the agrarian past more visible. This work established the full dimensions of the field, and allowed views of the river through the edited riparian edges, including views down a several-mile stretch to the southwest.

Following extensive vegetation removal, the field's newly defined spatial form and the views across it guided the siting of the house, drive, and vegetable garden and the layout of an extensive path system. The long, low-slung dwelling sits in the meadow, with its western face open to river views. Mown paths lead out from the house into the meadow to connect with a walk around the field's edges. Ultimately this network of paths will lead to boardwalks through the lowland woods and wetlands that now cover the spoils of the mining operation—a system that will make the site's unusual and varied history legible and accessible by uncovering and maintaining the features of former eras.

Despite its dramatic and brutal treatment, Reed Hilderbrand recognized the site's compelling beauty as worthy of preserving and interpreting. In certain lights and atmospheric conditions one can barely see the profile of the house on the horizon as one approaches from the entrance drive. The structure hovers lightly within the meadow's rolling contours; the stone boundary walls and treelines evoke the familiar agrarian pattern in this region, as if no recent effort had been required. There is a sense of connectedness—a harmonious continuum—between the new habitation and the property's earlier evolution. You feel that it was always there, waiting for the designers to wrestle out the character shaped by generations of mining and farming, and that it is now fitted to a new way of living on the land.

MIT North Court and Main Street

Pre-construction view of the proposed MIT North Court site with Koch Institute building envelope nearing completion. © Pictometry, 2009

The firm's commitment to extracting useful evidence from sites and reinterpreting broader cultural patterns also extends to educational institutions—and to intensely urban sites—as in the case of their work for the Massachusetts Institute of Technology. The American academic campus has evolved through a set of distinctive spatial types, many of which descend from European examples: quadrangles, courts, ovals and circles, yards, and street networks. Reed Hilderbrand's undertaking at MIT upholds and reflects these traditions while also making carefully studied departures from them.

At MIT the firm's study of the City of Cambridge and university context enlarged the vision of the site for the new Koch Institute for Integrative Cancer Research. Planning agreements with the city dictated that the new building form a block-long street wall. Parking covered a sizeable section of this part of the campus, obstructing desired pedestrian movement. The potential to improve a far larger area than that of the new institute became clear. As the firm's studies took shape, they made a compelling case for a project that would become the last significant quadrangle inside the superblock known as the MIT Main Group.

The Main Group—comprising neoclassical buildings that define courts organized along a long interior spine collectively known as the Infinite Corridor—is a well-known paradigm in the world of campus planning.

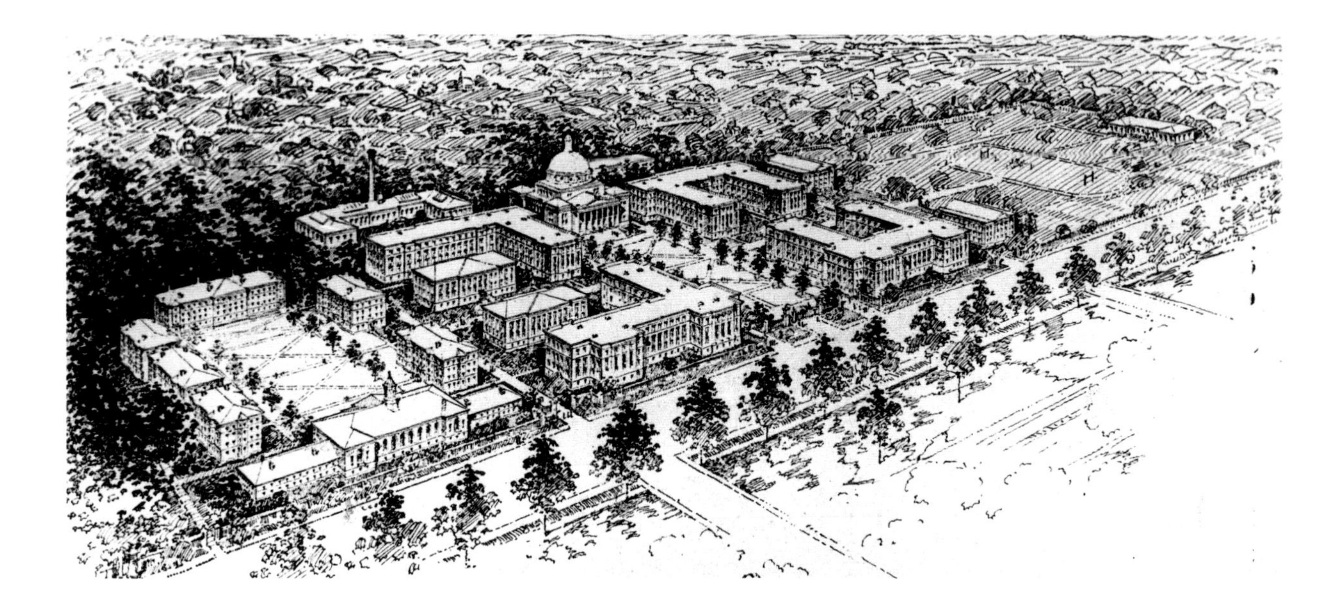

Unidentified artist, proposal for Massachusetts Institute of Technology campus, Cambridge, Massachusetts. Courtesy MIT Museum

William Welles Bosworth's original buildings combined an imposing classical scale and axial order with flexible arrangements for classrooms, laboratories, and offices. Nearly one hundred years later, an extensive tree canopy surrounds this colossal web of buildings and courts and has established an indelible physical identity for MIT's technology, science, and engineering legacy.

Reed Hilderbrand's documentary work also encompassed MIT's modern legacy. Between 1916 and 1960, additions to the Main Group primarily yielded rectangular courts of varying size. With 1960s expansion, buildings by I. M. Pei pursued allegiance to the orthogonal corridor but with such notable differences as the Earth Sciences building, a tower rising out of the university's building fabric. In the more open courts associated with Pei's work, two well-known designers planted London plane trees in single or double rows: Dan Kiley in Eastman Court, and Stuart Dawson of Sasaki Dawson & DeMay in McDermott Court. While Eastman Court evoked a Euclidean geometry of path and lawn, the slightly later McDermott Court was conceived as an open paved forecourt with a punctuating circular figure of lawn.

These simple iconic patterns, and their histories, formed the backbone of the Reed Hilderbrand plan to wrestle the irregular outlines of the proposed North Court into coherence. Two geometries came together: the historic orthogonal order of the campus, and a much older one—from the eighteenth-century alignment of Cambridge's Main Street—reinforced by the new Koch Institute.

The first move in organizing the court was the development of a wide promenade that forms a straight edge against the irregular shapes of Frank Gehry's cacophonous Stata Center, at once relieving the insistence of the building's geometries and material palette and grounding it in a larger context. The second strategy involved making an expansive lawn crossed by a network of walkways. Neither of these types—the promenade as an extended gathering space, nor the crisscross lawn—exists precisely within the traditions of MIT's spaces. Both make use of abstracted campus vocabularies, but they arise more specifically out of the circumstances of circulation requirements. Planting of the court makes reference to the traditions of the Bosworth, Kiley, and Sasaki periods of using canopy trees in linear arrangements to define space. The scheme's logic is clear: direct and shaded perambulation at the edges, and nonsymmetrical, irregular passage through the middle, open to the sky.

Together, these actions show the analytical rigor this firm brings to its work, leaving little to chance and producing emphatic, nuanced inventions rooted in type but adjusted or reinvented. Each insertion is studied for its relationship to found conditions and particular discoveries. Perhaps the campus is the place where this approach displays its greatest potency, since its inhabitants are transient. Populations come and go at a university, but memories endure, and spatial patterns evolve even as they remain rooted in type and history. The capacity to absorb and adjust while enhancing the public memory of a place is what this firm seeks, and what its work seems to achieve.

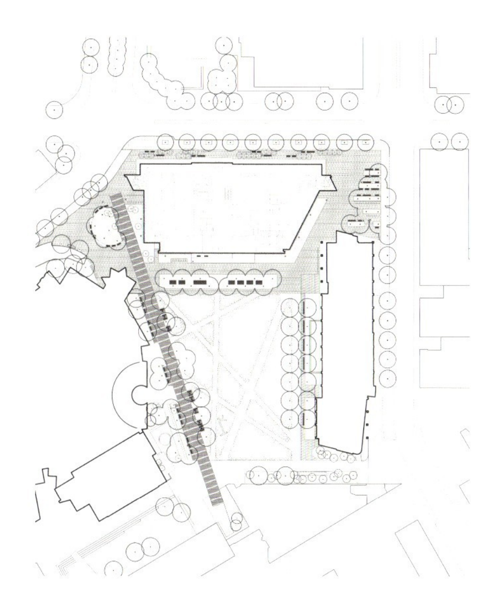

MIT's North Court promenade links the Main Group and Cambridge Main Street, in plan (below) and as executed (above).

President's Park South Design Competition

In May 2011 the National Capital Planning Commission (NCPC) announced an impressive list of finalists in a design competition for President's Park South—a 52-acre historic site, including the Ellipse, between the White House grounds and the Washington Monument.[19] Involved in the selection process were the National Park Service and the NCPC Interagency Security Task Force in cooperation with the United States Secret Service. The design brief emphasized the security of the president, First Family, and executive branch, while preserving the historic integrity of this highly significant landscape and tourist destination.

In his presentation, Gary Hilderbrand described this iconic landscape as having a "two hundred year period of significance," making it impossible to prescribe a preservation treatment that would favor any particular period. He professed the firm's long-held belief that landscapes of great heritage must accommodate change, as all landscapes must, and that contemporary adjustments can be made in ways that bring greater value to the heritage we inherit from prior generations.

The firm's approach to the competition was based on the belief that this site provides one of the most potent symbols of American democracy, the view of the south front of the White House, and therefore should convey as much free and flexible access as possible. They based their proposal on

19. Finalists were Hood Design Studio, Michael Van Valkenburgh Associates, Rogers Marvel Architects (the eventual winner), Sasaki Associates, and Reed Hilderbrand.

(above, left) *Aerial View of the White House Grounds, Looking Northwest.* Washington, D.C., ca 1986. Library of Congress, Prints and Photographs Division, HABS DC, WASH, 649-5

(above, right) Oblique aerial rendering showing the rehabilitated Ellipse and proposed pedestrian mall from Reed Hilderbrand's competition entry.

(right) Reed Hilderbrand's proposed site plan.

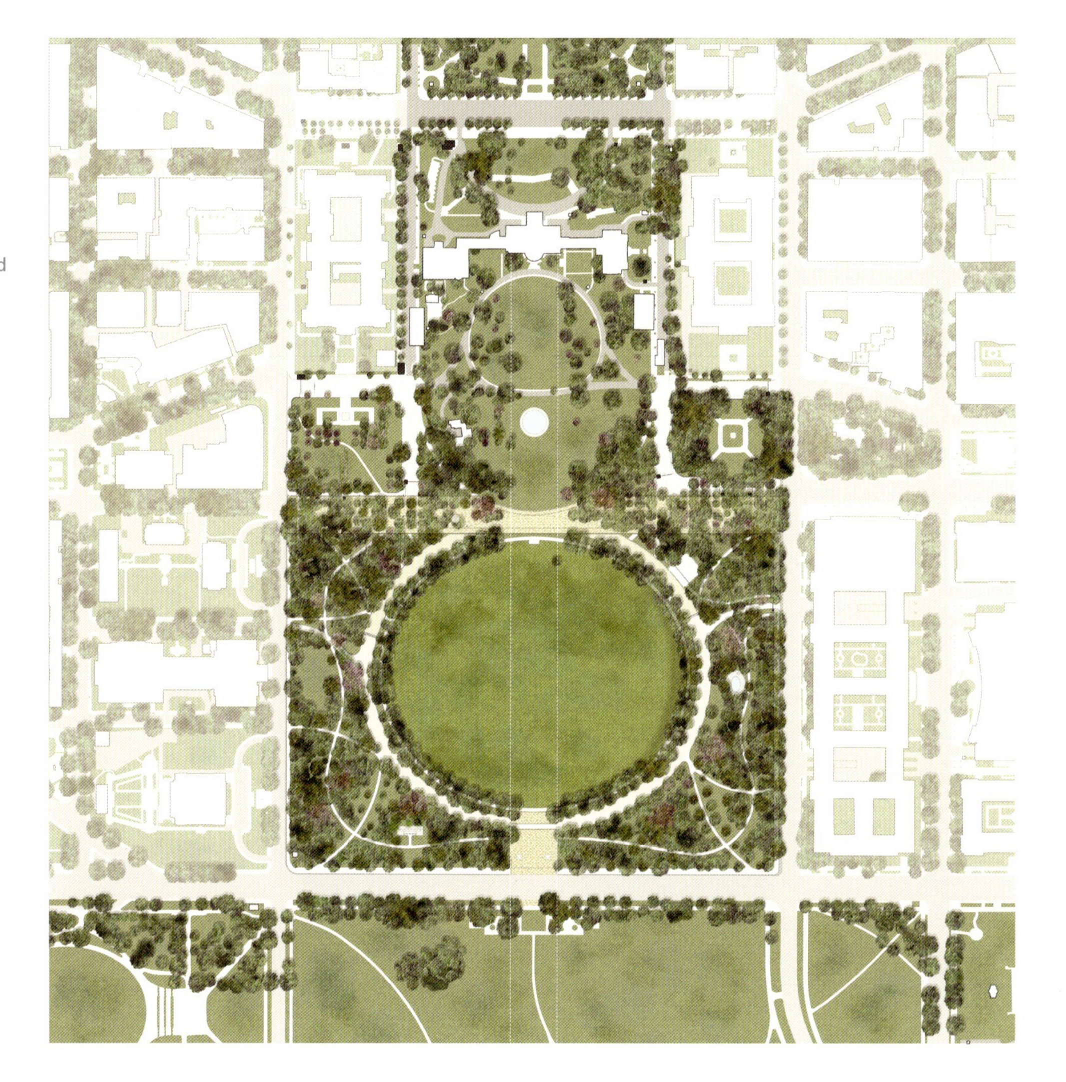

the promenade, a familiar urban form that supports public movement and gathering, civic gesture, and public decorum. Their solution resolves the present and the future demands for security and public access through the development of a new pedestrian plaza at the point where the southern end of the White House grounds meets the top of the Ellipse—"the place where the President meets the People," according to Hilderbrand—opening E Street to pedestrian and bike traffic. In essence, the promenade serves as the connective tissue that joins all of this site's diverse parts.

The scheme recalibrates the vast scale of the site by developing a pervasive tree canopy throughout the new E Street Plaza and by restoring the elms around the Ellipse. It resolves the potentially thorny conflict between access and security in a restrained and expansive space imbued with the character associated with the best of urban parks—diverse species of trees for seasonal interest, places for private conversations and group gatherings, and, most importantly, space for American and international visitors to photograph the White House from its most iconic and familiar viewpoint. The proposal combines these features in contemporary and sustainable ways that arise from the particular requirements and conditions of this location, thereby making a twenty-first-century landscape firmly rooted in tradition and embodying the democratic ideal.

Reed Hilderbrand's body of work, and the analytical and creative thinking upon which it is based, are testament to the fact that the deeper the exploration of a site's evolution—always the result of natural and cultural processes—the richer the designed landscape. Within professional practice today, I am not certain that the impulse to read the landscape as prelude to design has advanced so far as one would have hoped. And the use of that discovered "text" as a critical source of substantive meaning for design is even less common. As J. B. Jackson suggests, it is a matter of having the courage to speculate responsibly, and then the imagination to know what to do with the findings.

In the case of the work of Reed Hilderbrand the question *Is Preservation Design?* need not be asked. Design is the core of all the firm's projects, and the conviction is clear. They value history. They seek new paradigms of form, rooted in the history of a place and responsive to its new uses. Each site is a complex document. Only a careful and experienced reader knows how to mine the languages of time and place, and only designers with a thoughtful, creative, and synthetic approach can forge a refined and clearly articulated design expression out of a site's cultural and ecological stories. To read in this manner, one must be humble, one must be quiet, and one must have a sense of those places that have shaped one's own mind's eye. Doug Reed and Gary Hilderbrand and their firm read very well.

(top) Eugéne Atget (1857–1927), *Jardin du Luxembourg*, 1902, albumen silver print from glass negative, image: 8 11/16 x 6 15/16 inches, Gilman Collection, Museum Purchase, 2005. Image © The Metropolitan Museum of Art: Art Resource, New York

Traditional promenades, including the Luxembourg Gardens and the Tuileries, served as precedent for the proposed E Street corridor between the White House grounds and the Ellipse.

(bottom) Detail cross-section elevation of the proposed President's Park South Promenade.

Niall Kirkwood

On Making: Tectonic Clarity

At the beginning of a woodland path at the Sterling and Francine Clark Art Institute in western Massachusetts there is a telling moment: A wood and metal footbridge adjusts its shape and dimensions to account for the trunk of an existing tree. On one edge the gridded side rail stops short of the tree; on the other, the pathway's smooth wooden planks slide past it. A simple gesture, perhaps, which may go unnoticed by most who visit the Clark's grounds. Yet the form and material of the path invite us to directly engage an individual tree in the course of a woodland stroll. This is no accident, no slip of the designer's hand. Rather, it reveals close and intimate attention to what I will refer to here as a *tectonics* of construction—a studied interest in the expressive potential of construction's pragmatic realities, including the resolution of landform and drainage, vegetation, structure, and building material. The elaboration of a comprehensive design language rooted in making but deployed in the service of experiential qualities is a characteristic found consistently in the work of Reed Hilderbrand.

A footbridge fitted to existing trees marks the beginning of the woodland trail network at The Clark.

This one moment in the Clark's landscape also speaks of the firm's deep engagement with the construction process itself, of their devotion to building durably, and to their commitment to work closely with those who carry out the making of the work. Their approach encompasses issues of authenticity, the sensuous characteristics of materials, the craft of fabrication, and modes of assembly. This requires profound investments of energy, resources, and patience, and a deep understanding of design history and building traditions, leavened with as much practical experience on site as any designer can muster.

The work of Reed Hilderbrand always exhibits tectonic clarity, whether it is shaping an urban square, a city street, a campus, or a woodland path and footbridge. *Tectonic* derives partly from the Greek *tektōn*,[1] signifying a carpenter or builder yet connoting more broadly the 'maker,' in the poetic sense. My formulation, "tectonic clarity," suggests two meanings. The first refers to a design methodology in which one begins with a philosophy of construction and assembly, and only then reviews all decisions on a project so as to maintain consistency, quality, integrity, and a clear point of view about how things are made in the finished work. Kenneth Frampton championed this approach in *Studies in Tectonic Culture*,[2] where he argued that architecture's formal language is rooted in the evolution of structural logics and constructed material character; modernization, in Frampton's view, enables these logics to be adapted and expanded through advances in material science and engineering as well as through improvements in industrial capacity. Frampton was directly rebutting the prevailing focus at the time on the primacy of site, program, or spatial patterns in shaping form.

The second meaning of "tectonic clarity," one more closely tied to landscape architecture, derives from the deployment of carefully devised and integrated systems to reorganize surfaces and spaces so that they perform mechanically and biologically: the gradients and dimensional characteristics of walking and driving surfaces; the overt expression and systematic assembly of drainage and subsurface elements; the provision of moisture and soil structure to sustain the healthy growth of trees; and the assembly of these into larger integrated systems.

In the work of Reed Hilderbrand, one sees tectonic clarity in a broad range of landscape conditions, types, and project scales. I think of such individual elements as the translucent discs set into the lawn at Harvard's Naito/Bauer Laboratories to bring daylight to underground laboratories—shaped with such care as to reveal the complexity of a landscape built over a structure. The approach here relies on the coordination of elements on the laboratory's roof, including structural systems, utility networks, waterproofing membranes, the organization of structural and horticultural soils, and the precise layout and grading of surfaces such as brick paths

1. *Tektōn* is in turn closely related to the Greek *techne*, "artistic skill, art" and *technikos*, "artistically skillful, artistic, technical." See Eduard Sekler, "Structure, Construction, Tectonics," in Gyorgy Kepes (ed.), *Structure in Art and in Science.* New York: George Braziller, 1965.
2. Kenneth Frampton, *Studies in Tectonic Culture: The Poetics of Construction in Nineteenth and Twentieth Century Architecture.* Edited by John Cava. Cambridge, Mass.: MIT Press, 1995.

Surface qualities of wood and concrete at Boston's Liberty Wharf.

brick paths and grass panels. Ultimately this kind of applied rigor represents a reconsideration of terra firma, the makeup of a landscape's ground surface. While it does not relegate ecological considerations, economics, or visual/spatial values to the background, constructional logics prevail.

Central Wharf Plaza[3] in downtown Boston—that most common of public spaces, the urban plaza—demonstrates tectonic clarity through a highly ordered composition of common landscape components: a delicately graded paving field, stairs and ramps, seating, trees, and lights. The 14,000-square-foot plaza lies near the harbor, at the intersection of highly traveled streets and alongside the recently completed Rose Fitzgerald Kennedy Greenway. Its primary purpose is to serve as a platform for the heavy flow of pedestrians to the waterfront. A philosophy of "opening the works" guides the design: we are invited to regard the materials and their assembly as familiar, even timeless—yet carefully composed—urban fixtures. Here the designers are concerned less with economics (although they are still important) or approaches to consumption and sustainability than with a matter-of-fact approach to the individual refinement of each component part. Notably, canopy trees rise through a finished surface of granite paving setts without being surrounded by grates or tree guards, rendering a consistent stone carpet over the site, as if in reference to ancient paving techniques the world over. This surface is supported by a single engineered living-soil medium that performs structural, mechanical, hydrological, and horticultural tasks, allowing for the long-term maturation of two species of sizable oaks.

3. Central Wharf Plaza is an open space adjoining the Rose Fitzgerald Kennedy Greenway, the surface restoration completed as part of Boston's Big Dig, which transformed the city's downtown. While it is modest in size, the plaza's impact on this still confusing and incomplete civic district is important, demonstrating the potential of well-constructed urban space at the human scale. The project was completed with architects and urban planners Chan Krieger NBBJ.

Trees grow through a continuous field of granite paving at Central Wharf Plaza.

Step, wall, and rail connections at Harvard Naito/Bauer Laboratories.

These projects, and others in the firm's portfolio, exemplify a consistent drive both toward making new landscapes appear familiar and fitted, and toward reshaping mature landscapes so they may be seen anew. Their techniques and materials recall traditions; their interventions bring clear and incisive form to new uses without distracting from accumulated cultural value. These places—Central Wharf, Naito/Bauer, and the Clark's woodland walk—have a recognizable identity: assured and familiar, with a restrained material palette and construction vocabulary, but also astringent, sharp, and precise. The work, proceeding from explicit contract documents, is never quite removed from the act of construction itself. Detailed solutions to complex situations are often resolved in collaboration with contractors. Paradoxically, though, the firm's mastery of materials and construction techniques allows the designers to remain quite invisible. They seem committed to the task of making the complicated seem simple.

This balance of the assured and the astringent makes "constructional thinking" deeply embedded in their work, in both daily practice and personal aesthetic. The humility of their intentions reaches back into the traditions of landscape architecture, to common landscapes or the vernacular, even to such values as found in Shaker settlements, with their integrated and refined constructional language, in which buildings, furnishings, drainageways, boundary fences, production gardens, fields, and all the components of an essential infrastructure wring poetry out of economy and simplicity.[4]

4. The Shakers' dedication to hard work and perfection resulted in a unique range of practical design and handicraft styles. Their work is characterized by austerity and simplicity and has had a lasting influence on American design. By the middle of the twentieth century, as Shaker communities themselves were disappearing, some American collectors influenced by aspects of the modernist movement found themselves drawn to the spare Shaker artifacts and simple modest buildings.

Large oval storage box, probably New Lebanon, New York, circa 1820–1830, ash and white pine, original dark red paint, 12 x 20 x 15 inches, Jane Katcher Collection of Americana. Photograph courtesy David Schorsch and Eileen Smiles American Antiques

Carved wooden bowl, David Pye (20th century), collection of Robin Wood, United Kingdom

Continuity and Invention

Something else, too, is evident along the woodland path at the Clark: the influence of modernist ideas of landscape that speak directly to the logic of circulation found in the work of a master like Dan Kiley[5] and to Peter Walker's interest in surface manipulation.[6] This sense in the firm's work of balancing formal logics and historical grounding with an urgent, contemporary sensibility recalls the teachings of David Pye,[7] who wrote in the 1960s on ideas of workmanship, craft, and manufacturing in the post–World War Two industrial world. Even as he submitted to the formal and operational traditions of furniture design, Pye reframed the making of ordinary objects in radically modern terms, combining skilled handworking and machined precision. He considered the interweaving of the two as the embodiment of a truly modern approach to tectonics, distancing himself from the prevailing reliance on advanced and mechanized manufacturing. Pye is instructive here, for in Reed Hilderbrand's work one detects a similar balance.

There is an ease and comfort in this body of work that comes from seasoned experience, which makes the constituent materials on every site feel self-evident—the combined roughness and warmth of masonry revealed in how stone is shaped and set, the color and texture of spring vegetation enhanced through its placement against the horizon, or the patterns of light and shadow across a sloped grass plane. The firm's strenuous design invention encompasses editing, preserving, and manipulating ordinary landscape elements—acts that contribute to the work's sense of cultural continuity.

While these works are often grounded in traditional building practices and in the use of vernacular materials, each project subtly reinterprets constituent parts and construction methods in ways that make them visible, tangible, and meaningful once again. The firm does not fetishize materials; they explore them for their unique and enduring qualities.

5. Daniel Urban Kiley's (1912–2004), preeminent works have influenced both of the firm's partners.
6. Peter Walker, who taught both Doug Reed and Gary Hilderbrand at Harvard in the early 1980s, is one of the leading modernist landscape architects practicing today.
7. David Pye (1914–1993) was professor of furniture design at the Royal College of Art, London. For examples of his writings see *The Nature and Art of Workmanship*, Cambridge University Press, New York, 1978.

So much emphasis has been placed in our time on what is new and different that we overlook the expressive value of things that have remained essentially the same. By contrast, Reed Hilderbrand embraces the everyday characteristics of landscape and makes the ordinary and familiar exceptionally clear and contemporary.

The project at the Arnold Arboretum Leventritt Garden—its shrub and vine collection—for example, revises the New England fieldstone wall with tighter jointing and a more uniform vertical face. No less tactile or materially rich, the walls give the project historical context, yet mark it as clearly contemporary. They provide level ground for organizing the collection following the ancient technique of terracing. The walls' elongated, slightly rotated geometry and their crisply defined linear edges set flush with grade give presence to the site's gentle slope. The sloping walks recall the great tradition of making garden ramps for spaces of cultivation, promenading, and spectacle.

Immediately identifiable, these techniques seem to need little interpretation. In weaving old traditions into contemporary practice, the firm may claim to be defining new ones.

Fieldstone walls articulate terraces for production and sloping walks for strolling and garden maintenance at the Arnold Arboretum Leventritt Garden.

A granite wall marks the entry to new interment sites along the woodland walk at Mount Auburn Cemetery.

At Mount Auburn Cemetery[8], in Cambridge, Massachusetts, the long arcing space of new interment sites engages the visitor sensuously and intellectually, making explicit the terms in which Reed Hilderbrand has conceived the project—as a critical reappraisal of the history of arboreta, contemplative cemeteries, and strolling gardens. In a section of Mount Auburn with gently rolling topography, and sheltered by a pervasive canopy, what appears to be a precisely graded, curving path is itself a burial ground, inserting two hundred crypts under the lawn itself. The names of the buried are engraved in shared commemoration on four vertical granite markers along the path, defining a long narrow space within the less clearly ordered pattern of surrounding grave markers.

Offering a familiar experience of passage and reflection within feet of a busy city street, the walk carves through alternating groves of native trees and shrubs. The lushness of the enclosing vegetation and the sequence of carefully framed views of nearby Halcyon Lake promote introspection within a narrow edge of the historic grounds. Understanding the balance of integration and differentiation in this work gains power from familiarity with the symbolic and aesthetic threads that run through the cemetery—which contains the burial sites of the architect Charles Bulfinch and the

8. Mount Auburn Cemetery was founded in 1831. The founders, believing that the cemetery should be a retreat also for the living, embellished the natural topography with plantings, monuments, fences, fountains, and chapels.

painter Winslow Homer—paired with a conviction that Mount Auburn is a living, evolving landscape.

As the work at Mount Auburn illustrates, when faced with new project types and programs—or ones that are repeated—Reed Hilderbrand turns to rigorous research, studying what the firm and others have done before, to understand what continues to be meaningful today. To the visitor the resolution is simple and beautiful. But in the engagement of the visitor with the physical and conceptual orders of the work, there is more. In the firm's own words, there is the explicit integration of "responsible care for the landscape with the daily ordinary and extraordinary needs of modern life."[9] The approach is simultaneously rational and emotional, disciplined but pliant, structured yet adaptive.

Durability

That all constructed work is impermanent further defines Reed Hilderbrand's insistence on integrity, specificity, and durability. Local materials, vernacular details, and construction methods informed by patterns of use and qualities of weathering serve as potent antidotes to the homogeneity and superficial image consciousness of much of contemporary landscape architectural practice. Moreover, Reed Hilderbrand has little interest in wistful notions of craftsmanship as more authentic than contemporary landscape construction. Nostalgic or precious images do not pertain. They combine a value for true craft and the efficiencies of contemporary construction techniques to build well and for economy in the long term. Genuine usefulness, an economy of means, and an ethic of systematizing efficiencies of ongoing maintenance and repair are part of the work's tectonics—values that lead to cultural and physical durability.

The firm's approach to design practice has always had a certain moral tone. In the stark legibility of the built work, it is clear that Reed Hilderbrand refuses to take shortcuts. Despite constrained budgets, fast-track schedules, complex sites, or political pressures, they bring the same level of attention to each problem, searching for the most straightforward and consistent set of responses to the cultural and physical conditions of each project. A sense of stability of intention also derives from the fact that each decision is made with an eye to how it will define the practice as a whole. Yet the firm's values are not internalized and self-referential. Their work is driven by a sense of responsibility to the much longer development of the discipline—an explicit continuity with the past and conscious participation in shaping the profession's cultural significance for the future.

There is a commensurate seriousness with which the firm approaches their responsibility in shaping the public realm and the environment of

9. From the stated philosophy of Reed Hilderbrand, used in promotional material and on the firm's website.

Site furnishings as urban infrastructure at Liberty Wharf (left and center) and MIT North Court and Main Street.

the city. At Boston's new Liberty Wharf the designers have conceived the most vernacular of elements—boardwalk, railing, and bench—in new ways. Customized furnishings and urban fixtures, common in the firm's urban projects, impart a special character to each place and suggest that all problems cannot be solved in the same manner. At Liberty Wharf the sensuous qualities of weathered wood serve to link benches, decking, and rail cap. For the rail, simple steel fins support the gently turned cap, canted at just the right angle to comfortably support resting arms as one peers over the harbor. Crisply but simply detailed wood boxes, reminiscent of shipping containers, appear along the boardwalk as flexible seating—bench, table, gathering place. These speak to the harbor's history and to its contemporary use.

What we recognize in this work is that durability also derives from the strength of frank self-sufficiency. Drawn to the classic problems in landscape design—the reshaping or editing of landform, the reordering of natural systems, the provision of shade for rest and relaxation, and the patterning of the ground plane in a city square—Reed Hilderbrand finds meaning in making landscapes that perform culturally, ecologically, and technically without allowing overt references to performance to detract from the reading of the space for what it is: an inhabited landscape. This refusal to bend either to mere sentiment or to reflexive skepticism allows the firm to work in ecologically and culturally sensitive sites with rare authority.

The tectonic clarity, quiet functionalism, and continuity that characterize Reed Hilderbrand's work are rooted in traditional values of the discipline, yet are hard to find in much of landscape practice today. This body of work is distinguished by the intimate combination of the contingent and transitory with the eternal and immutable. It stems from forms that evolve intentionally according to function, drift, and need, and that are found in

Interpretive elements are integral components of the site design at the Boston Harbor Islands Pavilion.

patterns of human use as well as in nature. Through this work, the firm examines questions about the meaning of precision and rigor of construction, the significance of new assembly methods, and the professional context within which designers build projects. Since the founding of the practice the principals have worked with a growing freedom and command of tectonic clarity. As their attitudes toward the conventions and creative opportunities in building landscapes have grown more confident, the breadth of their expression has also increased, making their completed landscapes among the most direct, forthright, and familiar of designed works.

William S. Saunders

Afterword

The landscape art of Reed Hilderbrand is quiet and kind. Without demanding attention, it goes its way, as if there could be no other. It is assured, utterly grounded in place and tradition, and calmly removed from the jangling, mercurial design-media world somewhere else out there. Thus, although it may seem conservative and familiar, it is radical—searching for roots, for enduring, seemingly timeless fundamentals that those frantic for fame have left behind. A parallel practice in architecture might be that of the monastic Swiss perfectionist Peter Zumthor, who is equally dedicated to the sensuous and the essential. But Zumthor's free-standing objects are less rooted than is the work of Reed Hilderbrand, which eagerly digs into specific sites, becoming so contextual that context is content, not periphery.

This characteristic might suggest a kind of selfless surrender to the givens of nature and vernacular traditions, and, since firm principals Doug Reed and Gary Hilderbrand are captivated by New England's landscape, it might also suggest that their design interventions in that region are merely amplifications of the given, tidying it up and removing distractions in the slightest, lightest possible way (see, for example, the Manatuck driveway). Thus, invisibility of the designer's hand at work—the well-known gift, conundrum, and handicap of landscape architecture (which Hilderbrand writes about in this book)—could in itself be their goal: a highly active passivity, so to speak. But this would neglect the passion and assertion embodied in their work, along with its value to us. And it would suggest that we look at their landscapes as if they had just happened, when we know well that they are the fruits of long, hard labor; complex technical, scientific, and engineering analysis and construction; trial and error; and many slight adjustments.

So yes, there are paradoxes at the core of this work: great labor in the service of an appearance of effortlessness and inevitability; a resolute, even fierce energy about the need to be restrained; an implicitly deep engagement with several other modes of contemporary practice through a conspicuous exclusion (and thus rejection) of them. Present even if so obviously absent in one's awareness of their work are: landscapes embracing the transitory artificialities of popular culture, hip art, synthetic materials, and urban fashion; landscapes making sustainable ecological functioning their central focus and their instructive public face; landscapes working hardest to be places of vibrant social interaction; landscapes primarily asserting their status as works of art or design; and landscapes that exist to preserve and contemplate cultural (usually industrial) heritage.

As I see it, theirs is an attempt to maximize the felt presence of nature (everything not controlled and shaped by people), but only in a context that gratifies human desire. Theirs is a humanizing of nature, a taming of it just to the point (and no further) where it can offer people unthreatened comfort, pleasure, consolation, joy, and tranquility. Theirs is an act of generosity to the too-often-battered and careworn human species. This is of course a particular strand in the history of art, one in stark contrast to the ethic of facing up to painful realities, one that consciously and actively offers release from pain—Bach in *The Goldberg Variations*, Mozart in his Twenty-first Piano Concerto, Fra Angelico and Rafael, Shakespeare in *The Tempest*, Brancusi, Albers—and that embodies the comic, not the tragic, impulse. Yes, it is noticeable that contemporary examples are hard to summon. Recent high culture has much preferred being tough, cynical, raw, wounded, and unsentimental (think of the celebrated HBO series *The Wire*, about the brutalized lives of Baltimore's underclass; think of Peter Eisenman's stated desire to make people *un*comfortable).

Ultimately Reed Hilderbrand's work offers a measure of one's valuation of *beauty*. Not prettiness and not sublimity, but rather the mature, self-aware offering of consolation and joy.

What does this mean, more concretely, in the firm's work? A great deal of it gets as close as possible to nature and to vernacular landscape traditions, without surrendering authorial control. The rural New England landscape is its most frequent inspiration, both for the way in which raw nature is felt as relatively benign and for the way that so much of that landscape has been humanized. Very unlike the awe-inspiring, infinity-suggesting big sky and mountain spaces of the American West and the poignant lonely emptiness of the Great Plains, New England space is intimate, its hills close by and embracing, almost protective. Its terra is firma, undergirt with granite, relatively unabused by floods, mud- and rock-slides, earthquakes, scalding sunlight, killer storms, tornadoes, and the like. The only real threat to human life is winter's frozenness, and even that offers images of cozy houses nestled among hills. The firm's work incorporates these realities, encircling them in compassionate human constructs. Their rural work—which I think is especially poetic—employs a language of stone walls, fields, gentle slopes, unknown but unthreatening woods, intimate but not confined scale, and fabrications in dialogue with topography. Their urban work is also motivated by benevolence. A frequent gesture is to provide shade produced by tree canopies. This is not a mechanical act: Gary Hilderbrand is, so far as I know, the only landscape architect to have made a serious study of the qualities of the shade offered by different trees, presented in his 2009 article "Varied Tree Shade for New Urban Pleasures" in the *Harvard Design Magazine*.

One of the key images in this book is the aerial photograph of the firm's work at the Sterling and Francine Clark Art Institute's Stone Hill Center, in the Berkshires of western Massachusetts, where the designers revel and rejoice in this overshadowing yet beneficent natural and cultural landscape, finding it more glorious than anything they could make, and seeing their work as a tribute to it. But what have they done here? Their primary design element is the highly artificial arcing terraces north and south of Tadao Ando's building. Why terracing? Perhaps because it accommodates human desire even as it echoes the basic landform of the magnificent and locally iconic field lying just out of sight. Like steps, terraces tame slopes. Walking down steps or terraces is more comfortable than walking down inclines. At this site, terracing allows the designers to hide, organize, and absorb parked cars on the south. But on the north, terracing (even as it meets needs for an event space on top and, the next step down, below-ground stormwater storage) plays a role in establishing feeling, creating places of rest on the hill in a rhythm of controlling, then yielding—breathing in, then breathing out.

This is much more subtly and less functionally accomplished in the landscape for the Philip Johnson–designed Beck House in Dallas. There, the slope that Reed Hilderbrand terraced was slight and unchallenging for walkers, so the embodied meaning of the terraces says simply "this place is humanized." The comfort derived from a sense of order, regularity, and the very presence of human traces is what is sought. People are in charge here, even though they welcome the presence of off-balance trees in "their" world. The over 4,000 feet of concrete curbs and retaining walls, revealing a consistent 6 inches in height and 6 inches in depth at the surface, are clearly linked to the clean horizontal lines of the pool house on the property and to the exposed strata of the site's limestone bedrock. The terraces adapt to preexisting slopes and trees but make them serve people in a formal procession.

Sometimes, as in their regularly gridded groves (see their Dallas Museum of Art and Phoenix Art Museum gardens), the designers may lean further toward human satisfaction through control (in a minimalism that, like most minimalism, just avoids sterility). Here the modernist influence of Dan Kiley may be suppressing the firm's freer affection for the natural, the uncontrolled. More appealing, I think, are projects in which the natural is further integrated into the human, and the designers' touch seems very light, as in the Bennington College campus, where the mere act of mowing grass to make a path in a field becomes a modest accommodation to human need. The designers are also enamored of serpentine paths and roads, with their leisurely pace and gradual revelations. For me, the insouciance and relaxation of their design of a curving little rill for the Institute for Child and Adolescent Development in Wellesley, Massachusetts—free of the orthogonal—gives voice to their better angels.

The understatement and reserve of Reed Hilderbrand, and their eagerness to let landscape elements speak for themselves, make them ideal designers for new elements and programs in great older landscapes like those at the Arnold Arboretum and the Mount Auburn Cemetery, as well as on college campuses, which come with a character and design language that must be respected.

The firm's humanization of landscape, however complete, is not domineering. A kind of summarizing gesture can be seen at their Lowell Street landscape, where a stone terrace just behind the house is increasingly interrupted by lawn until, finally, two stones rest surrounded by green. The constructed edges shade off into the seemingly unconstructed: beyond the terrace is an exhilarating expanse of sloping lawn, opening toward a kind of symbolized "other." As at the great landscapes of many an English country house and Italian Renaissance villa, here we are offered the embodied idea of nature as benevolent and beautiful. And since nature has been "generous" enough to give us our moment of life, we have every reason to revel in the sensuous kindness of Reed Hilderbrand.

The works on these pages have been selected from more than one hundred fifty projects, completed over two decades.

Works

DO NOT
ENTER

A path through the Arboretum's historic linden collection provides one of two approaches to the garden.

While this project naturally falls at the head of an alphabetized list, it also stands as a formative and iconic project in the firm's history. Upon the invitation to join a limited design competition for a new research and display garden at the Arboretum—built in the 1880s through the collaboration of Harvard botanist Charles Sprague Sargent and Frederick Law Olmsted—Doug Reed and Gary Hilderbrand jointly submitted credentials and subsequently won the commission, with Maryann Thompson Architects. Over the five-year course of the work, as a young firm, we confronted formidable new territory on technical, programmatic, and horticultural fronts. The 3-acre site, just outside the boundary of the Arboretum's historic property, allowed us the freedom to develop a wholly new garden organization while fully integrating its circulation and spatial patterns into the Arboretum's larger collections. As a working garden it expands curatorial research and provides visitors opportunities to observe growth, habit, and culture for nearly 150 species of shrubs and vines. We employed terracing to reconcile 30 vertical feet of grade change while transforming the fallow north-facing parcel into a productive ground for cultivation. The terraces fan out to amplify the site's irregular outline; their varied tapering shapes diversify the scale and exposure of bedding so that plants can be organized by cultural requirements or taxonomic relationships. We thought of this ordering device as shaping a kind of organic parterre that exaggerates traditional bedding patterns and consequently heightens the garden's spatial form.

Arnold Arboretum Leventritt Garden

Boston, Massachusetts

The terraces are joined by a series of sloping paths, which provide accessibility to all portions of the garden.

(facing page) The garden is revealed along the primary walk from the Arboretum proper.

A reconstructed stream collects the site's formidable storm water along the edge of the garden.

The pavilion, designed by Maryann Thompson Architects, punctuates the upper terrace, affording views over the garden and serving as a venue for special events and outdoor classes.

The upper terraces display numerous vine species and cultivars.

The garden culminates in a long walk along the massive stone retaining wall that displays clinging vines.

An assembly of galvanized steel posts and gridded panels supports twining and clambering vines.

Terraces descend the 30 feet of vertical change and splay to fit the irregular shape of the site.

In a village faced with a stagnating economy, a dedicated philanthropist and former history teacher with deep ties to the area departed from typical preservation practice in an effort to quickly reverse a loss of industry and vitality. Her first request to the design team: think like entrepreneurs. As a result, we developed a series of targeted, privately funded projects that aim to transform underutilized historic sites into vital parts of the community. The outcome: six projects that have seeded a wider physical and economic revival. While in each case the landscape component of the project accompanied a building rehabilitation, we were able to expand the impact of each site design and to develop an identifiable community fabric by building upon familiar and beloved features that define this village along Cayuga Lake in the Finger Lakes region of Upstate New York—shaded walks and streets, lawn terraces stepping down to the water, long-lived hardwoods on lawns, and broad meadows.

Earthen terraces, which are a familiar device along the lake's edge, connect the historic French House—now a guesthouse—to the lake.

The village's landmark inn was rehabilitated to provide stone and lawn terraces for dining and entertaining along the lake.

View to an interior courtyard.

Cornelian cherry, mosses, and ferns define the intimate garden near the kitchen.

At this home in Baltimore's rolling hills, domestic life is shaped by intimate daily contact with both art and landscape. The design scheme locates the house and garden below the highest rise of the ridge to minimize the presence of the building and to offer carefully framed views of the landscape from an interior also punctuated by significant works of contemporary art. Outside, we extended terraces for entertaining, dining, gardening, and recreation directly from the interior living spaces, reiterating the order of the architecture within the native shapes of the landscape. We took the quiet, restrained, contemporary materials of the house, including concrete, quartzite, and metal, as the materials for our work, fitting robust and durable walls, walks, steps, and terraces into the site's undulating topography. The hilltop itself was gently reshaped, allowing Richard Serra's sculpture *Pink Flamingoes* (1995–1996) to further register and accentuate the arcing shape of the landform.

Stepped lawns articulate the hillside around the private rooms of the house.

The house, designed by Project-Space, and the regraded knoll with Richard Serra's *Pink Flamingoes* frame the arrival court.

A pervasive canopy of ginkgo and sycamore dotted with spruce marks the hillside approach drive.

For the site of Philip Johnson's 1964 Beck House, we elaborated several intentions that were already present in the architectural work but were somewhat hindered or even canceled, either by choice or by time. Examination of Johnson's original effort suggests that beyond siting the house adjacent to an existing pecan grove, the architect took only passing interest in the full development of the 6-acre site or of the processional opportunities set up by the scheme. Our effort, undertaken over a seven-year period after two decades of neglect, amplified the processional and spatial aspects of the house through a new sequence of arrival and engaged the full dimensions of the expansive site behind the house and across Upper Bachman Creek. By inserting a central stairway in Johnson's plinth and adjusting elevations at its base, we made the house more grounded and physically connected to the site; this also established a stronger visual linkage to the trees, lawns, and prairie on the east bank of the creek. To further unite the property on both sides of the creek, we inserted cast-in-place concrete risers to adjust grades for terraces, sculptures, and existing root masses that support the preserved cedar elm canopy. This tactic supported a larger ecological framework that eliminates invasive plants, returns health and vigor to the tree canopy, improves soils and drainage functions, and stabilizes the limestone banks of the creek. Sculptural works by Olafur Eliasson, Tom Friedman, Giuseppe Pignone, and Ulrich Ruckriem were sited during the project's final stages of completion.

Concrete risers, cast on site, provide level terraces for family use and for works of art.

Beck House garden front, with altered plinth. Johnson's double curved stair can be discerned through the transparent main hall.

View of the Beck House from the east side of Upper Bachman Creek. Johnson's restored bridge spans the creek's limestone banks.

The found space beneath the restored cedar elm canopy creates a setting for Tom Friedman's sculpture, *Outdoor Open Box*, 2009. Reverse view of the facing page taken from the altered plinth of the house's west front.

New Houses, by Kyu Sung Woo Architects, are fitted to the north-western slopes of a meadow, in the tradition of organizing the college's modern buildings around Academic Hill.

At Bennington we recognized early on that what gives this 450-acre campus a sense of cohesion is a layered mosaic of features that survive from a nineteenth-century farm, a turn-of-the-century estate, the early Beaux-Arts campus plan, and a series of distinguished modernist projects that engage the academic core, each with its own views of the surrounding mountains. Over twelve years we have participated with several architects in a rebuilding program that addresses academic expansion and landscape rehabilitation within a framework organized around these patterns of historic land use. We have engaged two scales of operation. Employing the regular schedule of maintenance, we have made the significant features of the property's heritage, including its memorable views of the distant mountains, more evident and integral through pervasive removal of undesirable vegetation. On a strategic level, we have developed plans that clarify vehicle and pedestrian circulation and reestablish the tree canopy to define large areas of distinct character; to address the college's growth, we have identified the iconic North Meadow as the space around which to locate the next generation of buildings.

(facing page) The Center for the Advancement of Public Action, by Tod Williams Billie Tsien Architects, occupies a knoll along the edge of the college's meadow and pond.

Views of Mt. Anthony in the Taconic Mountains, opened through the removal of volunteer and invasive vegetation, provide a memorable image of the college.

(facing page) Terraces at the student center by Taylor & Burns Architects and the library's Joan Goodrich Courtyard provide destinations for social interaction.

This project, which modified a recently completed park in downtown Boston, supports the thesis that urban parks may achieve cultural relevance, vibrancy, and sustainability with successive adaptations over time. It assumes that a park is a construct in motion. Through the insertion of a new program into a key segment of Boston's Rose Fitzgerald Kennedy Greenway—always envisioned but long in gestation—the pavilion provides a visitor contact center staffed by park rangers as the downtown gateway to the Boston Harbor Islands National Recreation Area. Strategically located opposite the public ferry dock, the project displays an intensified focus on the path of rainfall—coursing over the pavilion roofs, pouring onto a splash block below, filling shallow pools and then evaporating, or draining off through a system that provides moisture for the oaks nearby. We took great satisfaction in helping achieve the collective ambitions of an energetic and committed coalition, harnessed by the Boston Harbor Island Alliance and the National Park Service, with support from many adjoining institutions and the park's management entity, the Greenway Conservancy.

The lawn terrace is elevated from the street and shaded by swamp white oaks.

The project integrates with the materials and circulation patterns defined by the adjacent parcels of the Greenway.

(facing page) Rainfall is animated as it flows off the concrete canopies into a granite splash block.

Two pavilions designed by the architectural firm Utile house visitor services and engage passersby as they approach the harbor from Boston's historic district.

We have worked for over a decade within the distinguished legacy of modern campus planning that Eero Saarinen first conceived for Brandeis in 1948 and Harrison & Abramowitz developed in the early 1950s. The organization of the campus—built in conditions of steep terrain, pervasive ledge outcrops, shallow soils, and a canopy of oaks—had been substantially altered by continued development over the decades, and its coherence had been compromised. Throughout seven recent building projects by different architects, we have advocated for the role of the landscape as the unifying campus fabric, and we have demonstrated the cumulative value of incremental change in realizing larger planning goals. Our work has brought consistency to the essential components of the landscape, with economy and clarity. We have reordered circulation logics in steep terrain, reshaped open spaces along a central pedestrian corridor, and preserved and renewed the tree canopy. These have now begun to restore continuity and coherence to the experience of a campus landscape of complex and layered historical patterns.

The central pedestrian spine unites the residential zone with administrative and academic areas.

New housing is sited to fit to the undulating landform and pervasive mature oak populations.

The siting of new residence halls by Kyu Sung Woo Architects defines a positive and identifiable open space at the heart of the precinct.

A broad path joins the residences
with the center of campus.

The plaza grove and structures, developed with Chan Krieger NBBJ, create a strong vegetative presence along the otherwise open waterfront. Seen from above (left) and from the harbor edge, with Boston's Custom House Tower beyond (right).

The primary idea behind this project—to transform an urban square through creation of a canopy of trees where none had existed—reflected our devotion to a nearly timeless spatial type, the continuously paved, shaded urban plaza. Sadly, and needlessly, we commonly observe street tree failures in cities after a decade or so; here we aimed to develop technically sustainable approaches. We turned to emerging studies by scientists in the field of urban forestry and built a research base on which to formulate stronger arguments for the performance values that accrue—cooling, pollutant uptake, rainfall harvesting, carbon sequestration—when we achieve a healthy vegetative cover in the city. We saw the fully canopied plaza as a scheme that could absorb the busy energy of its surroundings and gain identity in contrast to the open expanse of the harbor and the adjacent Rose Fitzgerald Kennedy Greenway. Surprisingly, that instinct proved to be at odds with nearly everyone's expectations. But in a downtown arena with complicated jurisdictions and many stakeholders, our visionary client grew more enthusiastic for the idea of a grove, and made an unbending commitment to optimizing performance in the root zone and the canopy. Though it should have been obvious, it seemed like an epiphany: To foster urban trees, we need to see the evocative space we inhabit above grade, and the mechanical and biological mechanisms that support it below grade, as reciprocals. We cannot have one without the other.

(facing page) The plaza, pictured from reverse angles, gives commuters an unobstructed yet shaded connection between the harbor ferries and the financial district.

Set alongside arcing granite seat-walls that negotiate grade and enable universal accessibility, a garden area provides seasonal interest and intimate seating.

Small light fixtures hang from wires strung through the canopy, creating subtle pools of light in contrast with the glare of the surrounding streets.

At Boston's Spaulding Rehabilitation Hospital, we conceived of this project as a safe haven and active program area for those recovering from spinal-cord injury. On this 4-acre riverfront parcel all available open space had previously been used for vehicular circulation, ambulance traffic, service, and parking. No land remained for the hospital's critical rehabilitation programs or for areas that provide respite from the intense medical environment for patients, families, and staff. To accommodate these needs, the project finds landscape space at the edge of land and water and between public and private realms: an elevated pier and floating dock extend dramatically into the Charles River and overlook the most intensively developed portion of the river's Lower Basin. We developed large continuous channels of manufactured soils that hang below the deck to support a grove of honey locusts. Handrails, anchored directly to the substructure and free of the platform, are designed for maximum transparency and to accentuate the feeling of hovering over the water. The pier and dock, designed for therapeutic programs and as an outdoor space used simultaneously by patients and the public alike, realizes the critical aim of therapists to rehabilitate their patients for reentry into real-world conditions.

Experiencing the river: the pier and dock provide the opportunity for patients and visitors to engage the Charles river.

Spaulding's pier recalls the remnant piers and platforms of the river's industrial heritage.

Honey locust trees planted in long continuous troughs of soil held by the pier's structural beams make a comfortable place over the river for rehabilitation programs and casual use by the public.

The expansion of the Chazen Museum of Art advances the renewal of the Arts and Humanities District of the University of Wisconsin. Our associated project extends the East Campus Mall an additional two city blocks immediately between the volume of the new museum wing and the 1970s Elvehjem Museum building by Harry Weese. In doing so, it strengthens connections between the Arts District, the State Street Mall and Bascom Hill, the Memorial Union, and the active edge of Lake Mendota. Our plan transforms the mall's prescribed paving standard from a simple monolithic palette of concrete frames and insets, implemented on earlier sections, to a polychrome modular pattern that extends the gesture of the mall and integrates with the museum's expressive limestone character. A new arts plaza, with arrival areas for the Chazen (and eventually for the future music building) creates a new place for daily activities, special events, educational programs, and an expanded outdoor sculpture program.

Designed by architects Machado and Silvetti Associates, the addition to the Chazen Museum frames a new arts plaza, areas for sculpture, and a passage through the building's new bridge portal toward the State Street Mall and Lake Mendota. Between the original Elvehjem Museum and the new wing, East Campus Mall creates a promenade of broad and varied proportions.

Our work at the Sterling and Francine Clark Art Institute builds upon educational and stewardship aims as a philosophical foundation for expansion and renewal. The 140-acre campus is rugged, pastoral, and beloved—thus its lawns, meadows, ponds, and streams have gained devoted constituencies and garnered protections, paradoxically limiting its capacity for growth and change. These familiar tensions have shaped an ambitious but careful and sensitive plan to expand the campus. In a small and worldly place such as Williamstown, Massachusetts, the dialogue with members of the community—scientists and historians, conservation advocates, town officials, arts patrons—has made our work more rigorous and more fitted to context. Stone Hill Center, the first completed phase, opened in 2008. For the Clark's neighbors and patrons, the new conservation lab, gallery, and café terrace draw visitors out from the traditional museum complex to experience the full variety of the museum's landholding. Repeated earthen terracing brings new emphasis to grassland passages, restored woodland edges, distant views, and an extensive path network. Combining this with the work of the larger second phase of expansion, we will have revived and enriched the ecological, mechanical, spatial, and experiential aspects of the expanded campus as a set of interrelated systems with higher function and greater resonance. Ultimately, the visitor will experience a landscape that accords—in a vital, contemporary, and ecologically healthy manner—with the humanistic traditions embodied in the Clark's distinctive collections.

Stone Hill Center's meadow is part of a pattern that defines the northern Berkshires.

(facing page, above) The building emerges from the hillside, one story from the south and two stories of conservation labs facing north. A board-form concrete wall registers the slope and creates an open terrace for an outdoor café.

A network of circulation between the main campus and Stone Hill Center allows visitors to experience the swales, banks, and streams that shape the campus.

Seasonal parking demand is met by stabilized turf parking terraces set within meadow, designed to reduce paving and increase stormwater recharge.

The Dallas Museum of Art, designed in 1984 by architect Edward Larrabee Barnes with extensive courtyards by landscape architect Dan Kiley, launched a major urban recovery and situated the arts as a primary catalyst for social change in Dallas. The renowned Dallas Arts District is a place of enormous civic ambition that continues to accumulate noteworthy cultural institutions. For one of the building's original exterior courts, the museum commissioned artist Richard Fleischner to conceive a landscape work for the collections. The Fleischner Court was a notable example of the 1980s drive to take art outside the gallery—to engage living landscape material as the province of artistic practice. After two decades of growth and subsequent decline, the court needed renewal; we undertook a direct consultation with the artist to rebuild it. Fleischner's insistence on being faithful to the details of the original work proved challenging in light of the museum's program mandates for durability and nighttime use. In the end, his determination proved to be worthy: we revitalized the soils and drainage infrastructure, restored furnishings and masonry, and replaced all of the vegetation without significant departures from the original intentions, except for the substitution of cedar elms for the original Bradford pear bosque and the installation of small light fixtures suspended from catenaries in a manner entirely consistent with Fleischner's precisely squared, nondirectional design vocabulary. Though exacting restoration of landscapes is only rarely appropriate, in this case the artist's original work survives intact through a fruitful and rewarding collaboration.

Dallas Museum of Art

Dallas, Texas

A surface of decomposed granite over structural planting soil realizes artist Richard Fleischner's vision of a spare, non-directional groundplane.

New catenary light fixtures reinforce Fleischner's original geometry of squares within squares.

The lawn embankment that forms the edge of the park defines a shaded upper walk, a stage, and an area for play.

(facing page) The park incorporates a linear system of landform, walks, trees, and shrub gardens that connects to the adjacent streets and alleyways of the neighborhood.

Working within the City of Somerville's constrained budget, we developed a scheme that transformed an abandoned and littered lot into a heavily used community park. In this densely populated city, the park aims to foster neighborhood participation and to catalyze greater investment in the urban environment. We chose to prioritize the planting of large trees throughout, which establishes the park's spatial structure immediately and provides much-needed shade. The walks, trees, and garden areas, configured in linear bands, suggest visual connections to adjacent alleys and over neighboring yards. The park's program includes a garden of native flowering shrubs, a play area for small children, a reading circle, a walking loop designed with the elderly in mind, and a stage. Our public process elicited enthusiastic participation by local residents and received unanimous support by the city; it also initiated a plan for connections to a future transit stop nearby, spurred the extension of street-tree planting outside the park, empowered the reclamation of adjacent alleys for a public walking trail, and encouraged the improvement of adjacent privately owned parcels—green infrastructure for a greener city.

Edward Leathers Community Park

Somerville, Massachusetts

The lane cuts through the valley and along the side of the hill

The wooded site is punctuated by clearings containing hayfields, ponds, a domestic garden, and outbuildings.

This 50-acre property in southern New Hampshire epitomizes the region's familiar glacial pattern of drumlins rising out of lowland woods. Some twenty years ago, however, the lowland underwent a massive change: beavers dammed the drainageways, flooding the red maple swamps and permanently altering the hydrology, vegetation, and spatial patterns of a vast area. The owners revere this land and passionately believe in the transcendental power of nature to provide spiritual serenity and sustenance. They lead active lives primarily outdoors. Walking is a daily ritual. Habitat is nurtured. Produce grows organically. Family events are celebrated in the landscape. And at the end of their lives, family members will be buried on site. To bring the site's unusual variety more directly into their daily lives, we capitalized on the unique dynamics of the site's altered hydrology, managing the disturbed forest toward a more open and accessible condition, developing a series of ponds and wetlands, and constructing a network of boardwalks and trails throughout.

Water is ever-present on the site.
At this pond the top of the weir carries
a portion of the perambulatory path.

Renovated reflecting pool on the garden terrace.

When we first saw this 1982 Edward Larrabee Barnes house and the 4 acres of land behind it, invasive vegetation completely denied any productive or compelling connection between the house and its landscape. It was impenetrable. Extensive clearing revealed an undulating creek-carved landform of limestone bedrock covered with shallow soils, a characteristic of this Dallas neighborhood. We viewed this condition as a potent opportunity to develop a garden as a counterpoint to the rational language of the modern house and its stepped terraces. Through extensive grading, we accentuated the play of the architectural terraces against the dendritic pattern of the creek corridor and established a palette of moisture-loving plants of great textural variety. This hydric condition contrasts with a small patch of native Texas Blackland Prairie discovered at the upper elevation of the property, on the far side of the creek, which we have extended downslope to provide the focus of views from the house and its garden terraces.

On both sides of the stream, a network of footpaths is fitted within the site's dendritic land-form, weaving through woodland, along the stream banks, and across an area of prairie.

We surprised the owners of this remarkable landholding in the Berkshires when we landed upon a compelling question: What would it be like to create an observation pathway through the freshwater marsh, a place no one had traveled, except perhaps across the winter ice? Local approvals for a 2,700-foot-long boardwalk took nine months of negotiation. Conservation commissioners reviewed provisional field layouts in late summer and again in the following spring, slogging through the marsh, armed with waders and cameras. There were abundant concerns. With the commissioners and wildlife biologists, we tuned the walk's broad curves and narrow twists to navigate trees and snags, woody thickets, and beaver impoundments. We were asked, against our instincts, to vary the walk's gradient, warping the decking upward in places in order to mitigate shading across the perennial streams. Our response to this requirement turned out to be one of the project's most compelling physical attributes—adding to the varied lyrical character of the boardwalk. It helped form an unusual combination of immersion and exposure inside a special place—alternately dark and junglelike, then broad and high and open to the sky. Construction entailed removing invasive plants, but almost no other impacts; the walk was completed with handheld power tools. The project promoted a new kind of resource stewardship for the owners. Unanticipated benefits also seemed to accrue for wildlife; the path has become a favored route for foxes, coyotes, wildcats, and bears.

From the air, the boardwalk's strong sinuous line contrasts with the varied patterns of upland margins, wet thickets, matted grasses, and open water.

(facing page) Wildlife appears to enjoy the boardwalk's clear path of travel.

The boardwalk adjusts horizontally and vertically to engage the diverse conditions of the marsh while mitigating impacts on habitat.

The approach drive reinhabits a former driveway plantation of London plane trees.

The littoral drainage patterns of Long Island's East End have left a lasting mark on these 11 acres on the outskirts of East Hampton. The resulting topographic features—hill, valley, and plateau—and the complementary mature vegetation remaining from an 1898 estate are the primary components that have driven our approach to and design for this family compound. Two houses once crowned the hill at the center of the undulating landscape. From the outset we have taken an alternate approach to occupying the site. With the architects we developed an organizing framework for situating a building program on the plateau along the property's east and south edges, freeing the interior for expansive views of the valley and of the restored hill. The rational orders of the houses, courts, and pool extend into the landscape as self-contained gardens or alternatively as open platforms that flow into the larger site, their precise and restrained character taking on increased clarity in juxtaposition to the romantic and long-established character of the property. Hither Lane is one of those rare commissions where our work began alongside the architect's initial effort to design a single house and has continued as a fruitful collaboration with owner and architect for over twenty years.

Hither Lane East Hampton, New York

The house by B Five Studio occupies the east plateau and offers views of the valley.

The pool garden incorporates a grove of old sassafras trees that frames views of the valley.

(facing page) River birch populate the edge of the sculpture court.

A fence of stainless steel posts
encloses the pool garden.

In a compelling collaboration that provoked our most speculative design interests, we were captivated by a psychologist's profound and innovative idea that a garden could play a significant role in the diagnosis and treatment of children who have experienced trauma. This concept resonated with our deeply held belief that the garden can engender emotional well-being and help each of us understand our individual place in larger natural and cultural orders. The scheme draws from the patterns of natural dendritic water-courses to shape an intensively inward-oriented and evocative landscape. A rill weaves through a series of spaces that mirror the stages of a child's recovery from trauma—a cavelike ravine for the security of home base, a woodland for exploration, a mount for climbing, an island and pond for discovery, steep and shallow slopes for challenge, and a large glade for running and playing. Unfortunately, this clinic and garden were demolished in 2006 to make way for a new residential development.

The garden's landform preserves and engages landmark oaks.

Water wells up through a granite basin on the play terrace, then travels through the garden's rill to a pond.

The garden's narrative is built around a watercourse weaving through a ridge-ravine landform, past an island and mount.

The vision of this project's primary benefactor was to give Kansas City a vibrant new cultural center. In the associated rebuilding of a full city block between the downtown area and a newly revitalized arts neighborhood, we saw the opportunity to create an equally vibrant public realm. The project encompasses the public spaces of the arts center, the city sidewalks, and the roof of the underground parking garage that occupies the south half of the parcel. It was our instinct to develop a civic and parklike character throughout, with shady spaces for public gathering, networked circulation, and open lawns for performance, events, and recreation, as a way of extending the life of the center beyond performance times and to help foster a new community. The site's dramatic elevation change—more than 60 vertical feet—suggested a series of embankments and precise terraces that accommodate crossing ramps for universally accessible walks that span the block and connect previously separated adjacent communities. Underlying the entire project are innovative and sustainable stormwater solutions that define another practice of giving back to the community.

The arc of the entry drive as it passes below cables sets the geometry for the entire landscape. The building was designed by Safdie Architects.

Arcing site walls, planting beds, and rows of shade trees provide a framework for the garden terraces on either side of the performance halls.

EMERY. BIRD. THAYER CO.- WAREHOUSE

The garden terraces provide seating areas overlooking the parking structure's green roof and the thriving arts district to the south.

Our work in the Seaport District of Boston, in direct collaboration or coordinated overlap with other designers working with assorted private clients and government agencies, has resulted in a network of public spaces—streets, squares, parks, and promenades—that are emerging from old industrial properties occupying the filled tidelands and piers of Fort Point Channel and South Boston. Collectively, the projects are transforming an urban neighborhood that capitalizes on a revitalized transportation infrastructure and that will evolve over several decades as economic circumstances allow. Liberty Wharf, one of the earliest completed projects, has helped catalyze the Seaport's renewal. As with all waterfront sites in Boston, legislation required the pier's developer to provide a continuous public route along the water's edge—Boston's widely acclaimed Harborwalk. We devised a simple, continuous wharf surface in the tradition of grand piers used for shipping and for urban recreation. Structures on the waterfront require massiveness and durability—granite for seawalls and curbs, concrete for sidewalks and piles, wood for decking—but also lightness and transparency, in this case gained from the efficient strength of stainless steel stanchions, cables, and fastenings. With straightforward geometries and deliberately spare detailing, we aimed to capture the experience of exposure on the harbor: You cannot miss the ships and planes, the water, the light, or the weather, from the streamlined perch of Liberty Wharf.

Liberty Wharf Boston, Massachusetts

On the site of the former Jimmy's Harborside, a venerable Boston dining institution, Liberty Wharf's restaurants and cafés designed by Elkus Manfredi Architects once again command superb views of Boston Harbor.

NO SMOKING

While the reconstruction of the pier exploits private commercial interests on the working waterfront, the Boston Harborwalk provides unrestricted public access along the water's edge.

The 23-acre aggregation of Scenic Hudson's Long Dock Park, Peter J. Sharp Park, and the Klara Sauer Hudson River Trail has aided in the renewal of the historic waterfront in Beacon, New York. We approached this site with a frank recognition of strongly enigmatic circumstances: It is at once serene and tough. Projecting more than 1,000 feet from shore on a milewide stretch of river, the site embodies the unsurpassable pleasures of the Hudson Highlands' calm, pastoral beauty. Yet we found the site despoiled and degraded, formerly condemned to petroleum storage, industrial waste, and automobile disassembly. After a decade of remediation and recovery, the park provides some of the river's most peaceful experiences but also endures dramatic storm surges that occasionally inundate three-quarters of its landmass. It is more than a park for recreation. The site contains intertidal wetlands, newly created water storage and infiltration basins, new bulkheads and boardwalks, reused construction debris, and a gravel beach. The artist George Trakas hand-built a constructed marine edge that registers the estuary's 4-foot tides and provides fishermen and park visitors a unique engagement with the river's surface and flows. Programmatically, the River Center, Mill Street Studios, and a kayak pavilion diversify the park's functions. Portions of the site are reserved for a future hotel and civic plaza. All of these complexities and contingencies lead us to see Long Dock as a resilient living work that will continue to adjust and adapt to changing circumstances of climate, ecology, economics, and local culture.

Long Dock's structures include the rehabilitated Red Barn (left) and the new kayak pavilion (facing page, above), both designed by Architecture Research Office.

(below) Varied walks and perches take advantage of the river's intertidal zones.

The newly constructed beach, bulkheads, kayak pavilion, and a sculptural work by George Trakas frame a calm and placid river in summer, but they also withstand the tremendous force of ice floes during winter freezes.

Contrasting character: the expansive reach of the private side of the site and the contained urban qualities of the arrival court.

The unique qualities of this project are rooted in a real estate coup: the assembly of a series of lots at the interior of a block in the historic Brattle Street neighborhood of Cambridge. The unusual platting of the block enabled the owner to combine an alley, several backyards, and a shared drainage area into a contiguous landholding for siting a new home. We came to see that this strategy provided the opportunity to develop a private landscape that remains well integrated with its urbane villagelike setting and fully in keeping with the surrounding historically significant fabric. As a result we chose to exploit the sense of private retreat that the property allows by entering along the narrow street frontage and proceeding through a layered series of spaces to arrive at a compound of buildings. It is by moving beyond the house that one sees the surprising expanse of the property. Here, areas of lawn defined by shrub drifts further blur its edges. Employing a pervasive canopy of mature trees across the site, the design reprises a characteristic feature of the neighborhood and builds visual connections to abutting backyards.

A simple gravel drive ascends the ridge of a drumlin—accentuating the distinctive landform—through original stone fences and working pastures.

This 200-acre working farm in Stonington, Connecticut, with panoramic views of Long Island Sound, dates from the mid-eighteenth century. The site contains original stone walls, paddocks, fields, and ponds organized along characteristic drumlin and lowland Connecticut terrain that was shaped by glacial action. On a site with such compelling history, we were most struck by the power of a granite foundation wall some 600 feet in length and as tall as 10 feet—remnant of a former barn complex along the east side of the ridge. As a strategy to marry a contemporary home and modern life with fabric from earlier times, we took the high and long shape of the drumlin and the extended form of the remnant wall as organizing devices for the house and garden. From Main Street, a gravel drive ascends through hayfields and successive stone fences to reach a generous loop that circles around the nose of a drumlin to arrive at the front of the house on the east slope of the landform. Entry into the house reveals the long view of the valley. From here, the house, outdoor terraces, Cor-ten steel steps, pool, an original overlook, and vegetable and perennial gardens connect in dynamic tension with the remnant barn wall. Abstract, restrained, and decidedly contemporary, our interventions here avoid nostalgia, instead building upon the traces of centuries of farm life on this property to make its historical artifacts functionally and viscerally present in the daily lives of its current owners.

(facing page) The library offers views of the valley.

Cor-ten steel risers and lawn treads connect the house, by Maryann Thompson Architects, with the lawn terrace along the historic wall.

The remnant wall provides the boundary between the domestic zone and the farm fields.

The garden at the Robert McBride House is a quiet enclave in the dense fabric of Boston's Fenway neighborhood. It provides a place of respite and renewal for persons suffering from drug and alcohol addiction and HIV-related illnesses who live in an adjacent group home. To overcome the impact of parking and services in the surrounding network of alleys, we filled the available area with an enveloping grove of honey locust trees. Below their canopy we carved a network of paths and paved terraces out of a field of flowering shrubs. The density of the garden allows for individuals and groups to experience the garden without encroaching on each other's privacy. This project with the Archdiocese, coming early in our practice, became an instructive opportunity: It sharpened our resolve on the vital importance of the garden as a component of healthy cities and on the significance of shade—the urban tree canopy—as a fundamental requirement for metropolitan life. With this experience we found that questions about how landscapes perform urbanistically and ecologically became stronger drivers for us.

(facing page) The garden transforms the back alleys and parking areas of the block's interior into a place of respite and renewal.

A grid of honey locust trees shades an understory of mixed hydrangeas, holly, and spirea.

A series of commissions at the Massachusetts Institute of Technology challenged us to assimilate and extend campus spaces that originated as monumental and neoclassical, but which by midcentury had evolved toward distinctly modernist vocabularies—for us, a truly compelling design legacy. The David H. Koch Institute for Integrative Cancer Research opened in March 2011 with the mission of combating cancer by fostering collaboration among disciplines. Its placement on Main Street in Cambridge enlivens a campus threshold where MIT researchers and students intersect with some of the world's leading biotech and life science companies. Here we had a chance to carefully organize the everyday elements of a good city street: a broad sidewalk that allows both a clear path and room to meander, two scales of street trees, drains and lights, places to sit, and places to hitch bicycles. On the campus side, after completing a series of studies for rehabilitating portions of the 100-year-old "Main Group" complex, we realized that this new building and its neighbors—including Frank Gehry's 2004 Stata Center and I. M. Pei's 1976 Landau Building—would frame the group's last quadrangle. We spliced the circulation and spatial logics found in two traditional campus types, the promenade and the quadrangle. Together these produce a hybrid space for movement and gathering: a direct, broad walk that connects the street with the famed "Infinite Corridor," along with diagonal paths that dissect the lawn but don't interfere with large gatherings and campus rituals.

A new campus promenade draws a broad connecting space between the Main Street business district and the primary academic and research facilities on campus.

The project's east plaza introduces visitors and the campus community to North Court from the public transit system and Cambridge's ample bicycle routes.

The promenade and south terrace articulate varied characters. The terrace supports regular gatherings for the Koch Institute and is oriented directly toward the open lawn; the promenade is a movement space with seating providing multiple orientations.

(facing page) The Main Street sidewalk is unusually broad for Cambridge, exploiting the open and transparent character of galleries in Ellenzweig's building without interfering with a busy pedestrian flow between campus and surrounding businesses.

Existing cedar elms, live oaks, and pecans captured in the new space of the Long Garden.

It seemed something of a reach to us, as a very young firm, to be commissioned for a garden in a residential neighborhood in San Antonio, a place we didn't know in a part of the country in which we had not worked. But the challenge proved irresistible, the rewards exquisite and enduring. The project quickly gave us a devotion to working in Texas landscapes, which are hot and diverse and challenging, and always compelling. At Monte Vista, we fell in love with the live oak, the cedar elm, and the pecan—seduced by the opportunities to exploit beautiful spatial characters that result from the wildness of the trees' canopies, whether we organized them in geometric patterns or found them already there in irregular bunches. We alternately amplified or quieted the pervasive parallel orders in this project through the scale and repetition of trees. Varied, expansive qualities resulted: The garden spaces unfold sequentially, broad and open, narrow and elongated, irregular, gigantic, and intimate. We had an auspicious start in Texas.

Our work at the front of the property brought ordered simplicity to the ground plane, amplitude to plantings that surround the house, and improvements to canopy health for the mature hardwoods.

Long walks, low walls, and limestone steps overcame the problem of a four-foot elevation difference between the rear of the house and natural grade. Lake Flato Architects' renovation recaptured the second-story sleeping porch and an enormous screened room facing lawns and borders.

The arcing turf walk carved out of woodland provides two hundred burial crypts below its surface.

When it opened in 1829, Mount Auburn Cemetery solved a growing public-health concern: the need to find burial space for a rapidly expanding population in the Boston metropolis. The cemetery's founding doctors and engineers fused their plan for a pastoral burial ground with emerging scientific and popular interests in horticulture, leading to an urban landscape invention that many American cities would replicate almost immediately, the garden cemetery. Nearly two centuries later, Mount Auburn embodies a tremendous living record of our New World traditions of commemoration and interment, and supports our assorted customs of honoring the deceased through ritual gathering and visitation. But its mission also requires that Mount Auburn find ways to pursue more contemporary means of burial and memorialization, so that it remains a place of innovation and discovery. Moreover, the cemetery manages a historic tract of urban forest—a vast and differentiated botanical garden with heritage trees, a series of lakes and ponds and streams, and a wildlife habitat. Thus, each of the commissions we have approached here, large or small—a lake restoration, the almost surgical insertion of burial space beneath a new walking path, the provision of new visitor services, or the reorganization of the cemetery's horticultural and recycling operations—has required a mixture of curatorial discipline, economy and rigor in design, and the rebalancing of natural and human inputs that will lead to greater long-term resilience for the cemetery's ecology. The satisfaction that comes with working with the endlessly rich content and exquisite parameters of this context is immense.

This stretch along Halycon Lake provides an area of newly created wetland edge.

Understory shrubs of sweet pepper-bush, beautyberry, and coralberry blanket the banks of this area of the lake's perimeter.

(overleaf) With the lake dredged and its lawn edge reestablished, the reflection of the Mary Baker Eddy Memorial on the water's surface is restored.

Narrow footpaths allow the visitor to walk near the lake's edge.

The addition to the original structure, by Pirie Turlington Architects, is embedded within planting and is almost unseen from the drive.

Reorganizing the weathered refuse of Stony Creek granite tailings for this coastal Connecticut project provided surprising discoveries for us. The sizable vein known locally as Old Quarry had been exhausted by the 1940s, and in the subdivision that followed, most homeowners buried the evidence of extraction and smoothed the land to produce waterfront plots with extensive lawns and gardens. The original owners of a 1952 modernist house by the sculptor Tony Smith responded differently. On this parcel, which partially floods during tide surges, the house was raised on *piloti*, and much of the rough post-extraction condition remained. In 2009, the property's new owners completed an exacting restoration of the house and added a wing with a quietly contrasting character. While collaborating on the restoration and addition, we focused on exposing the rock—it was inescapable—and reordering it in various ways to sharpen one's awareness of the found conditions of stone pits, stacks, walls, and rocky plains. We chose a specific soil mix and select palette of coastal plants to withstand tidally influenced upwelling and occasional surface inundation. In the project's planting and circulation, for the most part, we suppressed any overt figuration or strong geometries. Only the two jettylike stone paths align orthogonally with the house within an otherwise meandering, episodic field of rocky or vegetated shapes. This was a real departure for us: the vigorous pursuit of the irregular.

The original Tony Smith house to the right and the pavilion to the left, with remnant granite along the edge of Long Island Sound.

(facing page and above) Granite gathered on site takes on multiple characters and functions—at times highly ordered, at times slightly edited as found in the remnant borrow pit.

One of two linear stone paths connects the drive to the stairs to the front door.

On 116 acres of rolling farmland in Virginia's Piedmont, an 1820s farmhouse with recent additions is perched along the edge of a ridge and at the head of a sweeping valley. The owners sought to develop expansive areas around the house for outdoor living that would celebrate views of the farm while accommodating circulation around the house and into the valley. Drawn to the owner's deep attachment to the region, we chose to root the design's expression in its restrained and direct design traditions, in local building materials, and in specific construction practices of this area of the state. One of those traditions seemed especially relevant to providing level ground for the active areas around the house: the innovative and expressive earthen terracing undertaken by Virginia plantation owners from the eighteenth century onward. We thus designed long earthen terraces held by lawn ramps and stone walls that extend from the house, reflect the shape of the ridge, and orient to the valley and the lake beyond. The terraces incorporate shaded lawns, paved areas and walks, parking and service areas, and flower and vegetable gardens ordered with geometric precision to play against the rolling Piedmont landscape.

Lawn terraces extend from the house along the length of the ridge to offer views of the valley and lake.

Canopy trees of sugar maple and sycamore, the property's namesake, surround the house on the hillside.

The sculpture garden is organized along a central walk that extends the full length of the court.

The full-block site of the Phoenix Art Museum has historically served as the cultural center of the city, including a theater and originally the public library. The previous and most recent expansion of the museum defined a new central courtyard surrounded by buildings of different periods, character, use, and elevation. Our task was to develop a public landscape that would provide a venue for special events, serve as an outdoor gallery for sculpture and museum exhibitions, and unify the disparate buildings and programs that surrounded it. We conceived of this courtyard as a counterpoint to its urban context and to the surrounding fragments of desert landscape, an internalized space with cooling shade in the tradition of the cloister but motivated by the qualities and characteristics of oases found in arid landscapes. The garden's components are organized to provide contrast of sun and shadow, the sound and reflection of water, the fragrance of foliage and flowering plants, and the rich shade of canopy, evergreen, and ornamental trees that are heat and drought tolerant. Underlying it all, we shaped a continuous folded groundplane, which enables universal accessibility, provides flexibility in programming events of different sizes, and ties into buildings at three different floor elevations.

The museum expansion by Tod Williams Billie Tsien Architects completed the enclosure of the 1 1/2-acre court for the display of sculpture, dining, outdoor classrooms, and special events.

(facing page) A bosque of willow acacias frames the court's central lawn.

The museum's varied program requirements are accommodated in spaces organized along the perimeter of the central lawn.

The Chicago headquarters of the Poetry Foundation gives physical expression to Harriet Monroe's founding vision of *Poetry* magazine as an "open door" that would increase poetry's profile in society, help poets pursue their art, and cultivate public interest in the form. Working seamlessly with the architect, we conceived of the building and landscape as an interwoven series of spaces and thresholds that would break down apparent barriers between the foundation and the public, between inside and out. A transparent screen with an open corner wraps the property and identifies the facility. Within this frame, a glass curtain wall moves along the edge of garden and interior rooms, visually joining the two together. A concrete floor extends across garden and first-floor rooms to the sidewalk edge. Paradoxically, we saw abstraction and spatial ambiguity as powerful strategies to support the clarity of the larger planning concept. This project reminds us that it is only through an intense meeting of the minds with the architect and client that a project can achieve a conceptual, spatial, material, and tectonic cohesion and richness.

John Ronan's elegant metal construction expresses both solidity and permeability at the corner of Superior and North Dearborn avenues inside Chicago's Loop.

The garden establishes an outdoor room between the perimeter scrim wall and the building, and offers a sequence of experiences on the way to the front door.

Interior rooms, the garden, and the street are joined through transparent and translucent enclosures.

At this early modernist home in a community north of New York City we recognized almost immediately that the design intentions of the architecture, which included a compelling open plan and strong visual connections between inside and out, had never been equally realized in the landscape. The property also reflected stylistic conventions of the 1960s, particularly the use of ornamental evergreens planted in masses along the house foundations and along property boundaries, obscuring the relationship of the building to the rolling terrain and restricting the perceived expanse of the property. Careful analysis of landform and vegetative systems uncovered potential relationships between the architecture and the shallow valley in which the home lies and indicated that editing and a rearrangement of vegetation could be more effective at initiating connectivity than would wholesale change. Our targeted interventions established a network of walls, paths, terraces, sites for sculpture, and planted forms, all extending orthogonally from the house along the length of the valley, to accentuate the irregular terrain and unite the building with its site.

On the private side of the property, outdoor areas for entertaining, dining, and play extend from the house.

On 43 acres of lowland woods, wetlands, and meadow along the Westport River in southeastern Massachusetts, we have worked for over ten years to develop this contemporary home, rural retreat, and small farm operation. In this site we were drawn to the subtle yet powerful patterns of a riparian landscape coupled with the remnants of both agrarian practices from the nineteenth century and destructive mining operations of the twentieth century that had rendered this an uncharacteristically flat expanse of land. The work we have done—primarily extensive removal of invasive vegetation—has made these spatial patterns visible and accessible for daily experience, and they now form the principal structure of this landscape. The uncovered fieldstone walls and hedgerows and stands of trees along the river give clarity to the edges of the meadow and accentuate the horizontal expanse of the low-lying land. Native vegetation has regenerated as a result of reduced competition. We chose to set the wood and glass structure at the edge of a gentle rise in the meadow's rolling topography to engage the most expansive views of river and sky. Into this indigenous pattern we have inserted path circuits that extend from the house to reach points of historical, botanical, and topographical interest.

The house sits at the edge of a 19-acre meadow.

(facing page, above) The only cultivated area extends along the east and south edges of the house designed by Maryann Thompson Architects.

(below) Interior forms, materials, and furnishings are conceived in sympathy with the tones and scale of the meadow.

The house is located 200 feet from the river's edge, in accordance with the Massachusetts Rivers Act.

The wet meadow's diverse perennial vegetation is managed through mowing.

A perimeter path extends along
the length of river frontage.

These varied views—of the house from the public roadway, the tennis court and orchard trees from the drive, and Somes Sound from the great sweep of lawn—preserve Rosserne's storied place in local culture.

As the most distinguished house completed by widely acclaimed Northeast Harbor architect Fred L. Savage, Rosserne epitomizes Mount Desert Island's long tradition as a prosperous coastal haven and celebrates the island's legacy of patronage. The character of the 6-acre site derives from a limited palette: gently shaped landform, landmark trees, native spruce forest, and an emphasis on the surrounding water and sky. Precise grading brings forward the land's great strength and the house's proud westerly aspect. Orchards, cutting gardens, rescued outbuildings, and walking trails have been added. The great expanse of lawn overlooking Somes Sound—which requires significant maintenance—is a local point of pride and is thus considered an essential part of the owner's fidelity to Rosserne's storied past. We employed a discreet hand, emphasizing careful editing as much as quiet intervention. Rosserne proves the value of a curatorial approach to a historically significant property, where our work aims to honor and extend venerable local traditions.

A path of salvaged stone in the woodland garden.

(facing page) The central lawn panel extending from the rear portico has always been a significant feature of this garden. Its prominent position is maintained and enhanced by brick paths and perennial gardens on either side.

At the Taft Museum, we faced the task of rebuilding a much-loved garden whose fabric had endured serious decline and which could not be adequately preserved in the context of the museum's expansion plans. The original property, home to prominent Cincinnati families—generations of Longworths, Tafts, and Sintons—was identified in the mid-nineteenth century as the American Midwest's grandest agricultural estate. The 1820 Taft-Sinton house is acclaimed as an outstanding example of Federal Period domestic architecture, and Taft descendants possessed one of the nation's premier collections of American and European paintings and decorative arts. When the house became a museum in 1932, landscape architect Henry Fletcher Kenney developed a garden that would come to embody part of the Taft's identity. After rigorously documenting the story of the garden's origins and alterations over time, we predicated the design of the garden upon four principal intentions: preserving the site's domestic character and scale with intimation of its rural heritage; complementing the finely scaled proportions of the building's rear porch in the garden's lawn and borders; balancing symmetrical and asymmetrical features in an irregular four-part organization; and restoring vistas toward the distant hills that were once part of the agricultural landholding. We added to these intentions one inescapable, overriding aim: to create a new garden that could seem at once new and familiar to the Taft's devoted community.

Our work transformed annuals plantings into a four-season garden and, to improve canopy health and long-term viability, altered the pruning regimes on the original aerial hedge.

Boston's Christian Science Plaza stands as one of the nation's few outstanding examples of mid-twentieth-century heroic modernist urban spaces. As a response in the late 1960s to disinvestment and decline along the seam between the city's Back Bay and South End precincts, The First Church of Christ, Scientist and its designers—I. M. Pei, Araldo Cossutta, and Sasaki, Dawson & DeMay—created a lasting civic achievement that welcomes all citizens to engage its buildings, spaces, and vast reflecting pool. Though we can be critical today of the devastating impacts that came with clearing entire neighborhoods before this project's completion, the work embodies a commanding monumentality and clarity of expression that have been deservedly admired. Its vegetative orders, though beautiful in conception, were considered by many to be limited and disengaged. Our work, some thirty years later, brought a new level of vitality and stewardship to the site's public horticulture. We devised a management plan to restore health and vigor to the site's immense two-hundred-linden aerial hedge; changed the plaza's annual planting displays to a more sustainable perennial garden that corresponds with the gigantic scale of the reflecting pool; and inserted an intimately scaled sitting garden at the Massachusetts Avenue entry to the Mary Baker Eddy Memorial Library. This rehabilitative work reflects the steadfast commitment of a private institution to sustaining the city's active public realm and its significant urban design legacy.

The entry garden for the Mary Baker Eddy Library creates an enclosed corner as a contrasting feature to the monumental plaza. The glass library entry was designed by Ann Beha Architects.

The regionally predominant pattern of walls along rectilinear fields and beside old country lanes defines the relaxed and restful quality of this 16-acre parcel of gently rolling lowland in New York's Westchester County. In these vernacular patterns, we saw an opportunity to give order and logic to new building projects while celebrating the simplicity and utility of the region's traditional farmsteads. Repeating these vernacular geometries, four new stone retaining walls stretch across the site and systematize the entire program for the property, including the main house with its arrival court and outdoor terraces, recreation building, pool and pool house, tennis court, and casual play areas.

Circulation and parking in the arrival court is organized by a row of tulip poplars.

(facing page) Two fieldstone walls provide level areas for the pool and tennis court and retain the knoll for informal play.

Removing invasive vegetation revealed the historic lane that separates the fields.

Successive layers of remnants and contemporary life: old boundary walls, lane, pool house, knoll, and house.

Mowed lawn frames taller meadow grasses, inverting the typical suburban condition.

The site-planning strategy for this 2-acre Long Island property, which sits near the ocean along a potato field and overlooks Wainscott Pond, eschews the standard organization of most residential development. Instead of placing the house near the street to afford a large backyard, the plan sites the building program along the edges of the rectangular lot and frees the interior for an expansive yet private garden to accommodate a growing and active family. We saw the agrarian character of the context—its flat horizontal reach of crops and meadows, familiar hedgerows and shaded farmsteads—as providing a potent language for the design itself. Our scheme employs simple lines of trees to frame the two long edges of the property; a figured meadow that fills the center of the site; and, as a point of contrast, lines of ornamental trees that run across the width of the lot to suggest subtle divisions within and to define spaces for various outdoor activities.

Wainscott

Wainscott, New York

Plantations of poplar and honey locust create enclosure and subdivision in the garden.

The east perennial garden extends from the house, designed by B Five Studio, at the base of the preserved knoll.

One of the firm's first commissions provided the opportunity to shape an unoccupied but sizable landholding into a home for a young couple whose loyalty to the firm has extended for twenty years. Fashioned on the unique American model of the agricultural estate, this rural retreat some forty-five minutes north of New York City embodies the couple's values through land stewardship, a dedication to horticultural and culinary experimentation, and the implementation of innovative sustainable practices. Our work here has been incremental, developing the site based on a master plan that has preserved the topographically rich landscape and its historic features of stone walls and hedgerows as its organizing structure. Our plan has sited all of the buildings and related program on the sides of a prevailing ridge in order to preserve a series of four high knolls as open meadow. Shrub gardens, flower gardens, and herb and vegetable gardens envelop the house and reflect a restrained and precise order that is both classical and modern, as well as resonant with the agrarian character of the landholding.

Shrub gardens near the house lead to the south lawn, which arcs around the knoll.

Since the origins of Reed Hilderbrand, the firm has experienced the obvious but still remarkable transition from drawing and modeling by hand to digital projection. Landscape work requires four-dimensional thinking, and our tools for this are increasingly empowering—allowing us to depict how landscapes work in space and time and delineating some things about how they will change. But in a completely digital culture, we have only increased our interest in drawing plans that embody the primary site influences and ideas behind the work. The plan is an ancient device that, in landscape architecture, embodies an irrefutable conceit. It's a time-stopped view that describes the world partly as it exists, partly as envisioned. Because of its comprehensiveness, designers rely on the plan quite naturally—and often uncritically—based on conventions that evolved in cartography and exploration, archaeology, architecture and planning, manufacturing, and design. Whether depicting our interventions and their contexts on small sites or many city blocks or hundreds of acres, the plan carries the unrealistic burden of representing too many conditions; what counts for us is deciding which things to emphasize so that we convey something of the ideas in the work itself.

Plans

0
140

Aurora Aurora, New York

0 750

0
240

Baltimore Hills Baltimore, Maryland

0 150

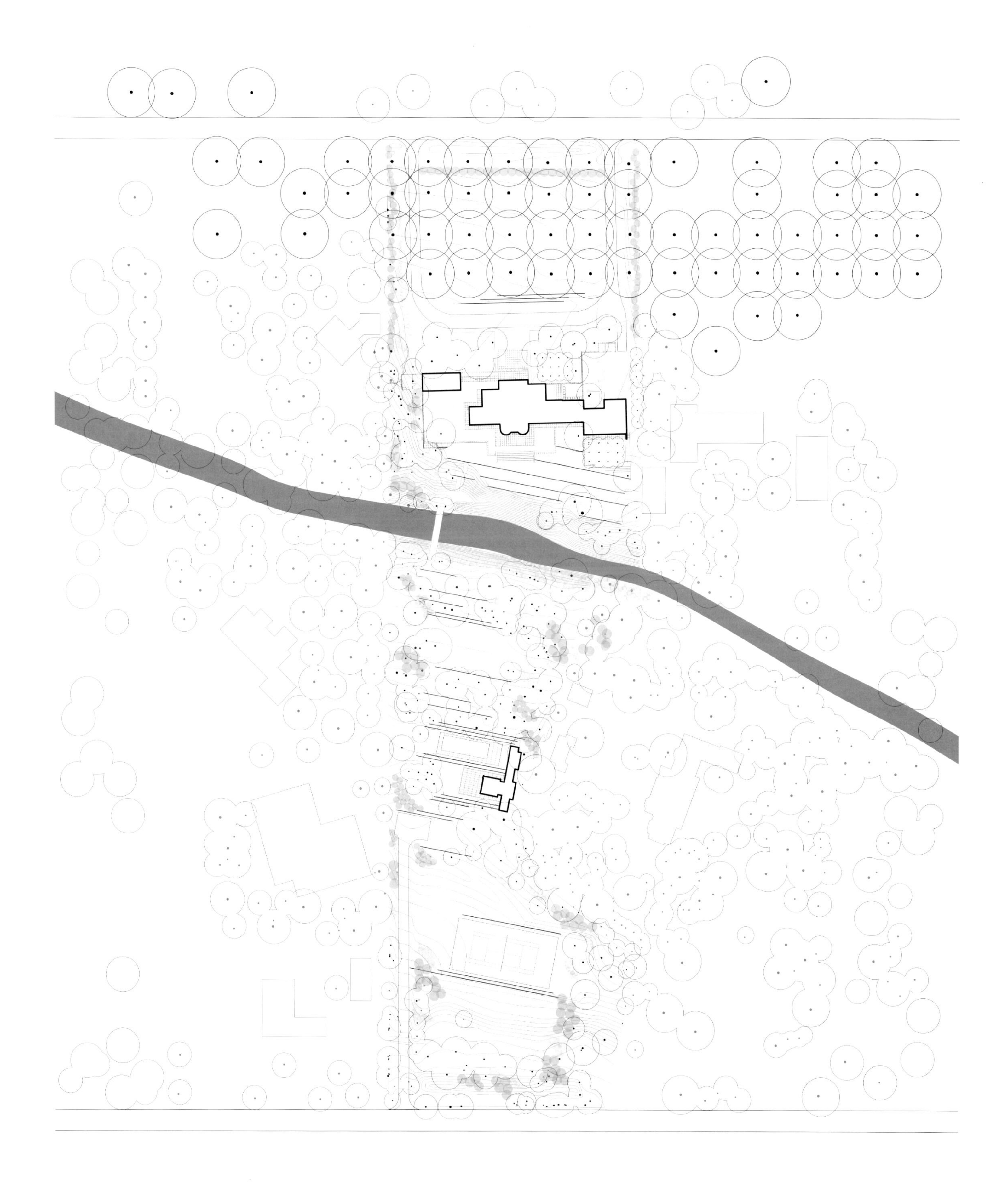
0
150

Bennington College Bennington, Vermont

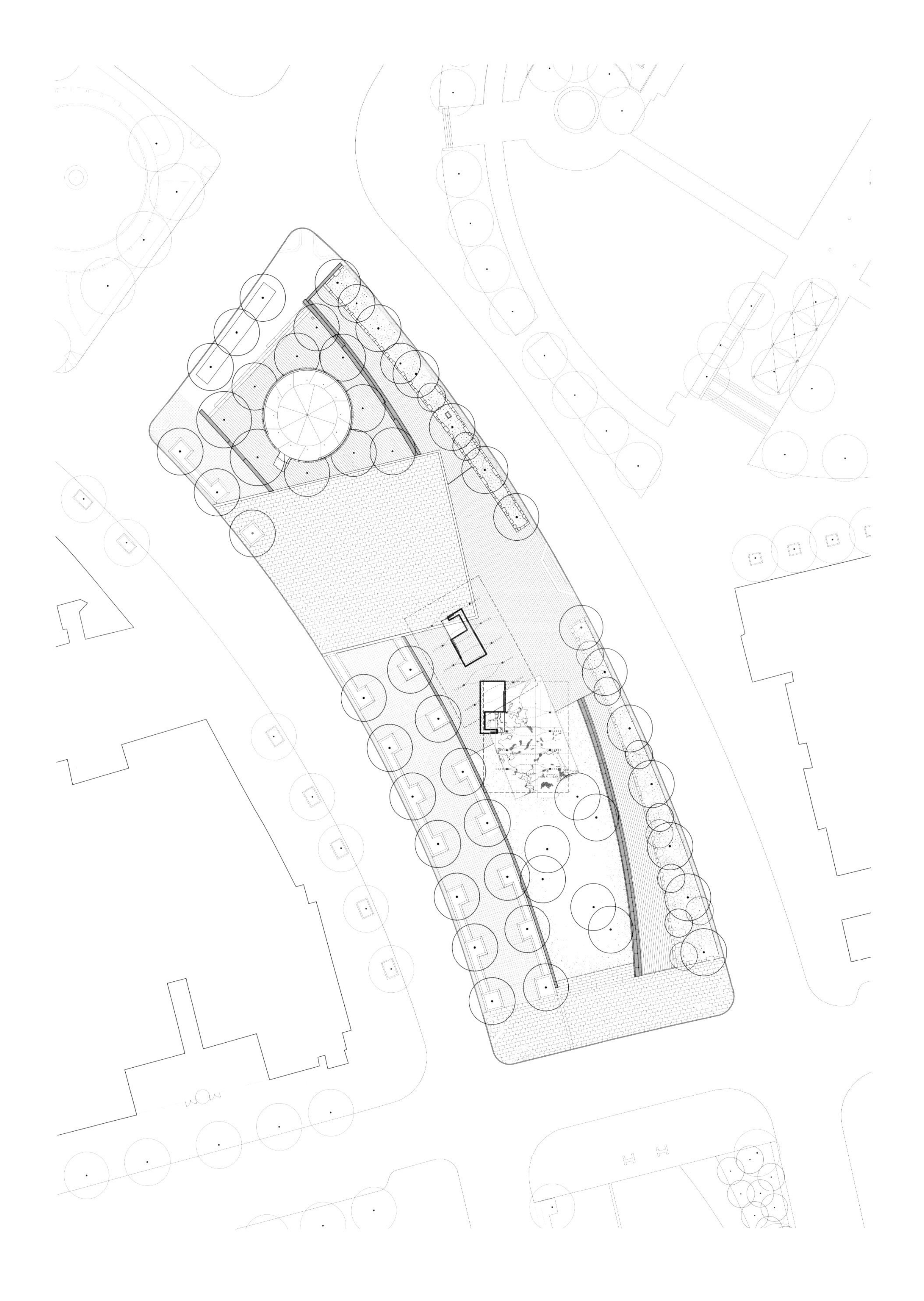

0 70

Brandeis University Waltham, Massachusetts

0 600

0
80

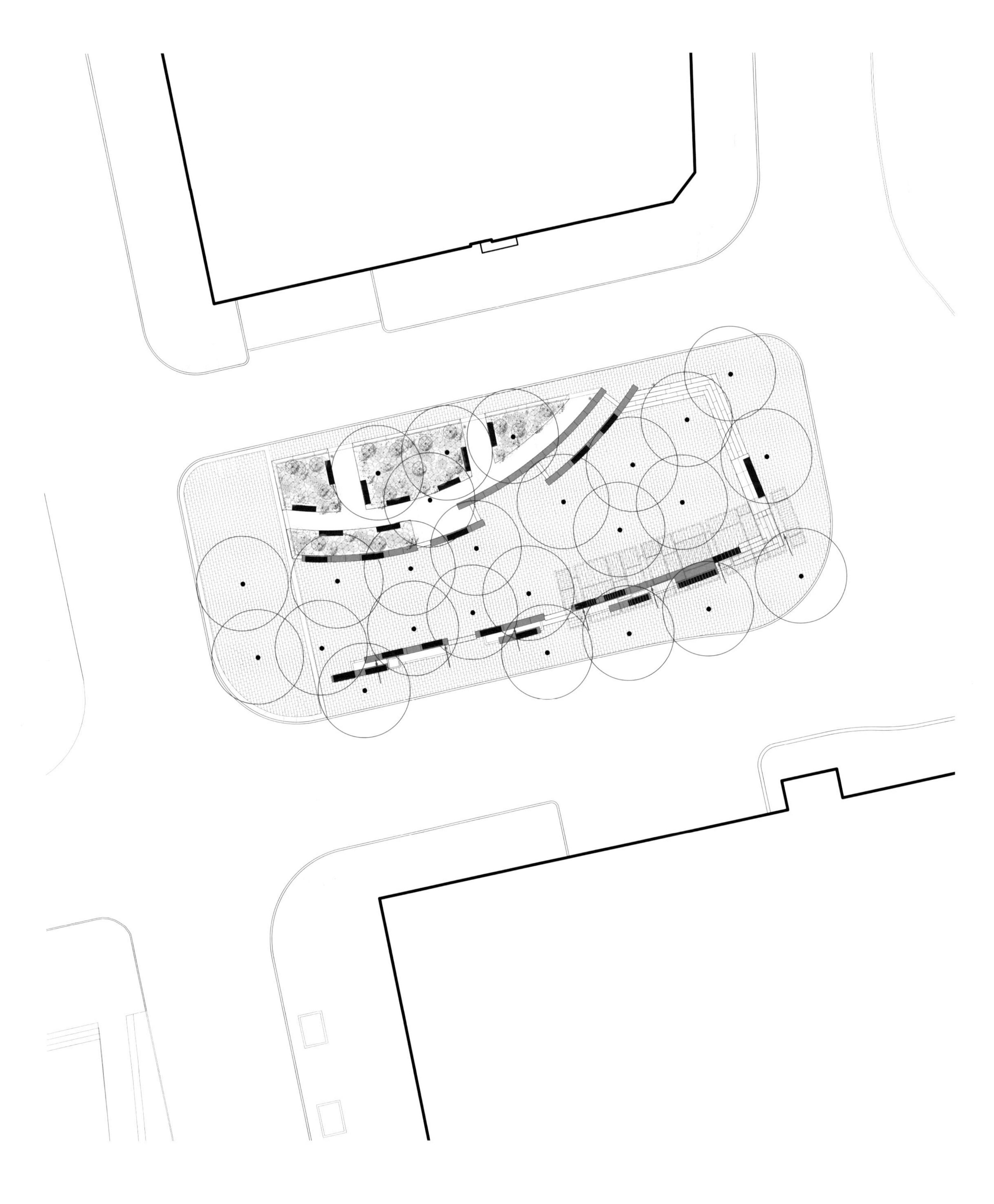

 Central Wharf Plaza Boston, Massachusetts

0
100

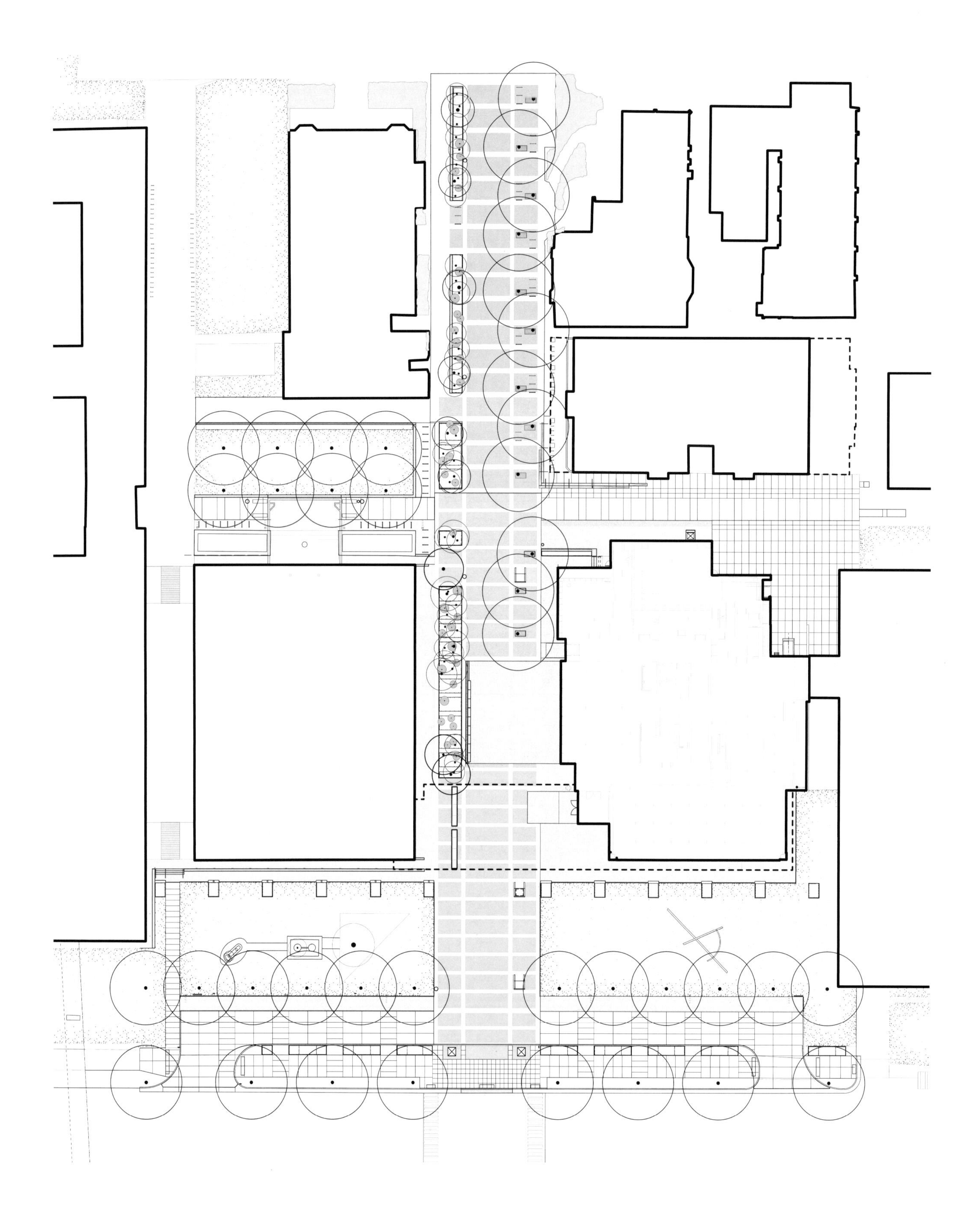

 Chazen Museum of Art Madison, Wisconsin

0 70

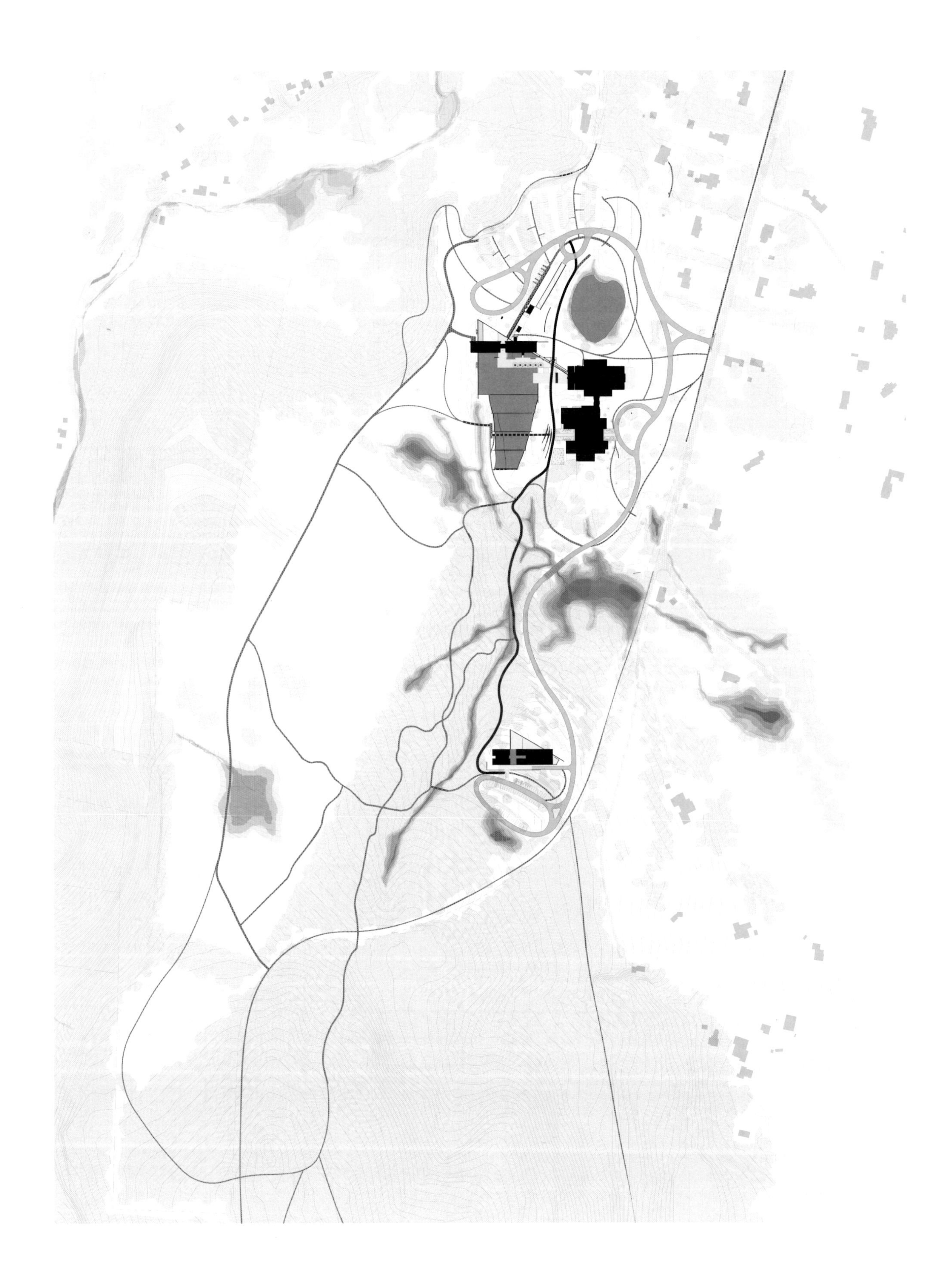

0 500

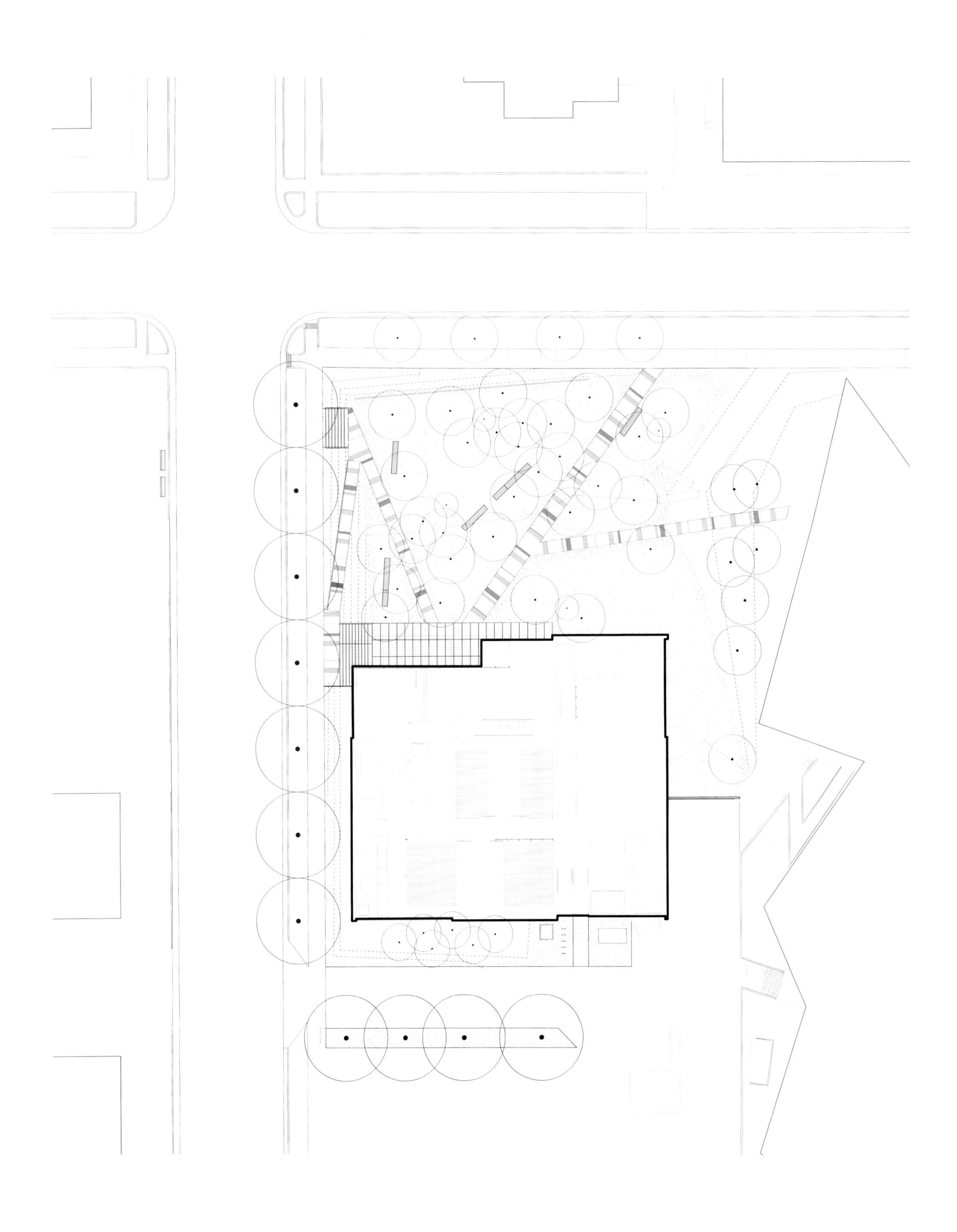

Clyfford Still Museum Denver, Colorado

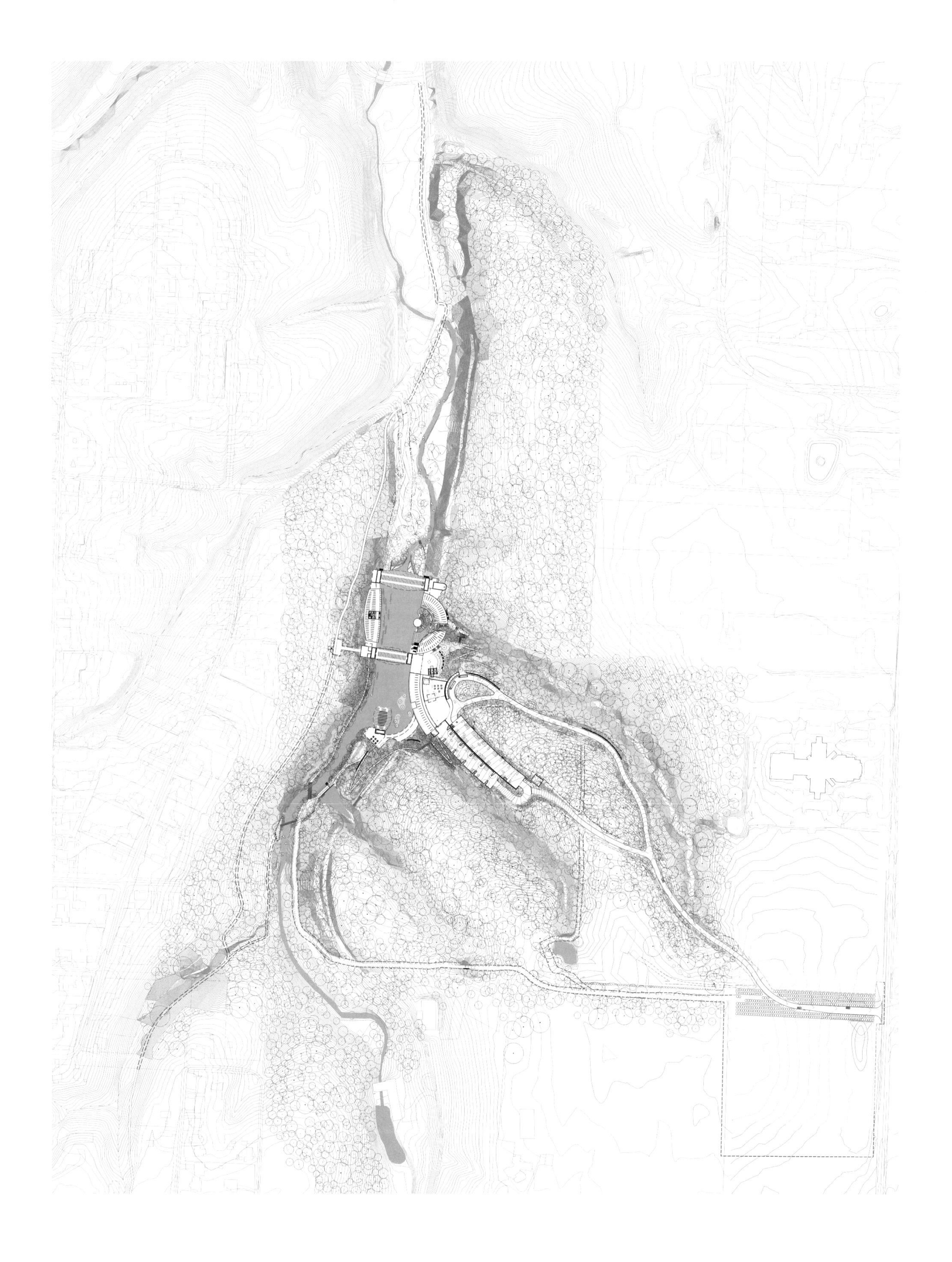

0 500

Bentonville, Arkansas Crystal Bridges Museum of American Art

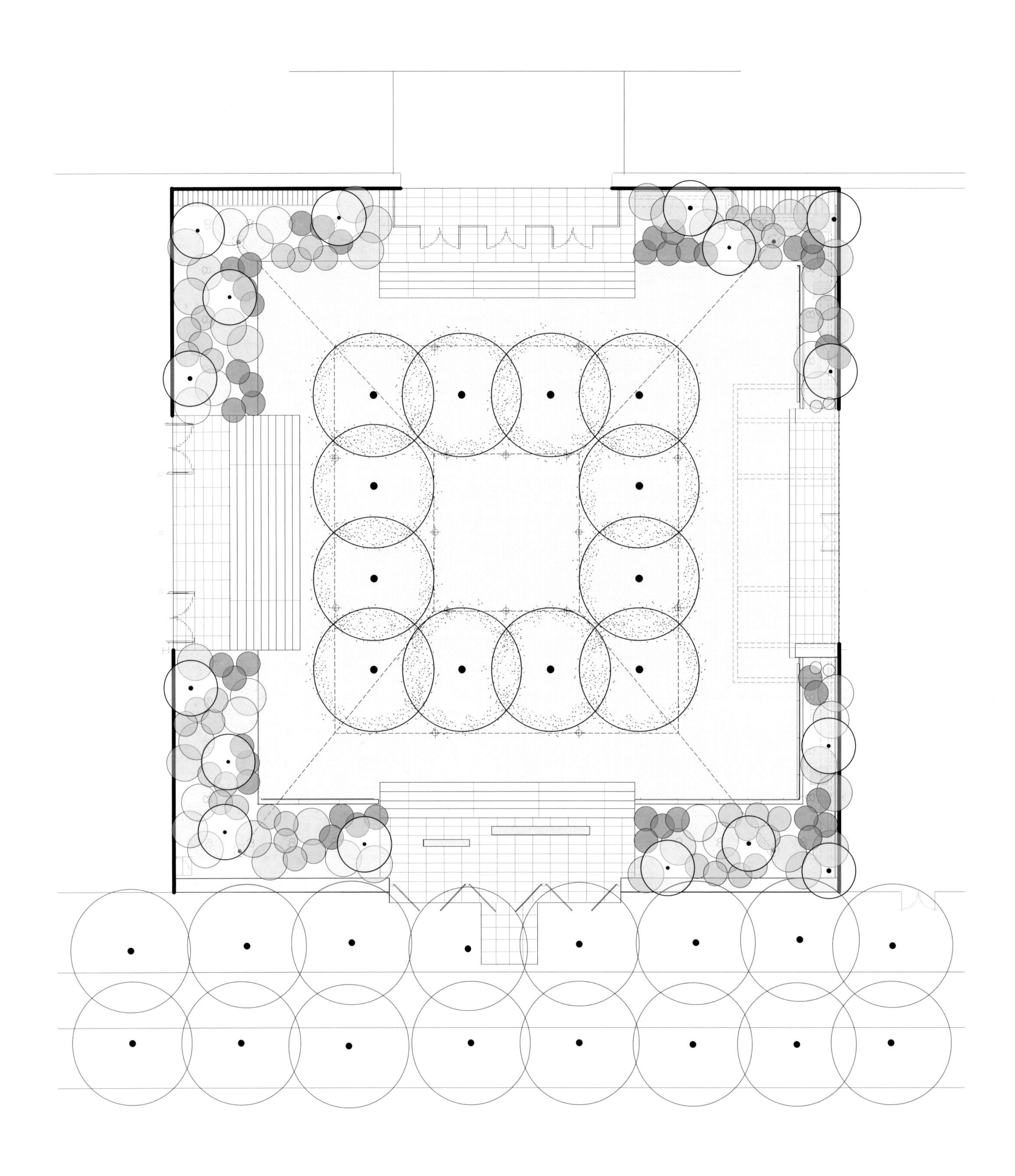

 Dallas Museum of Art Dallas, Texas

0 20

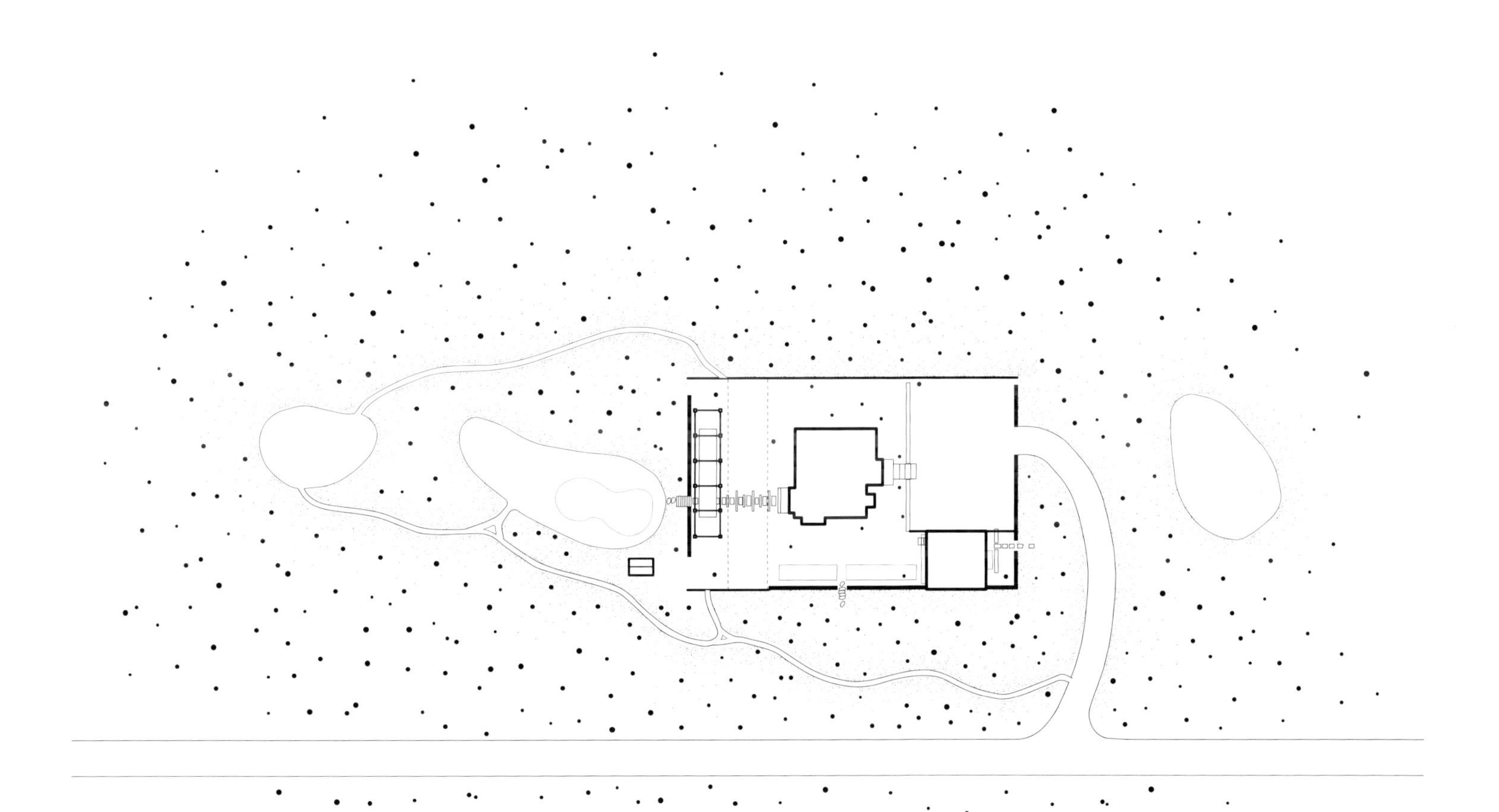

0 70

Duke University Campus Drive Durham, North Carolina

0 200

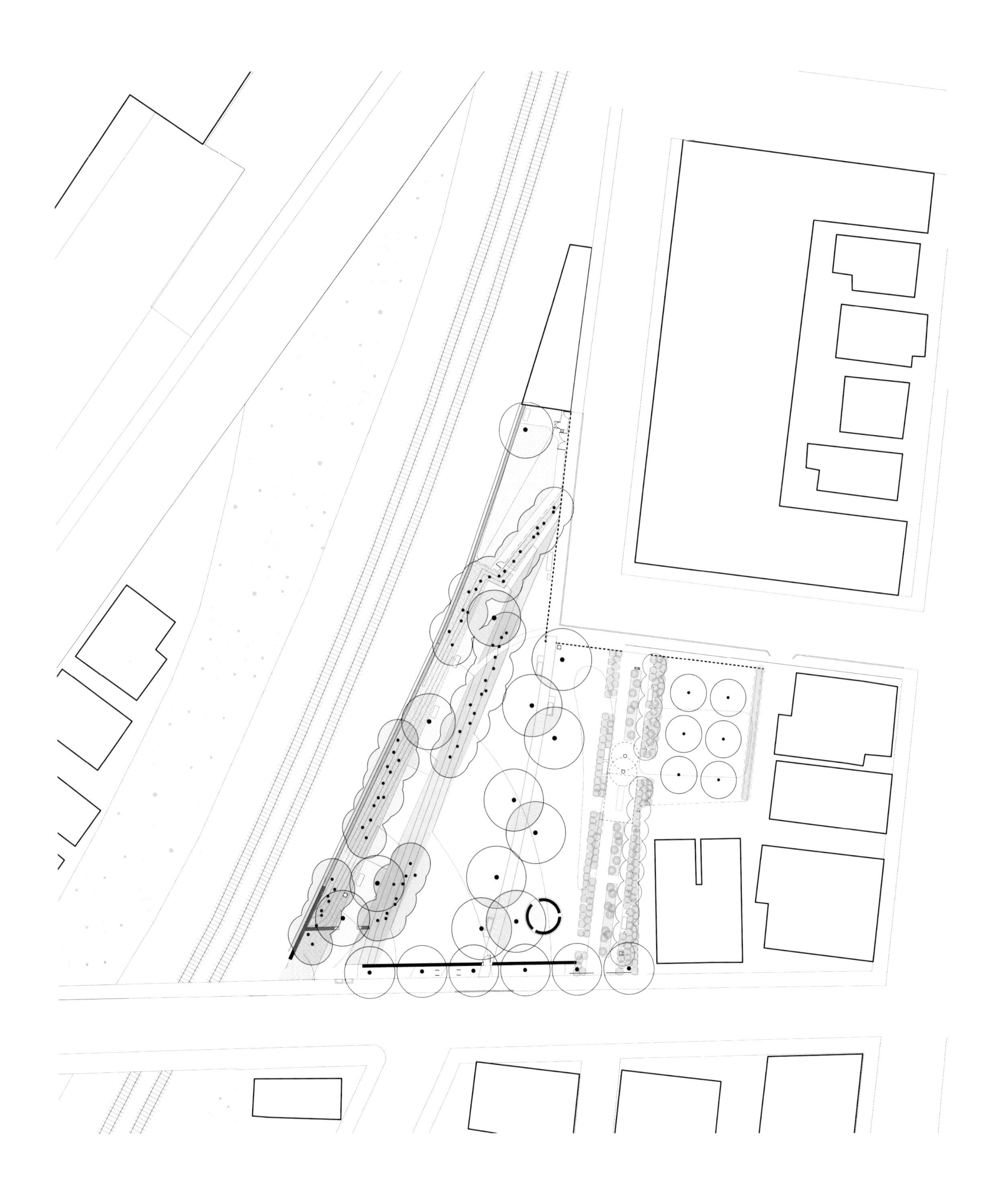

Edward Leathers Community Park Somerville, Massachusetts

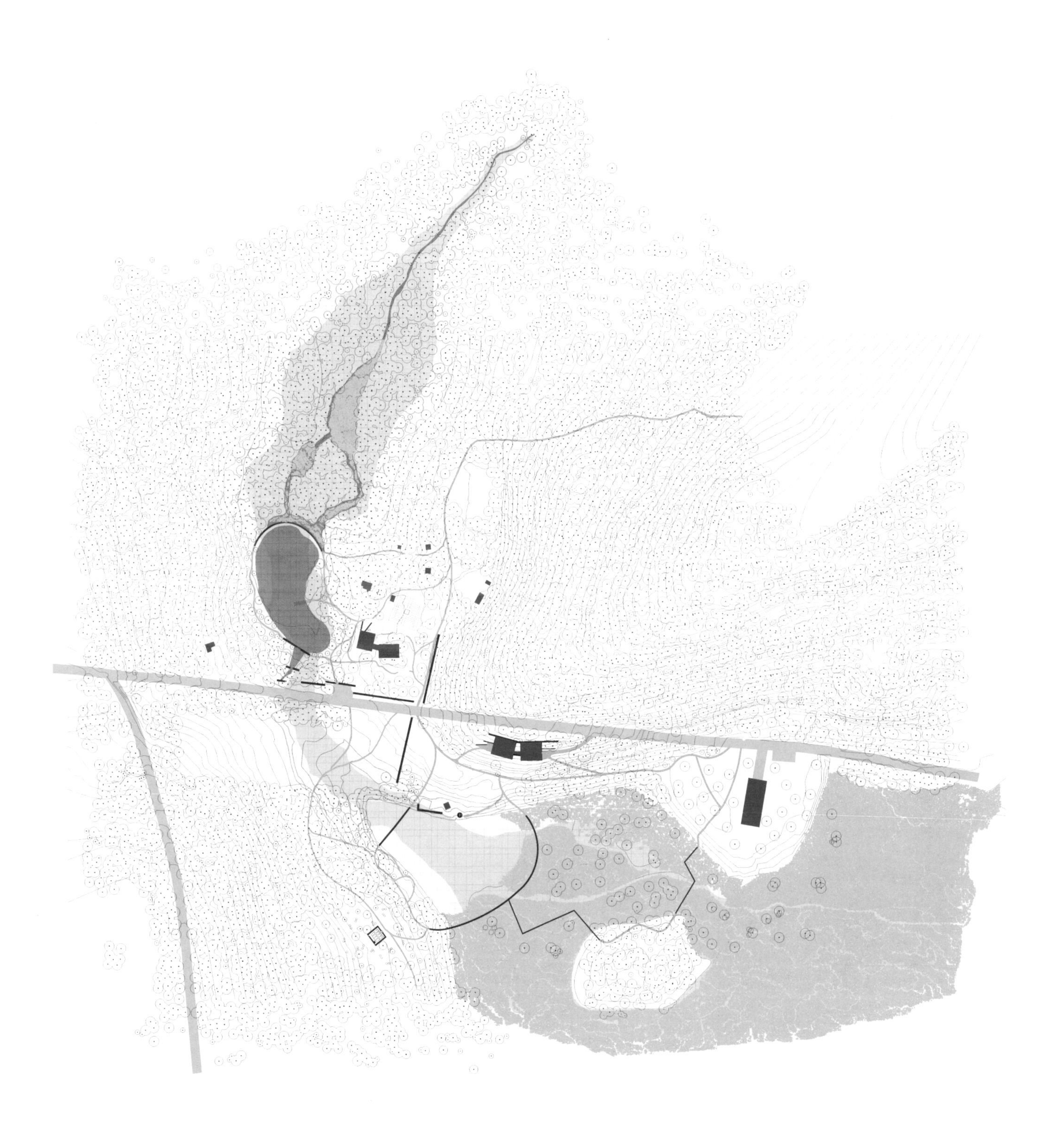

0
300

Greenlee House Dallas, Texas

0 100

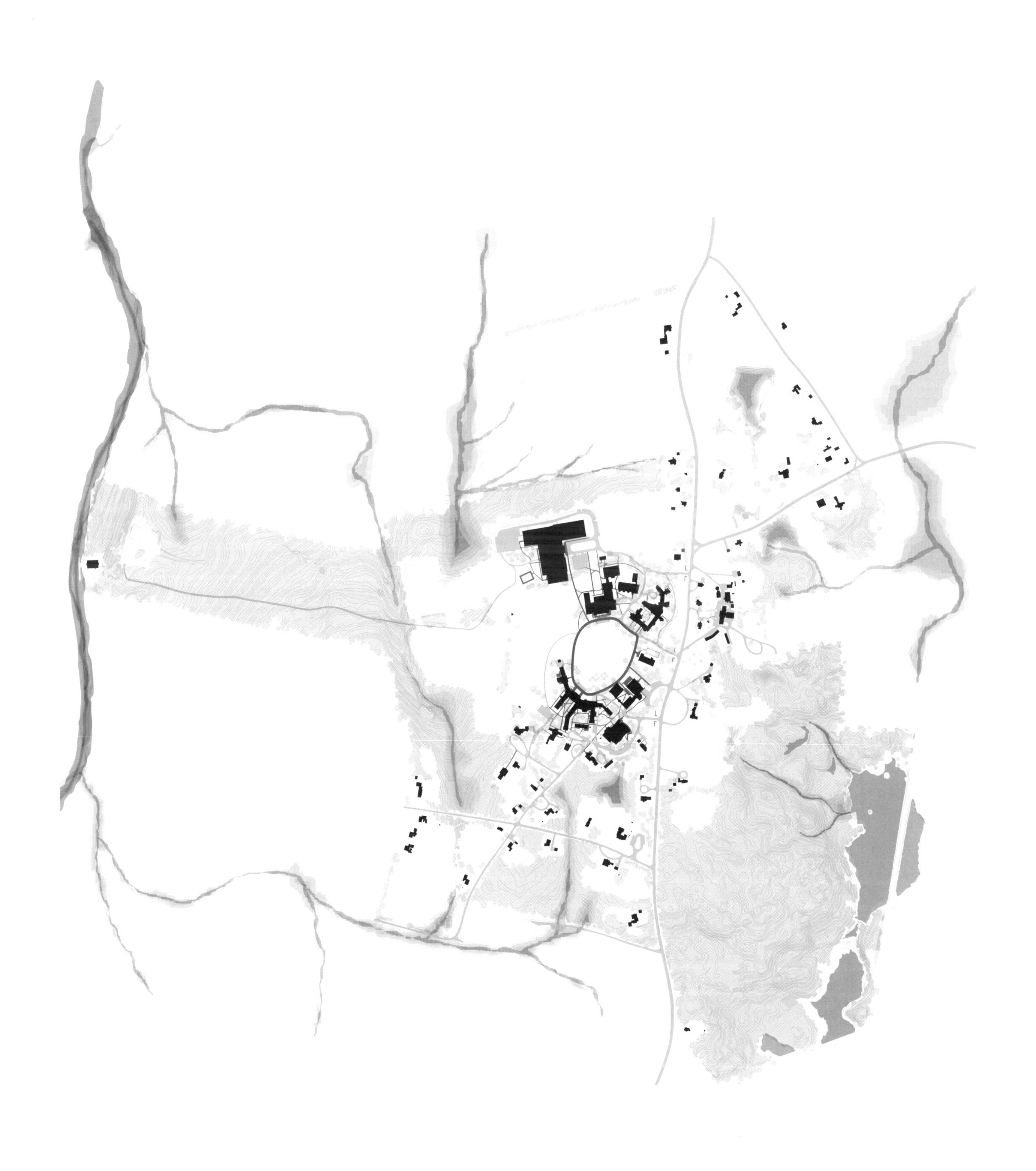

Groton, Massachusetts

Groton School

 Half-Mile Line Stockbridge, Massachusetts

0 400

Boston, Massachusetts

Harvard Business School

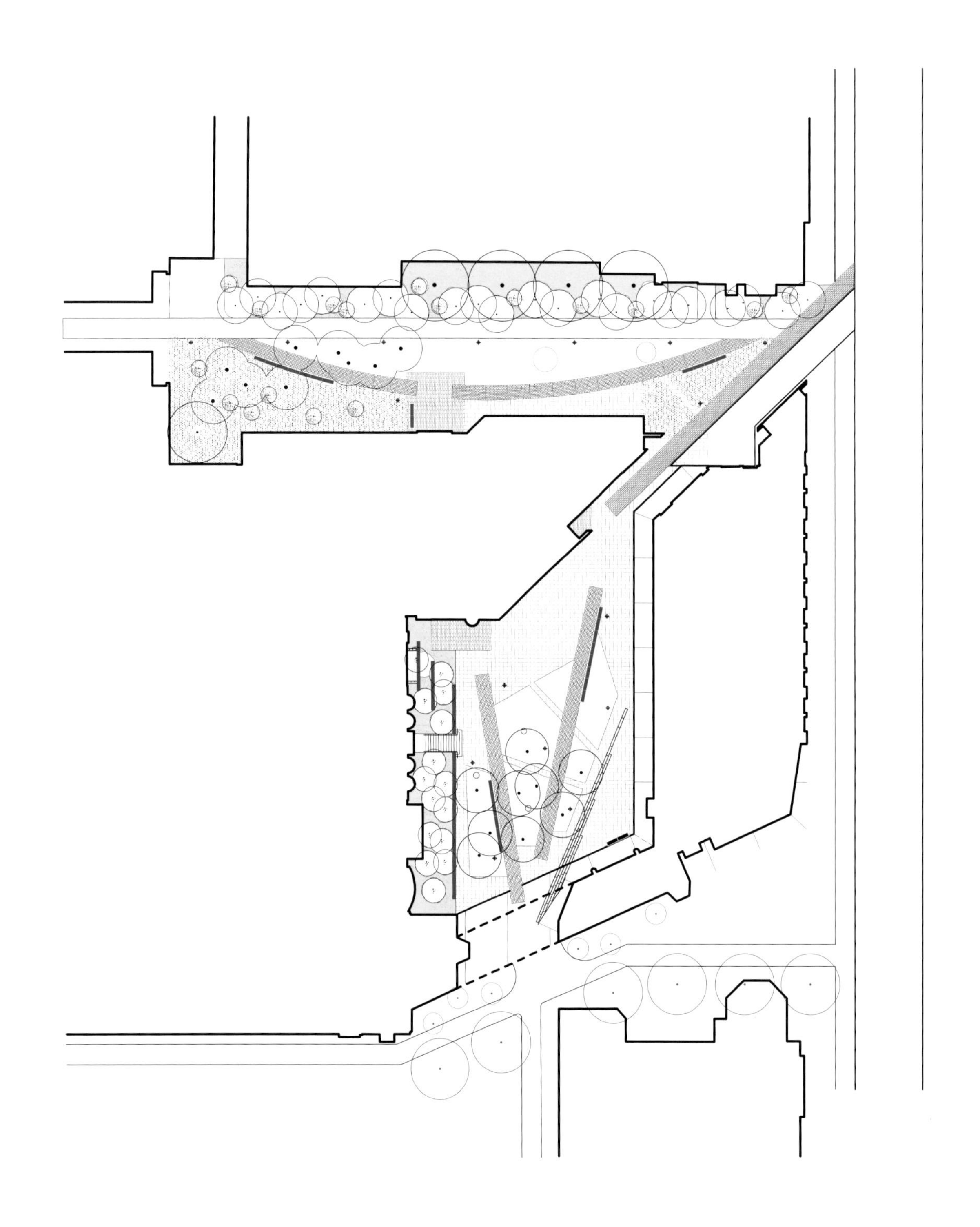

 Harvard Naito/Bauer Laboratories Cambridge, Massachusetts

0 80

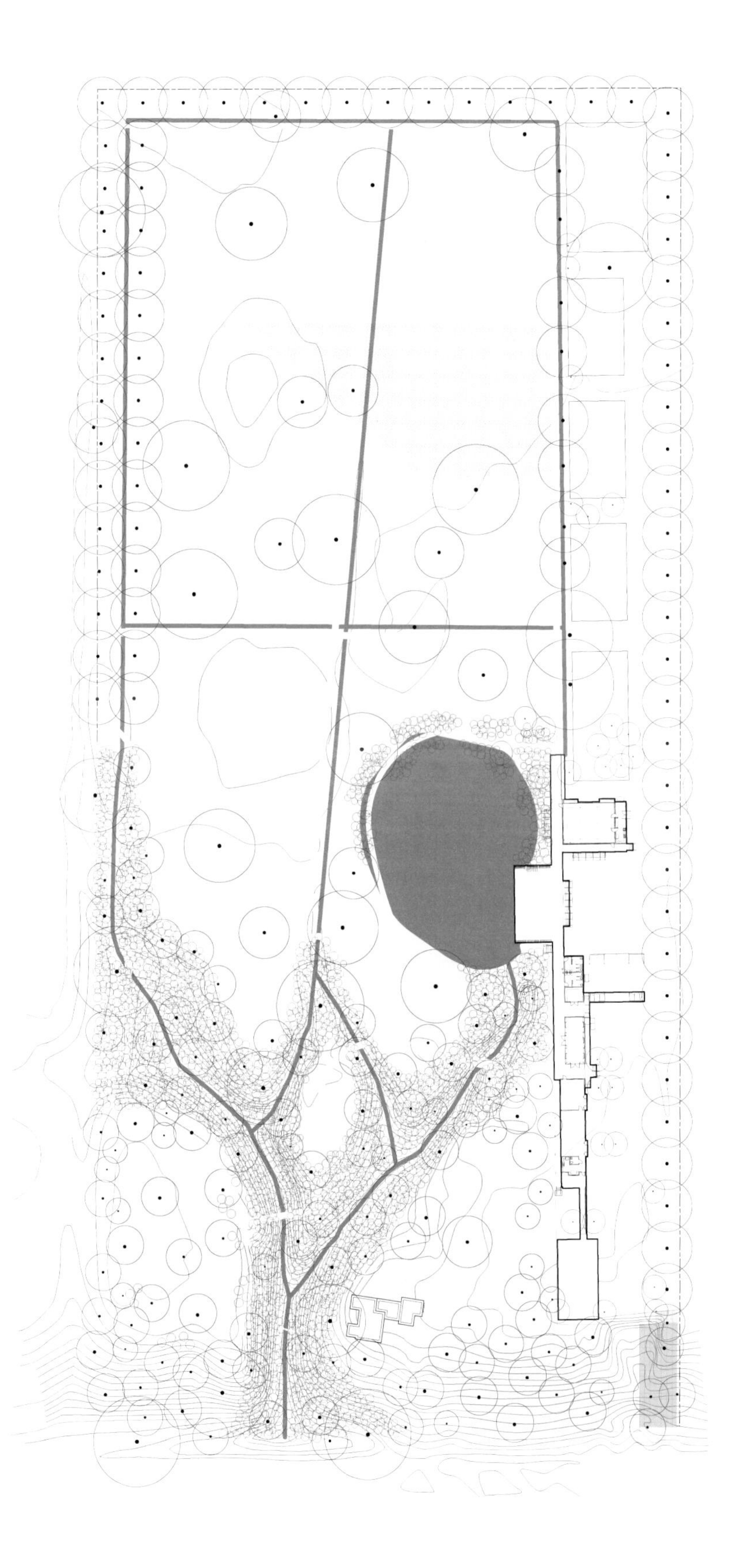

Baton Rouge, Louisiana Hilltop Arboretum

Hither Lane East Hampton, New York

0 120

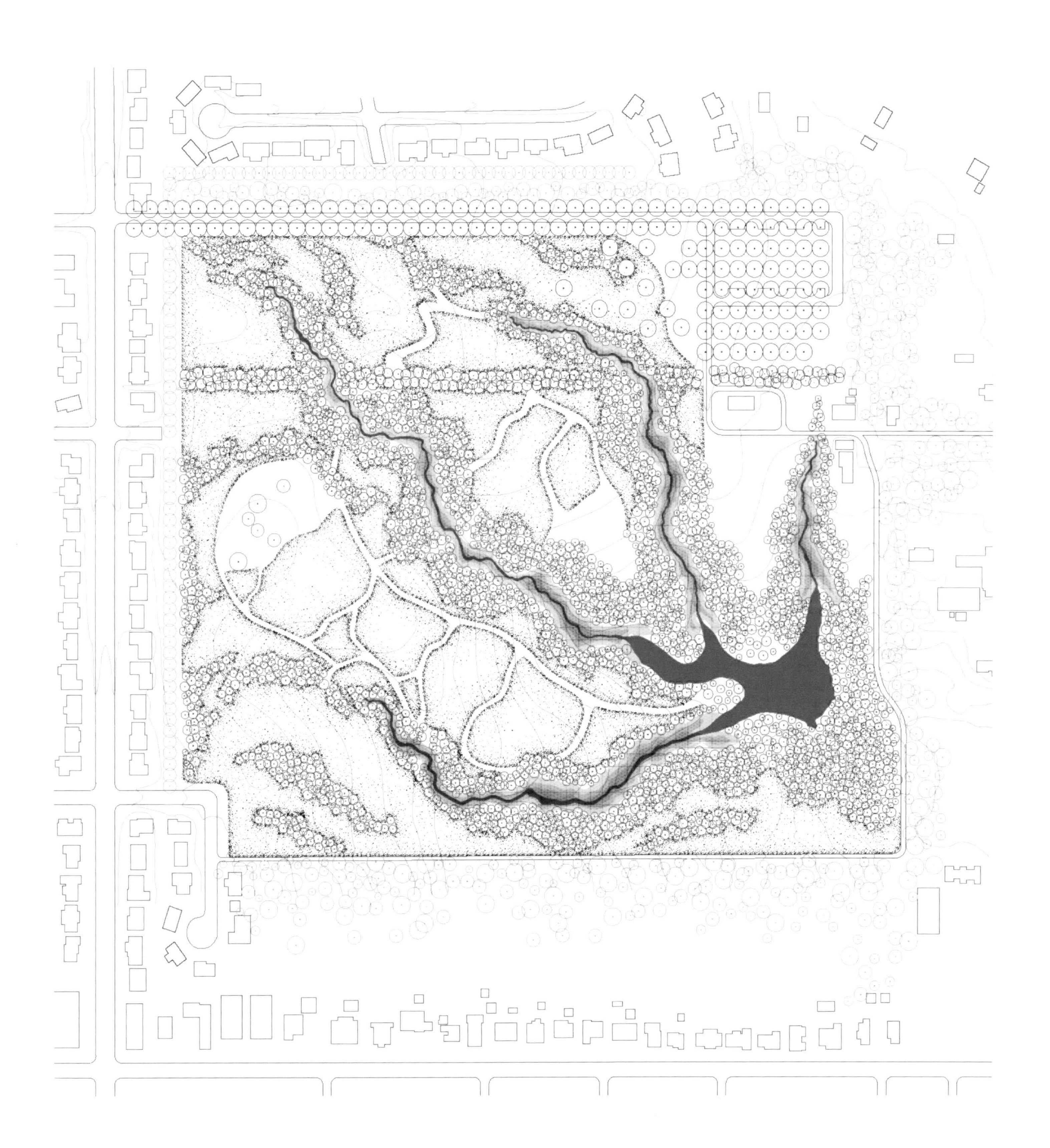

Troy, Ohio Hobart Urban Nature Preserve

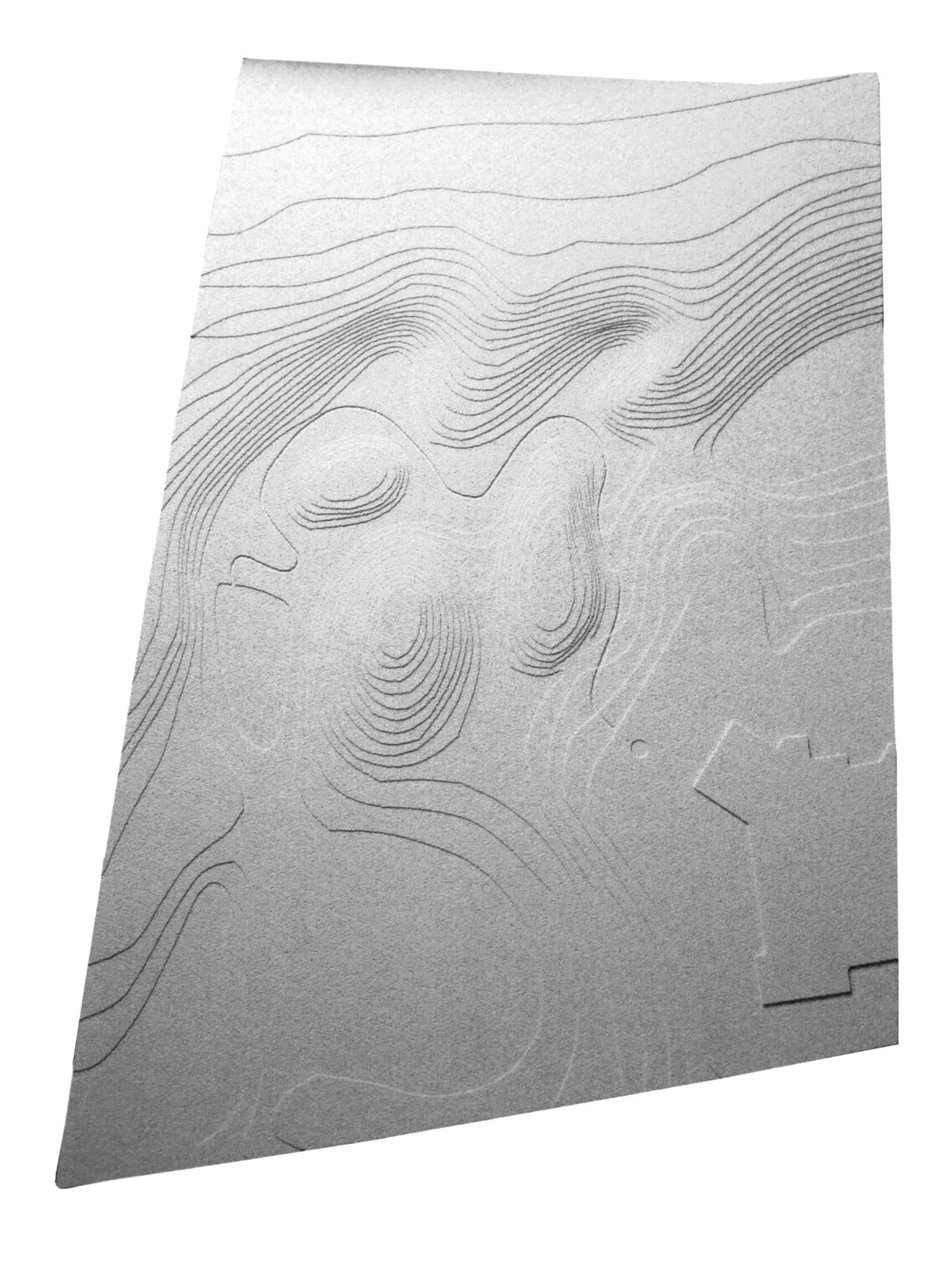

Institute for Child and Adolescent Development Wellesley, Massachusetts

0 50

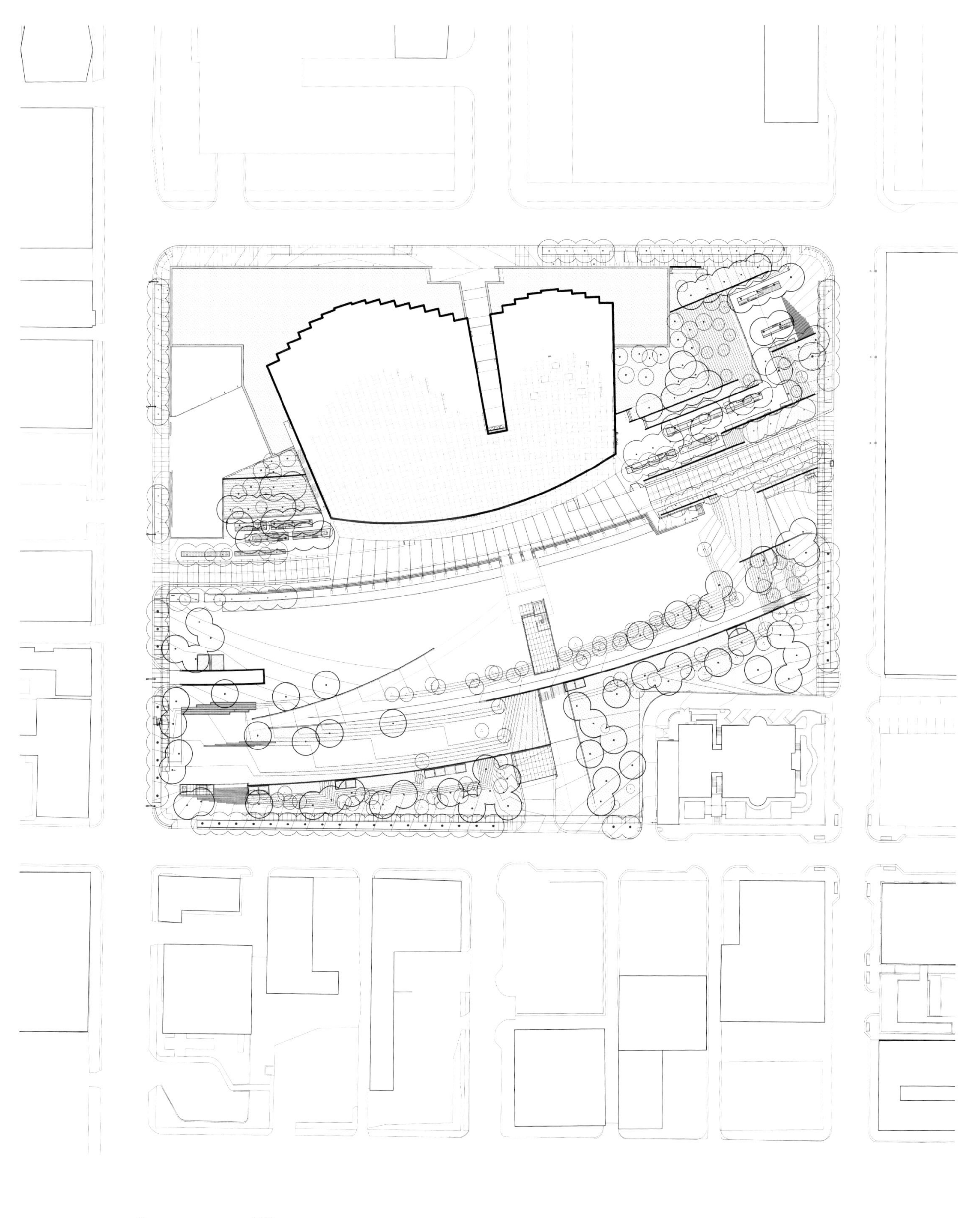
0
150

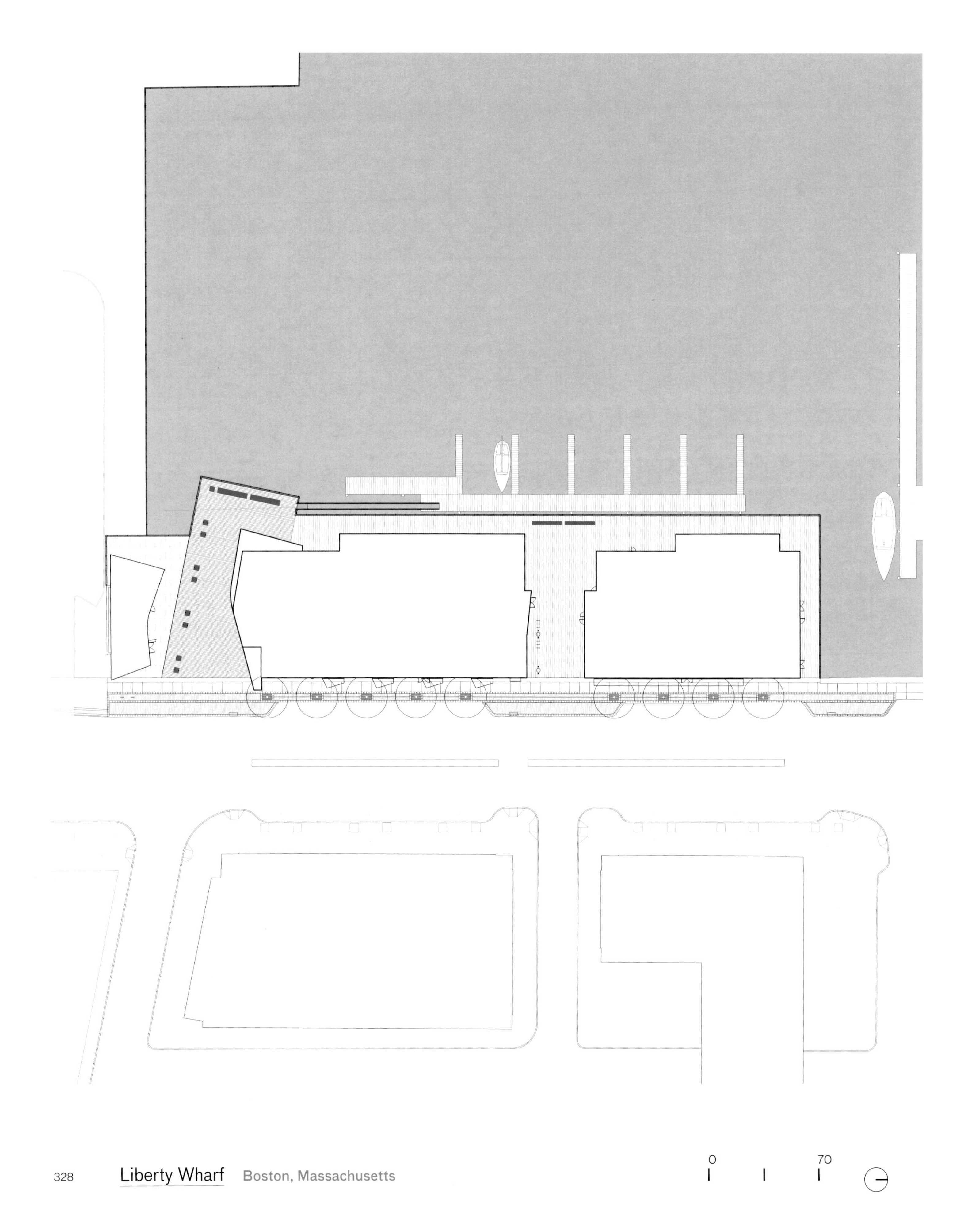

 Liberty Wharf Boston, Massachusetts

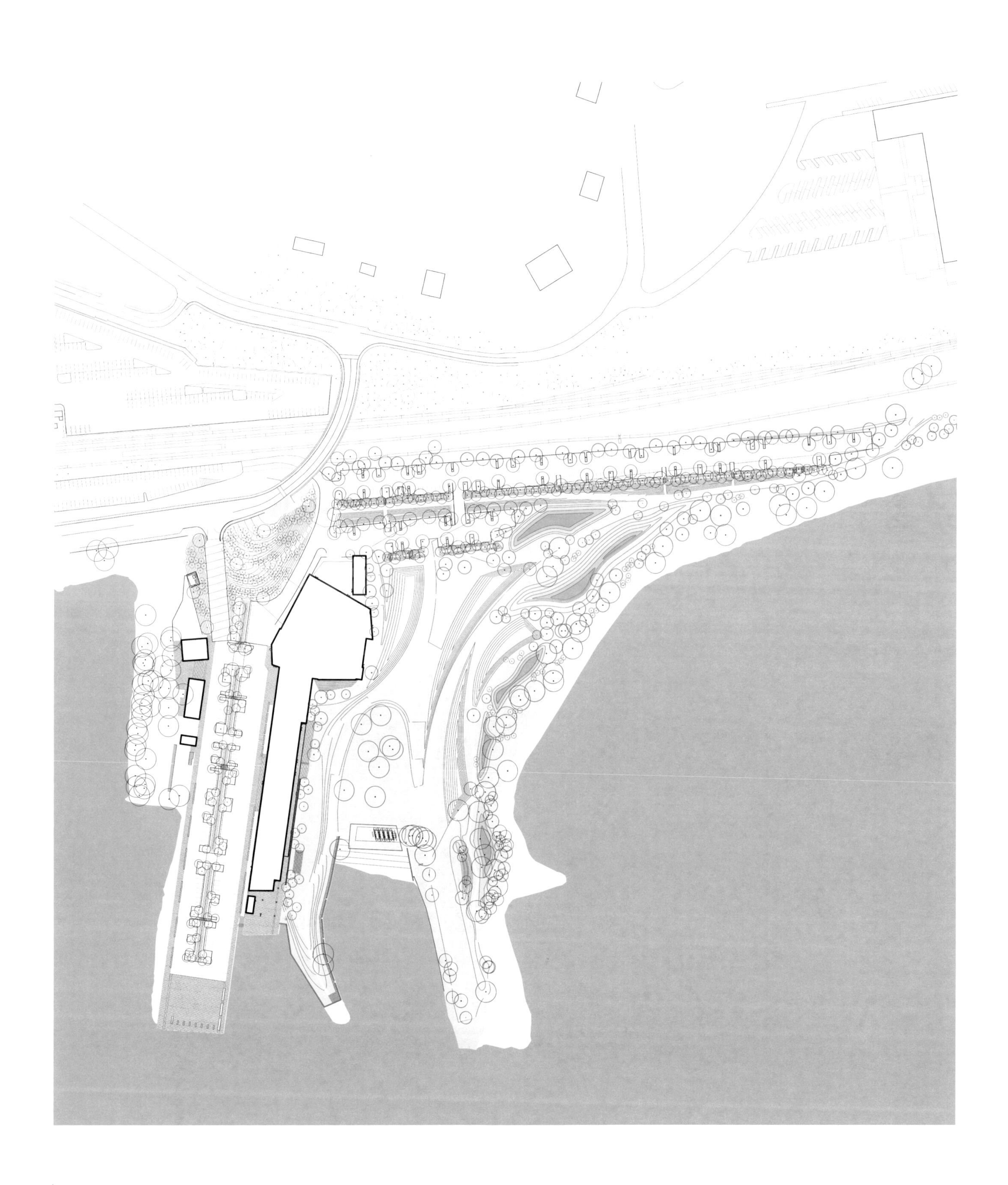

0
240

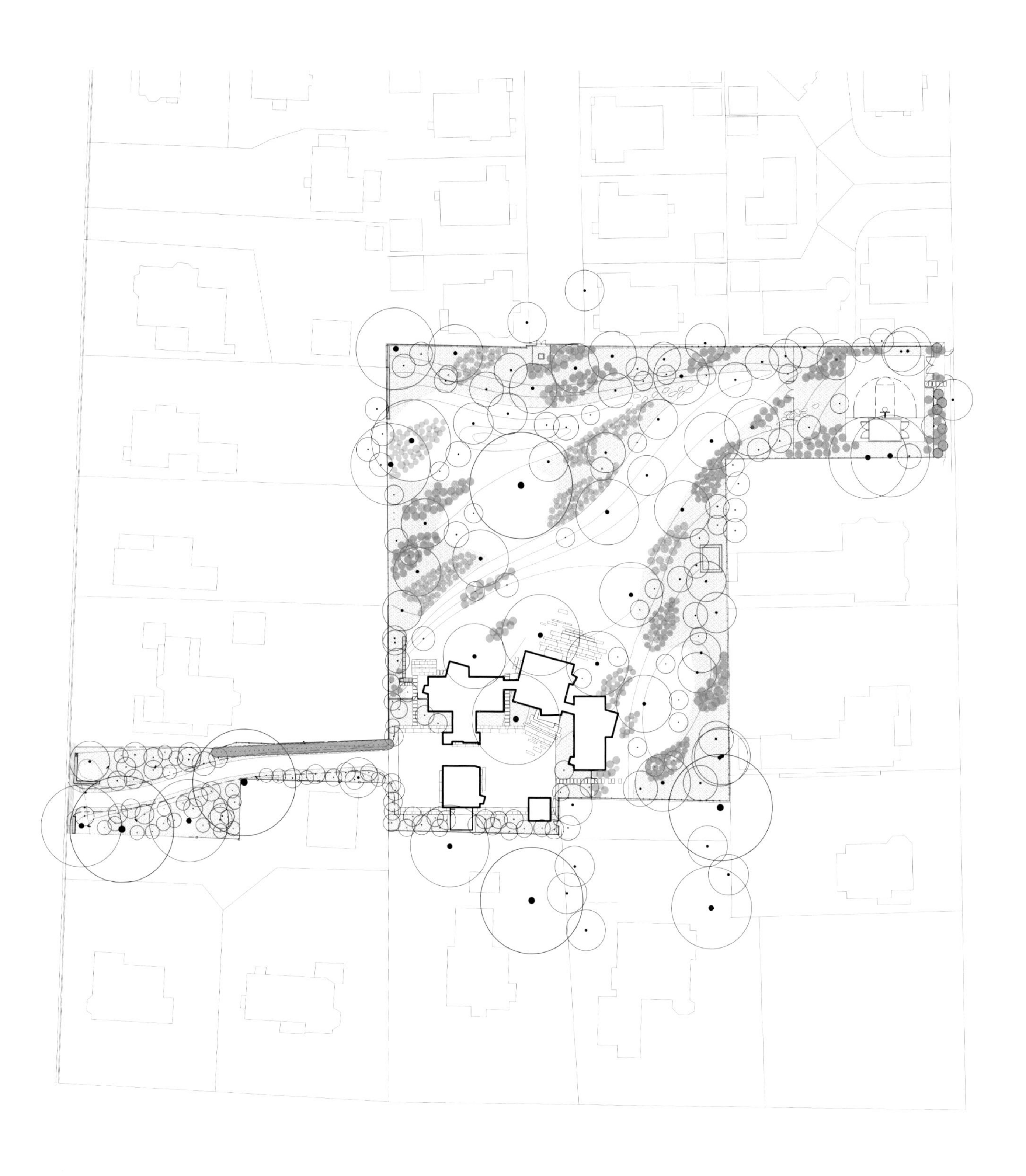

Lowell Street Cambridge, Massachusetts

0 80

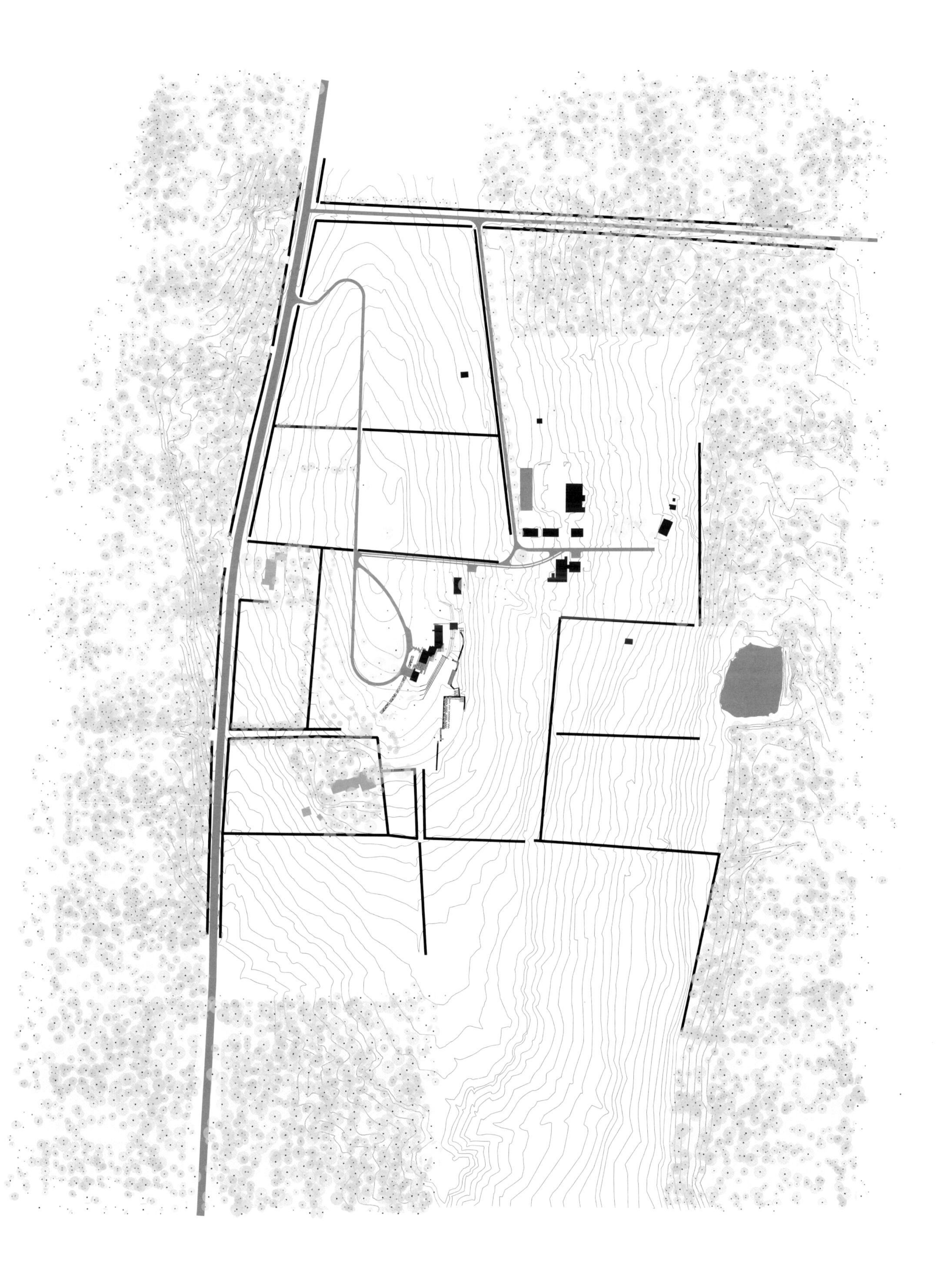
0
400

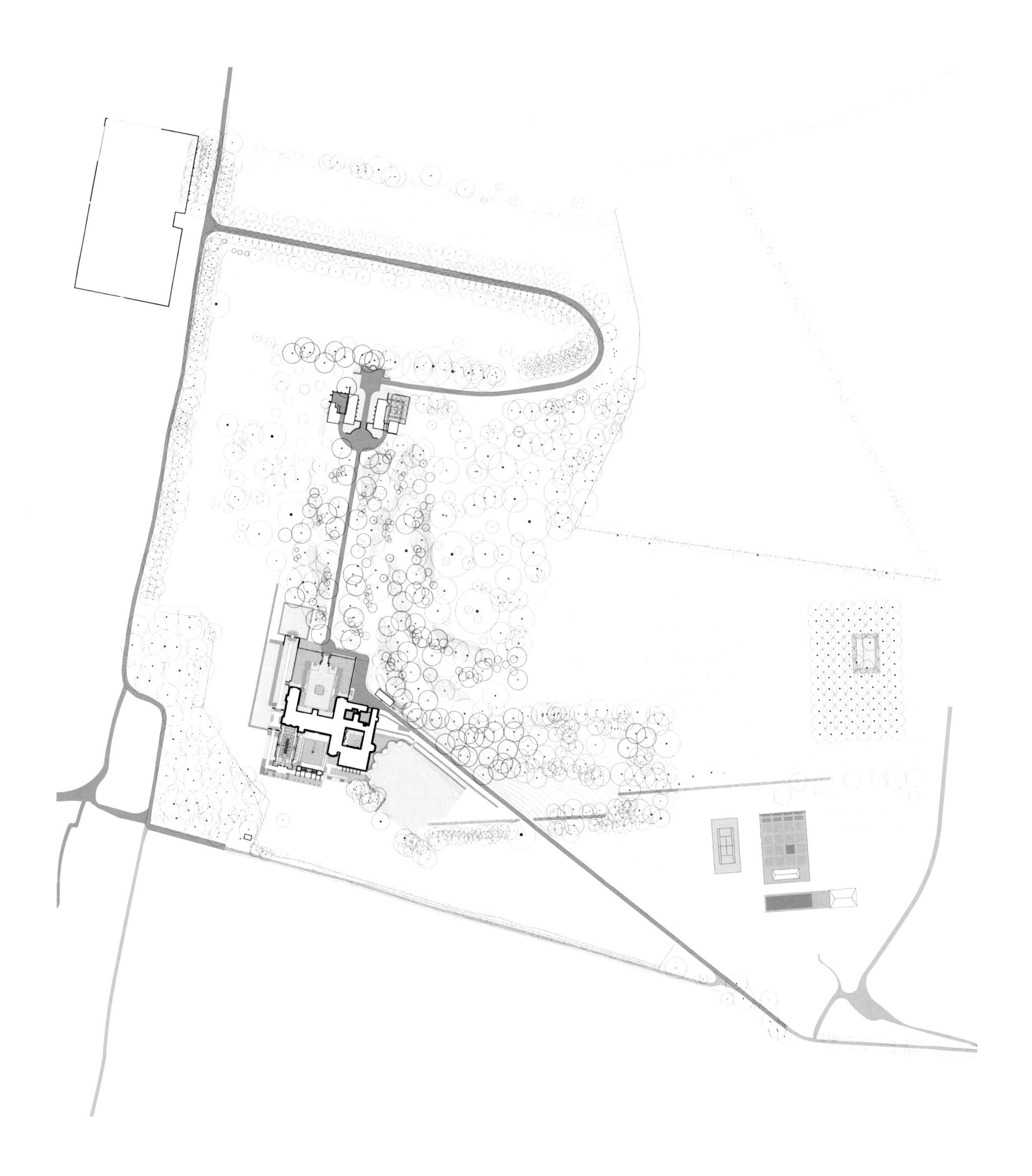

 Marsh Court Stockbridge, Hampshire, U. K.

0 400

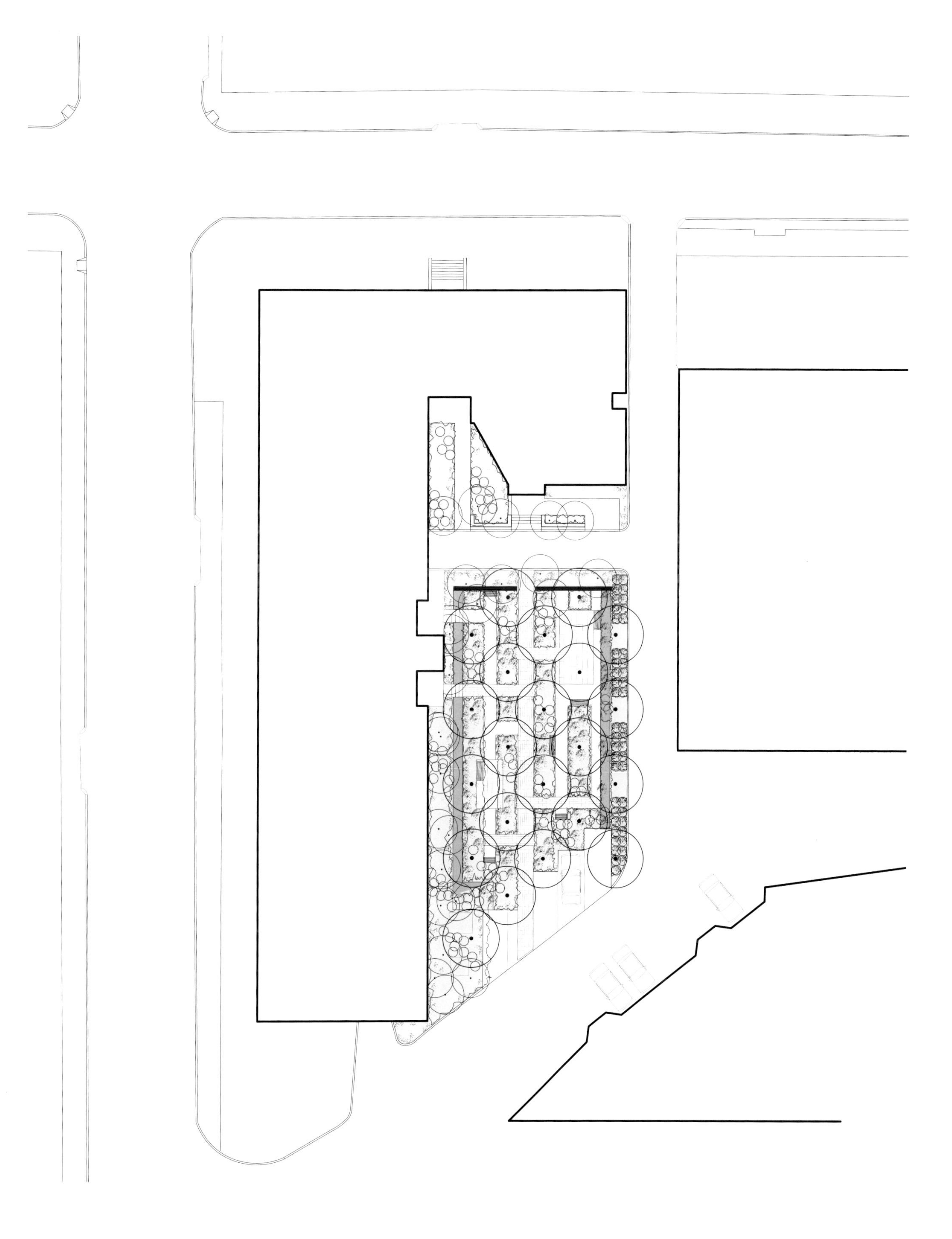
0
40

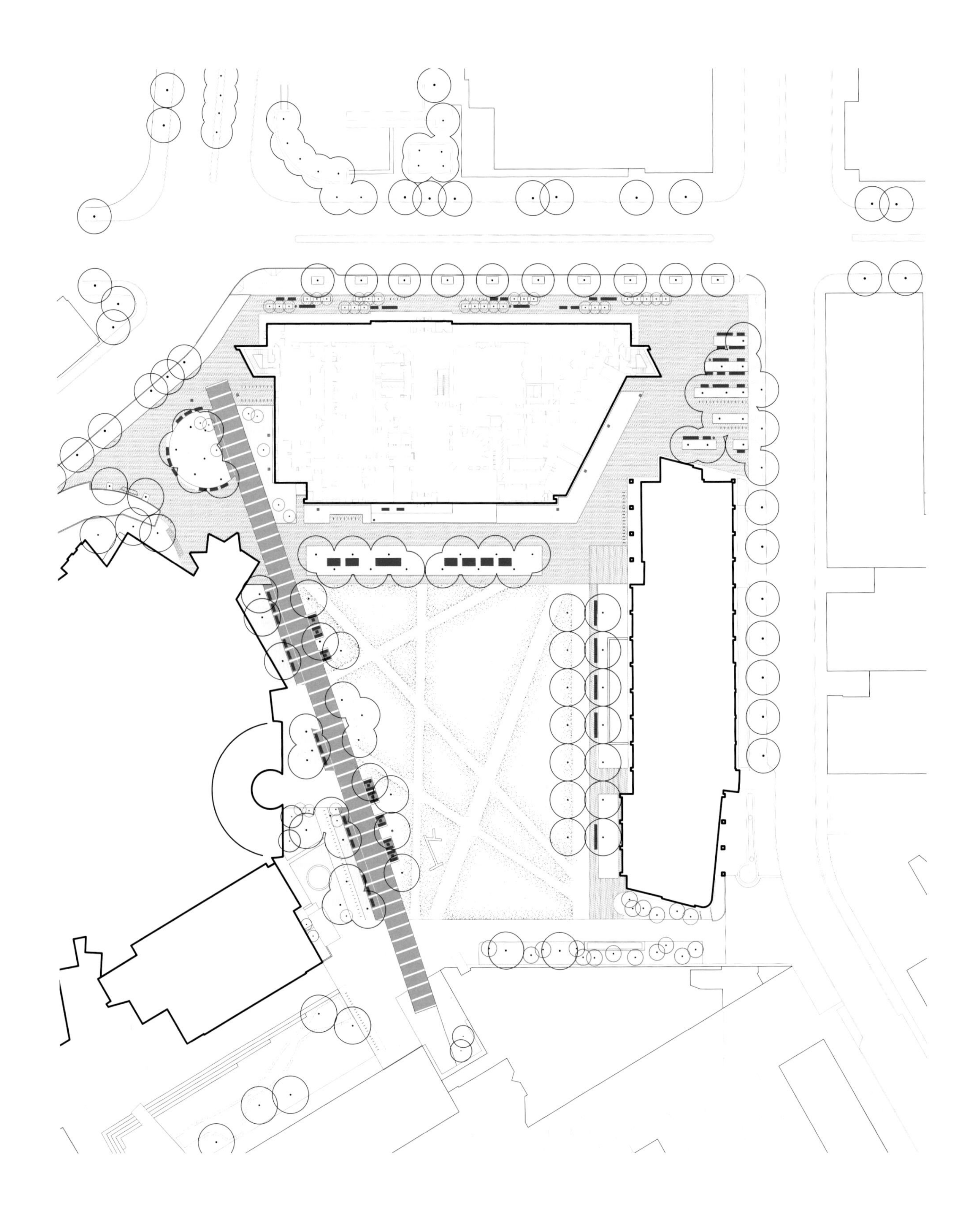

MIT North Court and Main Street Cambridge, Massachusetts

0 100

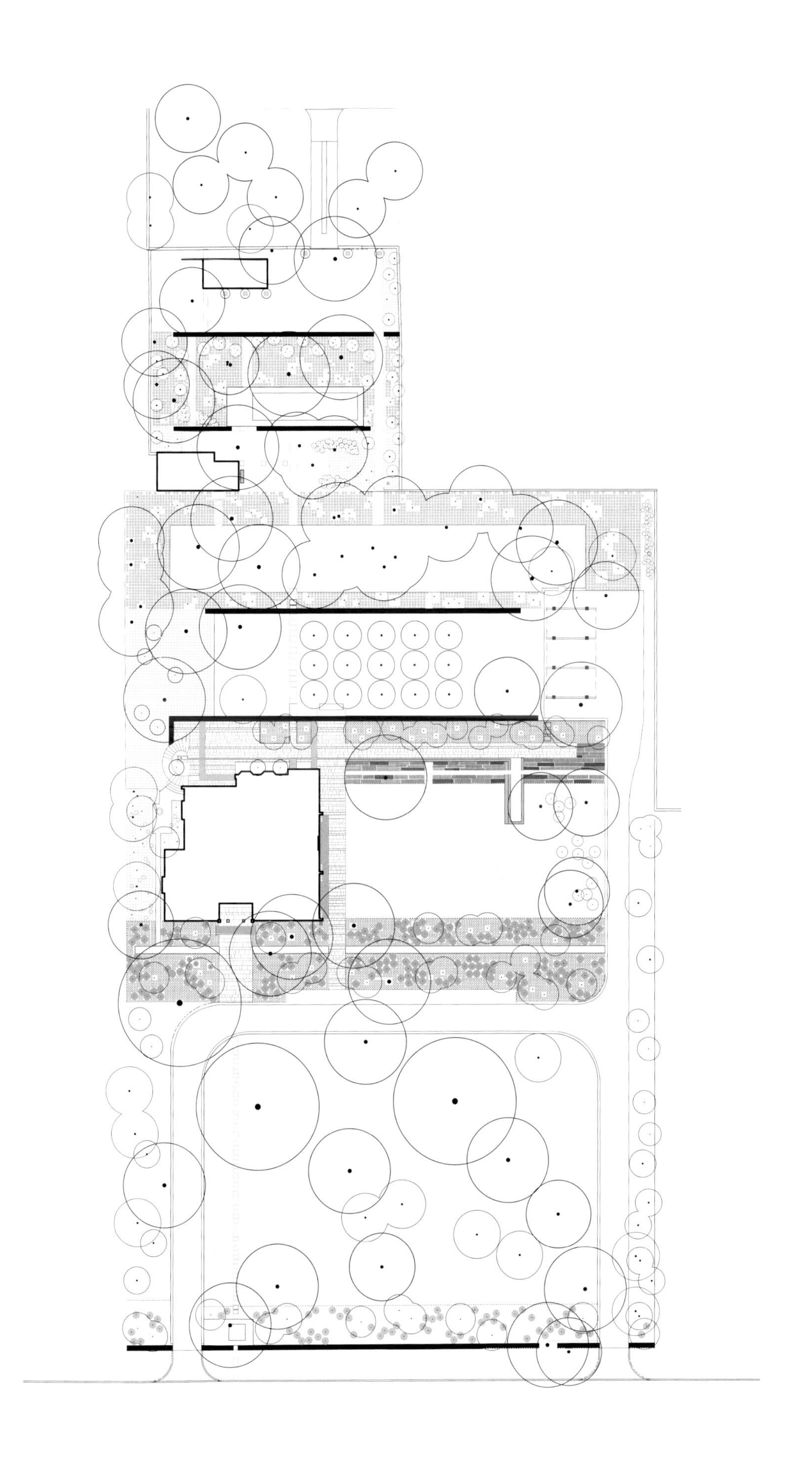

0 80

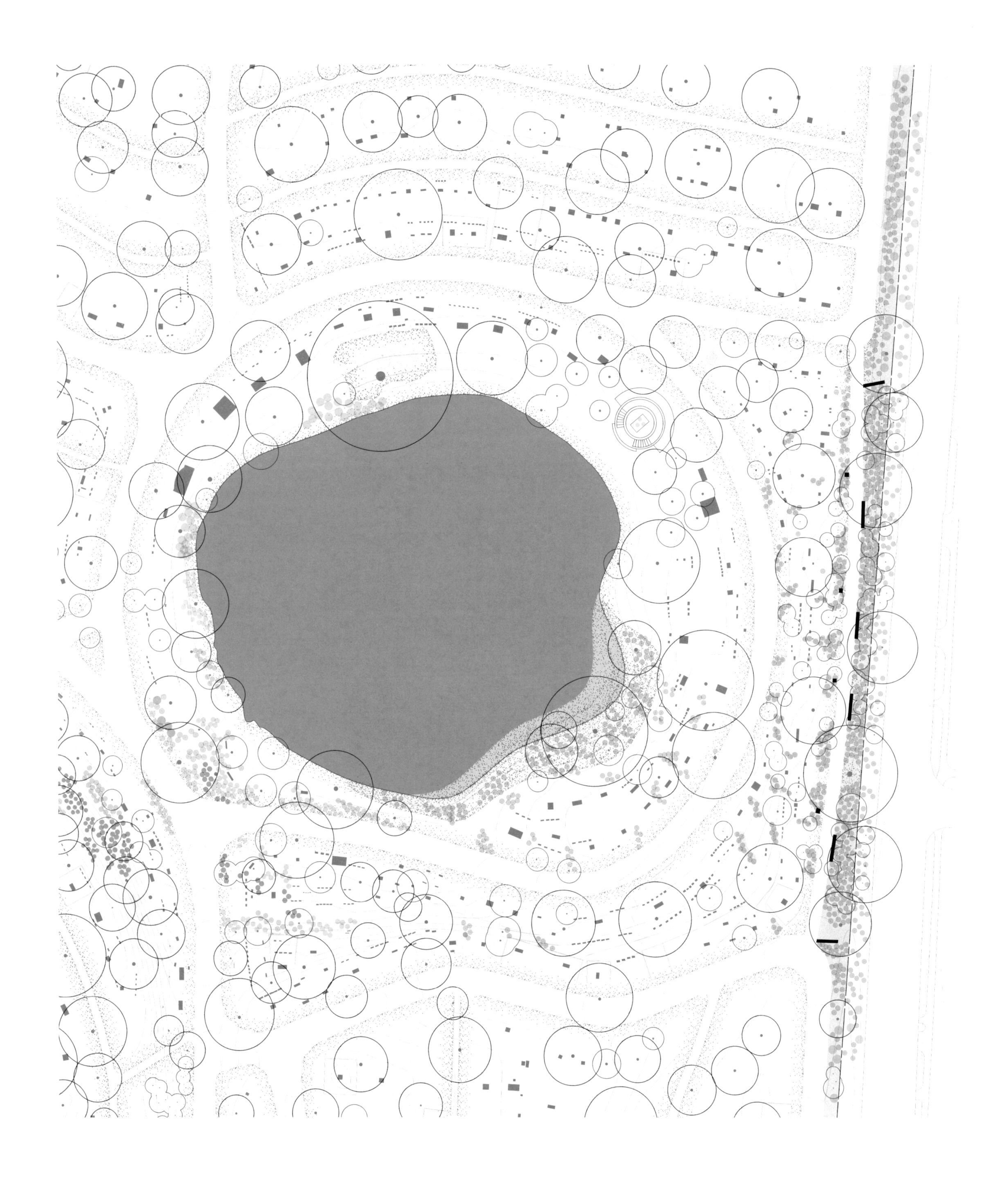

Mount Auburn Cemetery Cambridge, Massachusetts

0 80

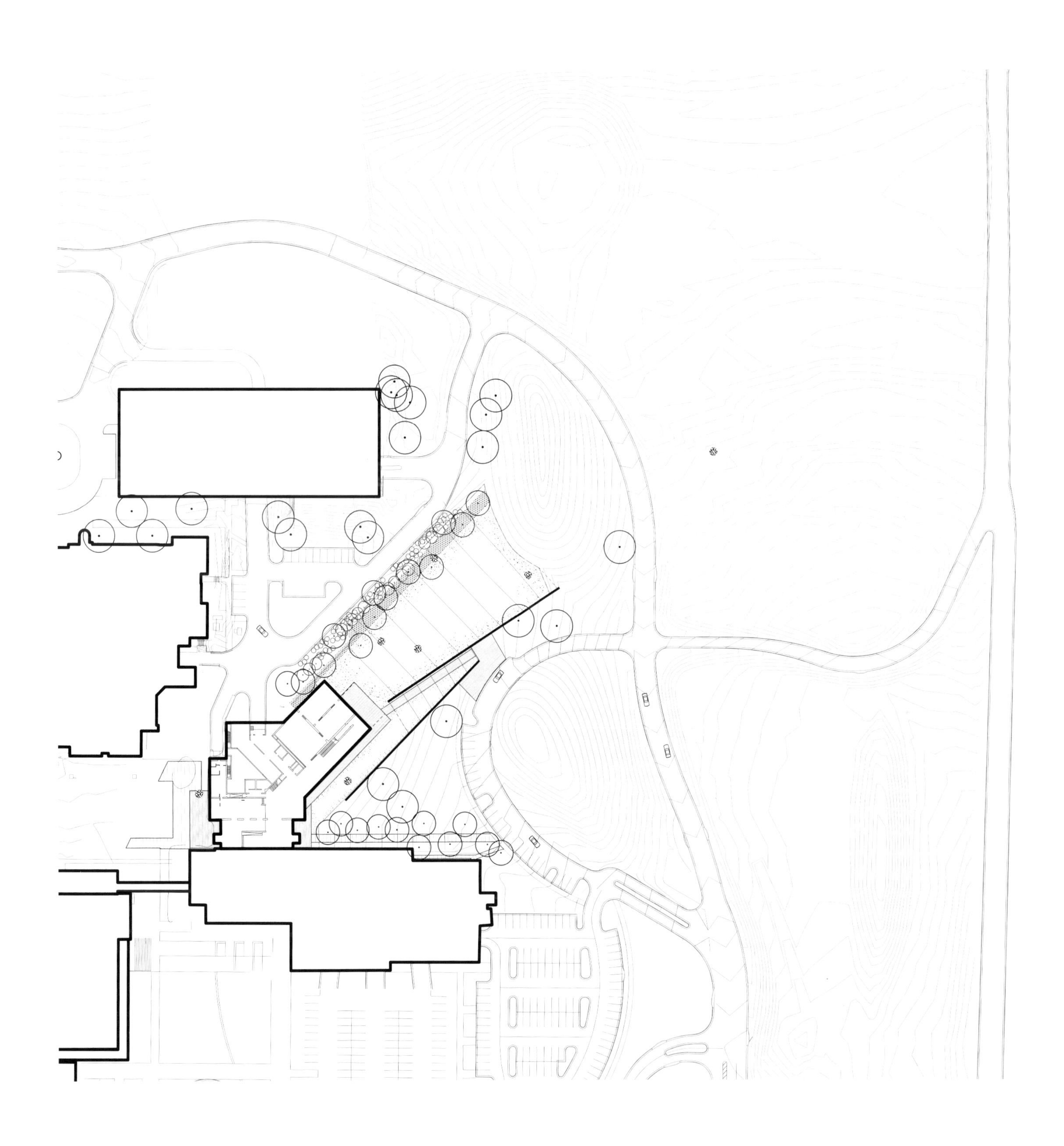

0
160

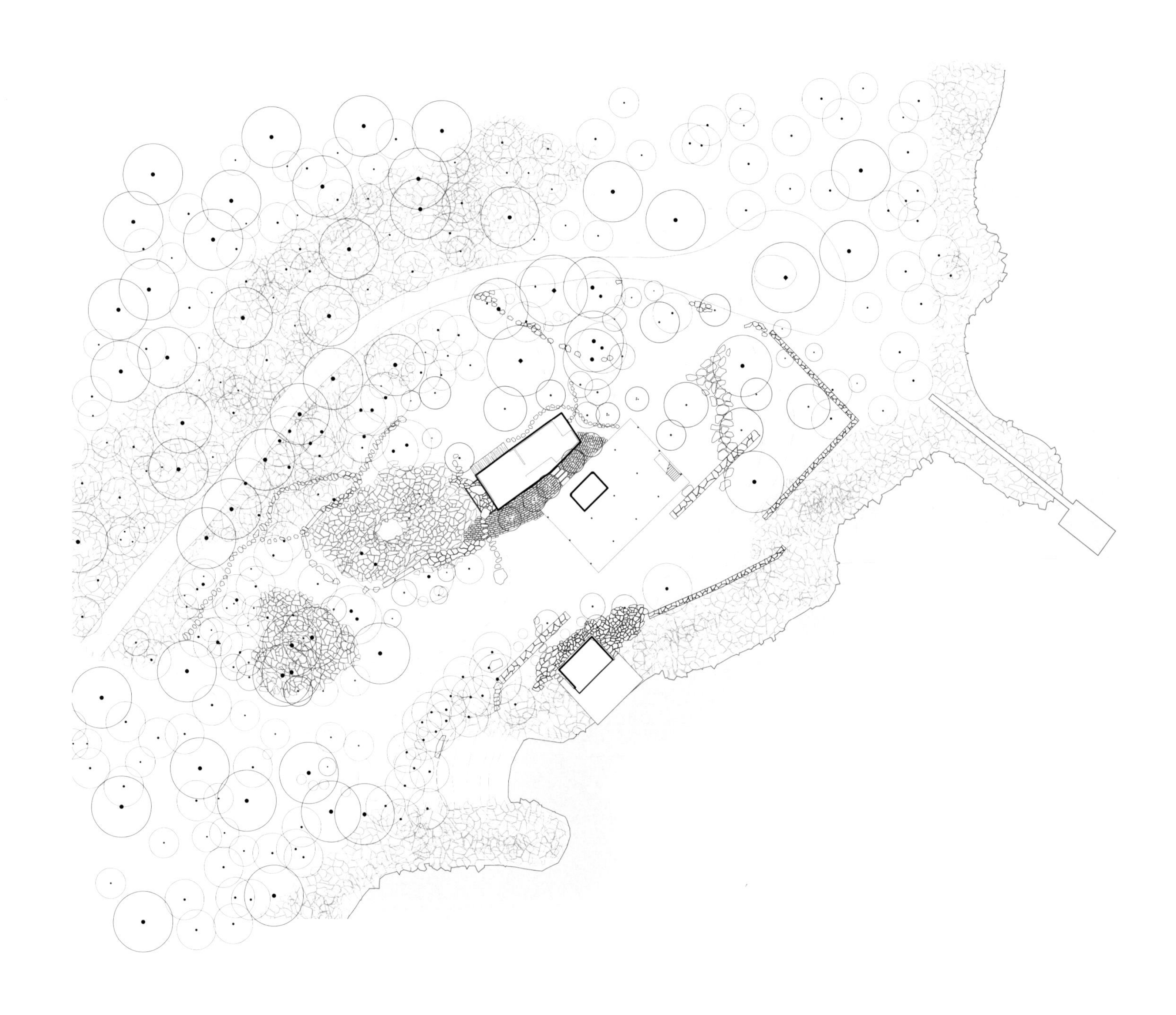

Old Quarry Guilford, Connecticut

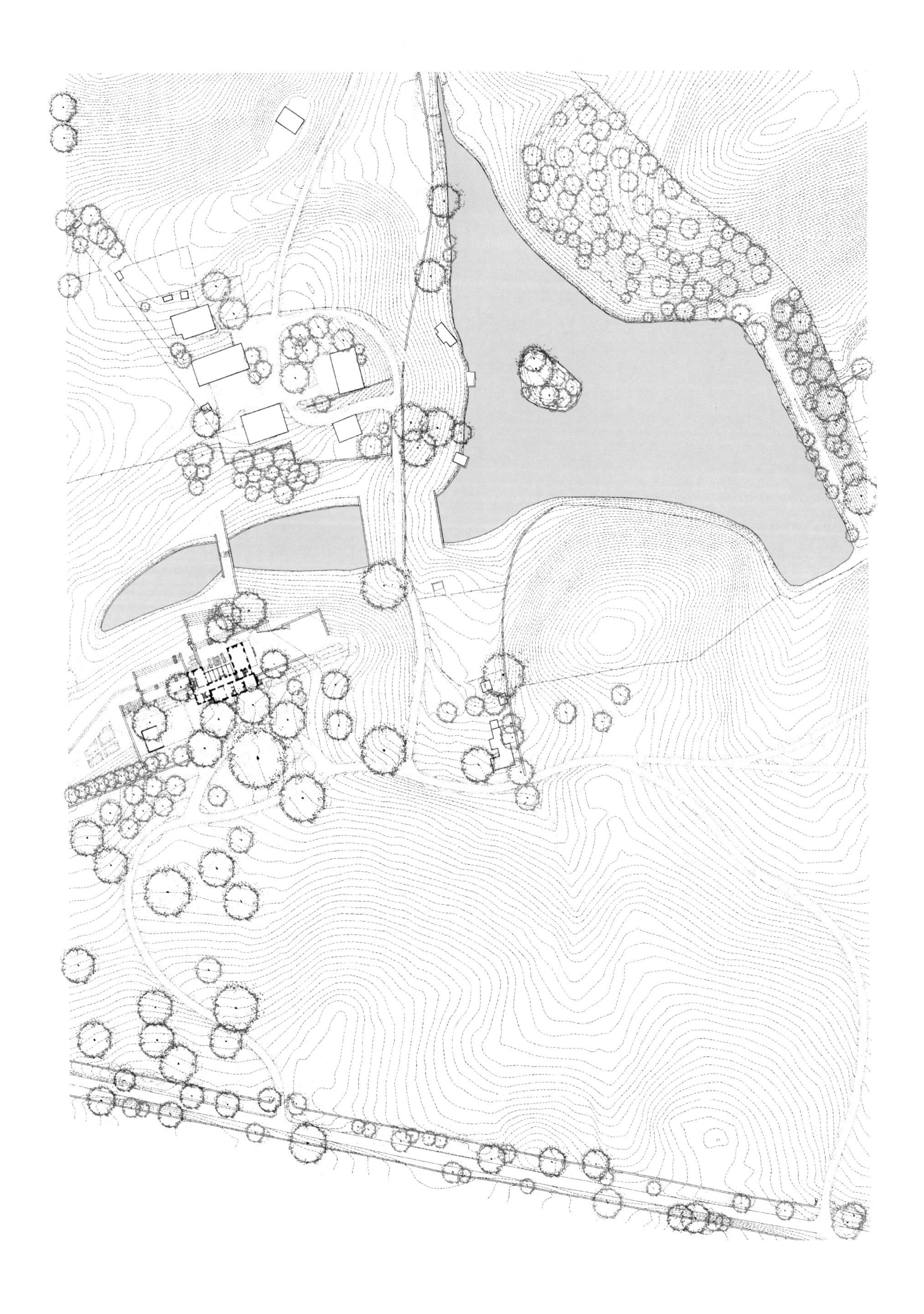

0 180

 The Ohio State University Columbus, Ohio

0 600

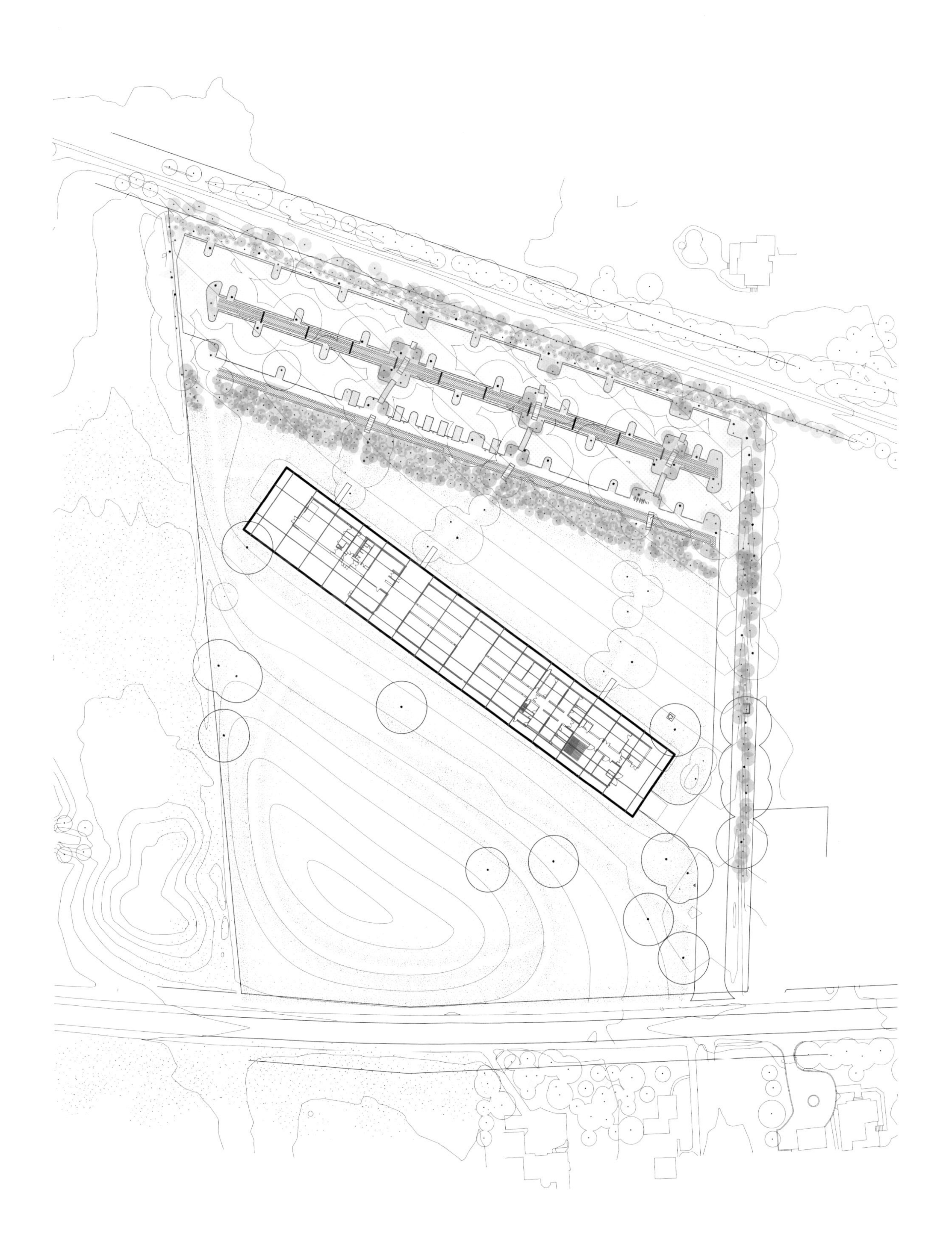

0
150

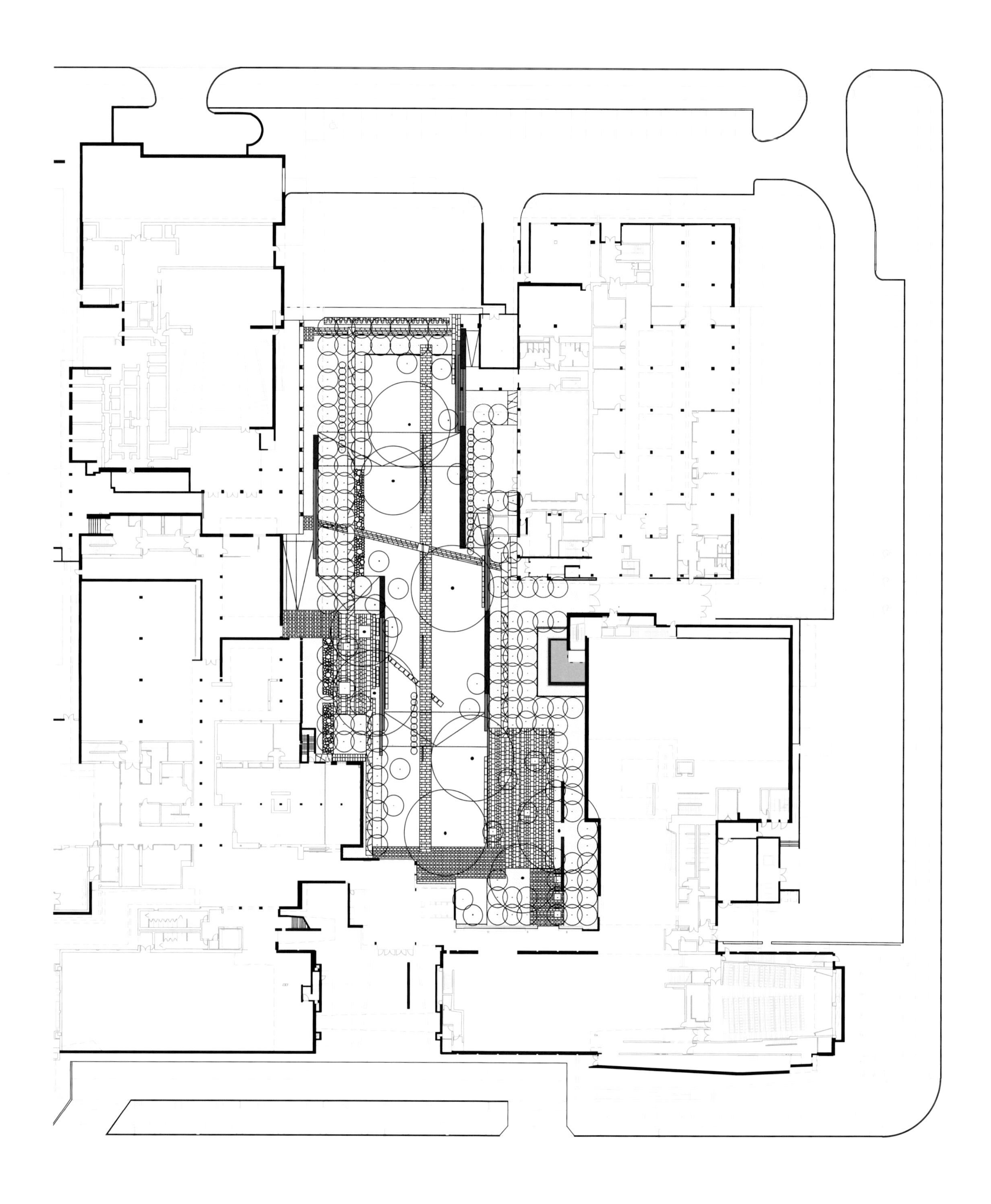

 Phoenix Art Museum Phoenix, Arizona

0 1000

Baton Rouge, Louisiana Plan Baton Rouge

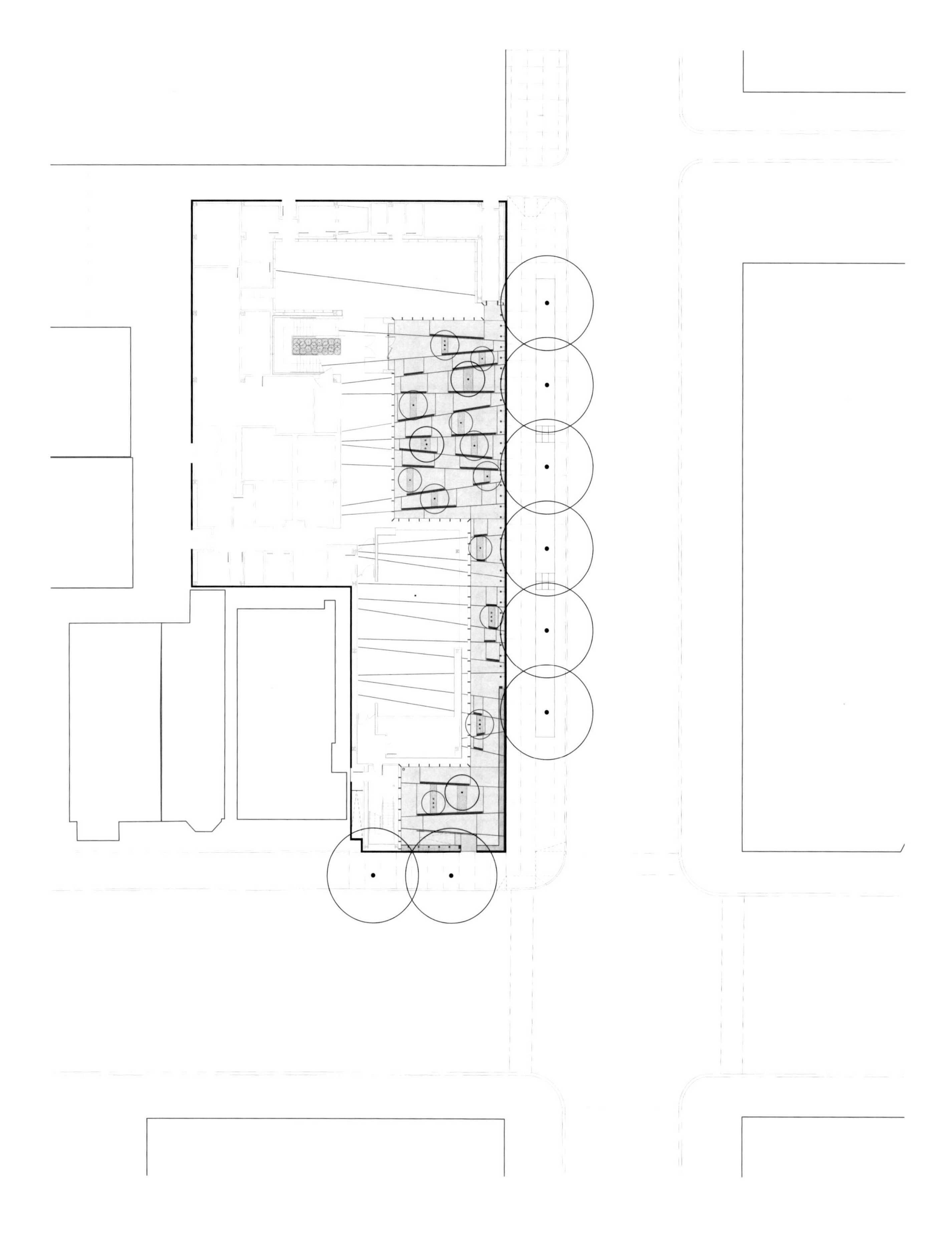

 Poetry Foundation Chicago, Illinois

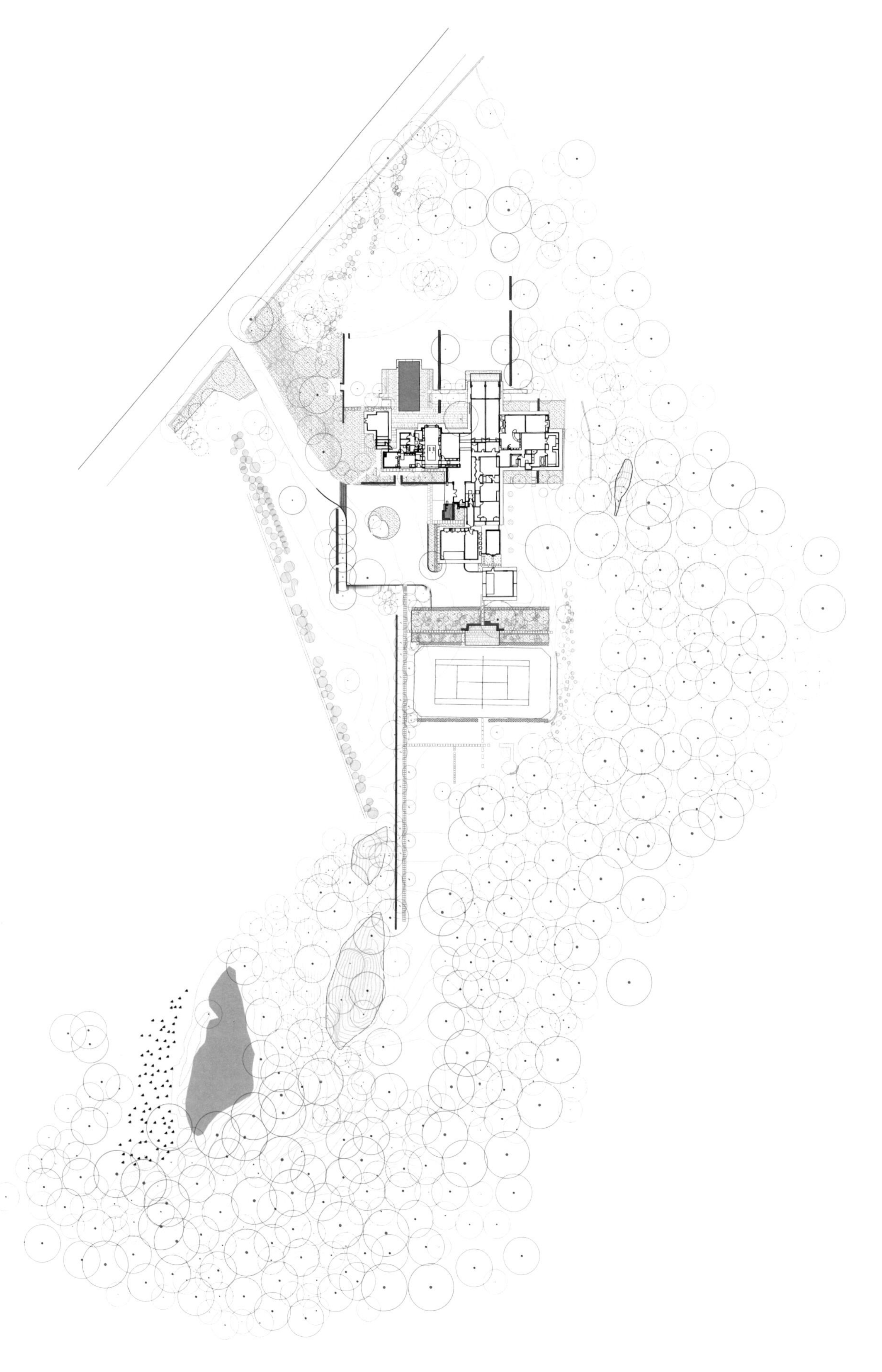

0 120

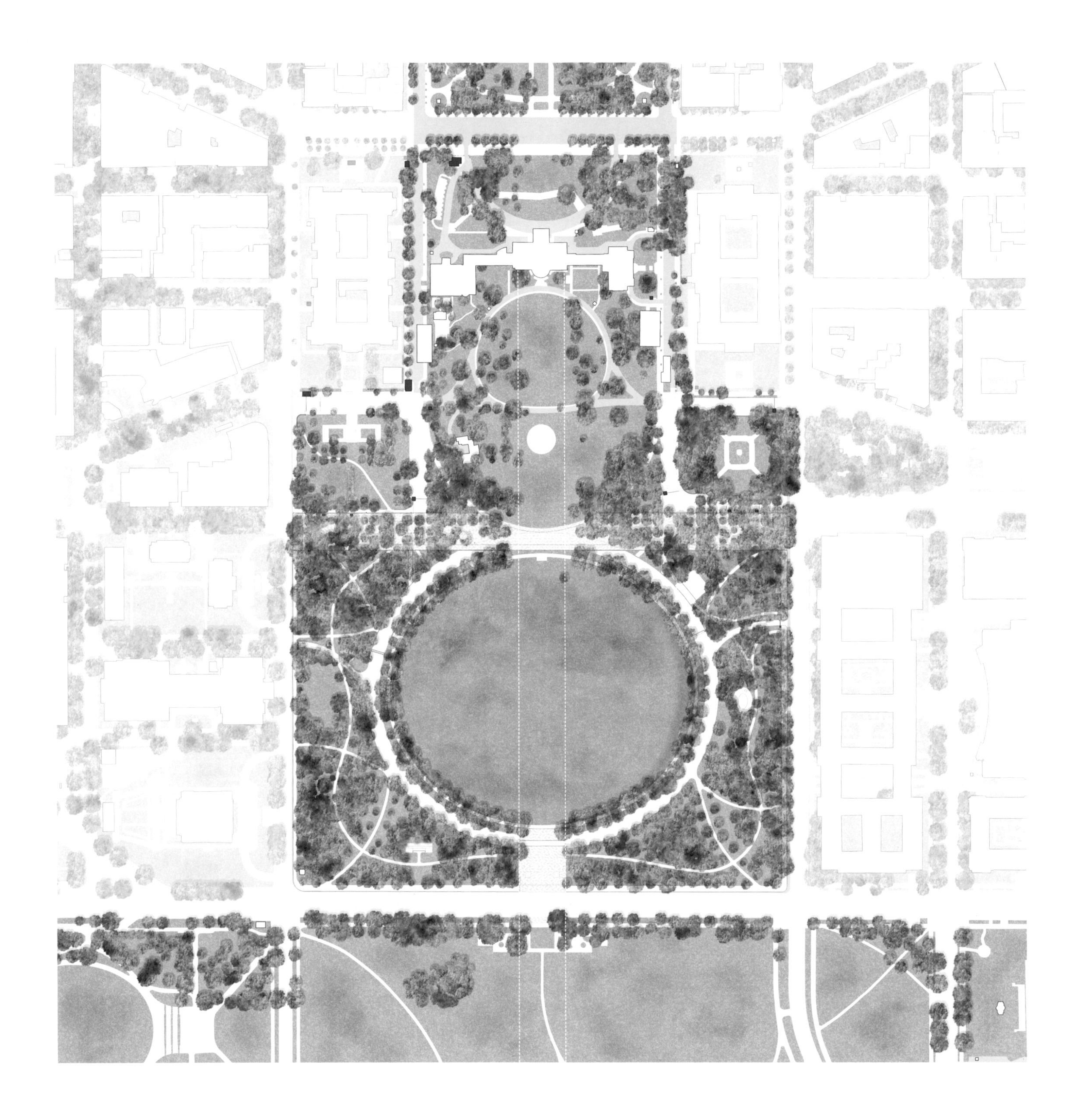

President's Park South Design Competition Washington, D.C.

0 300

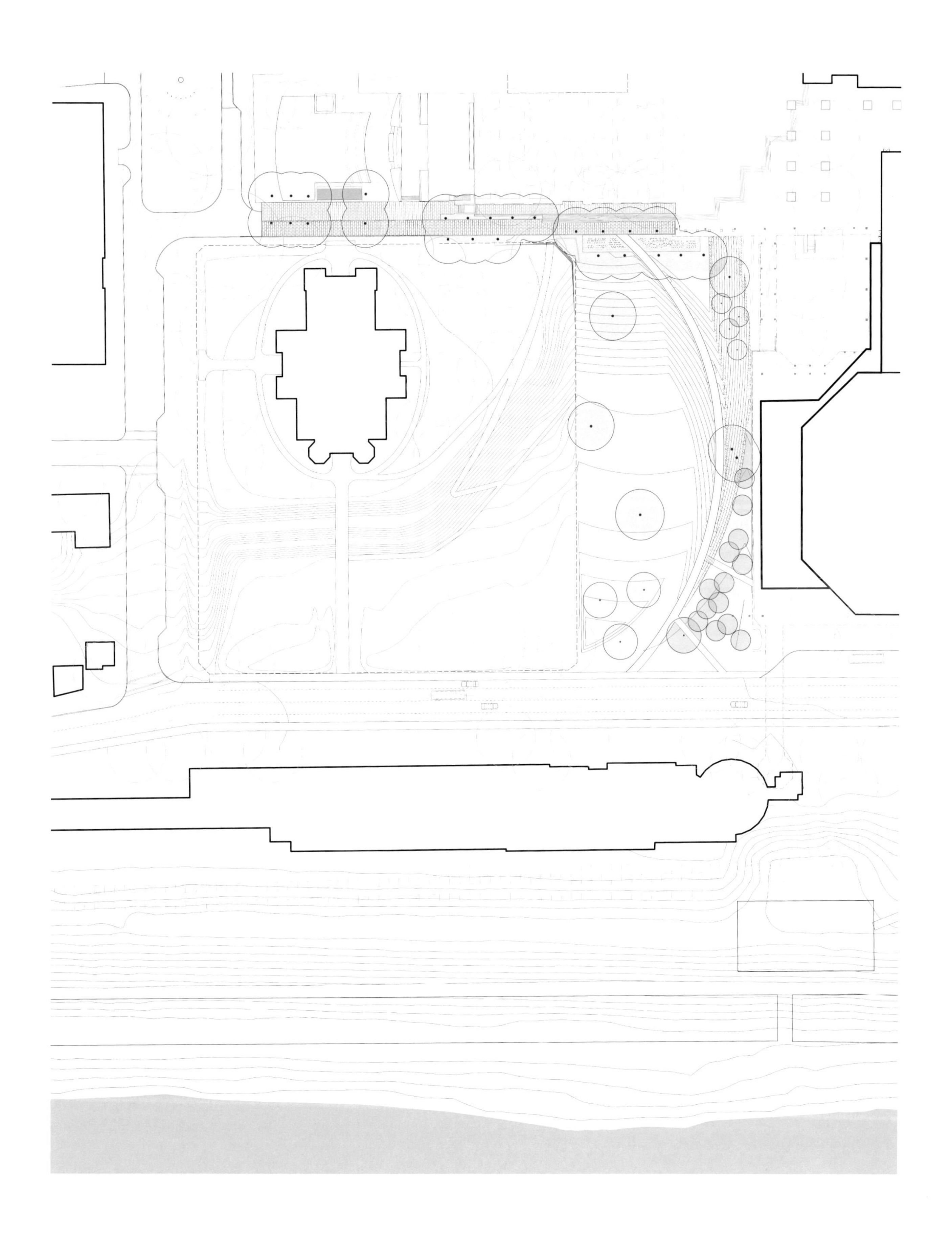

0 120

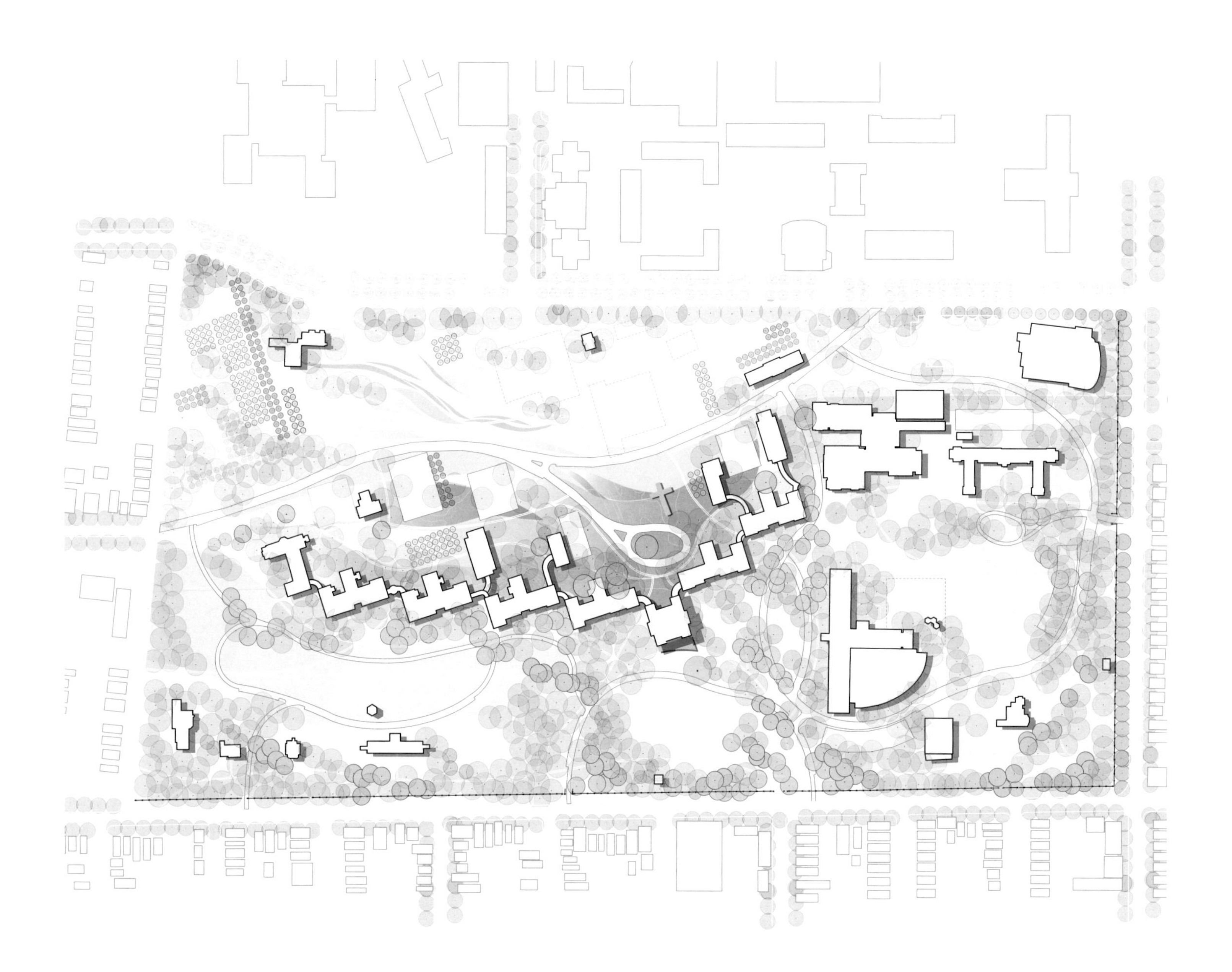

Richardson Olmsted Complex Buffalo, New York

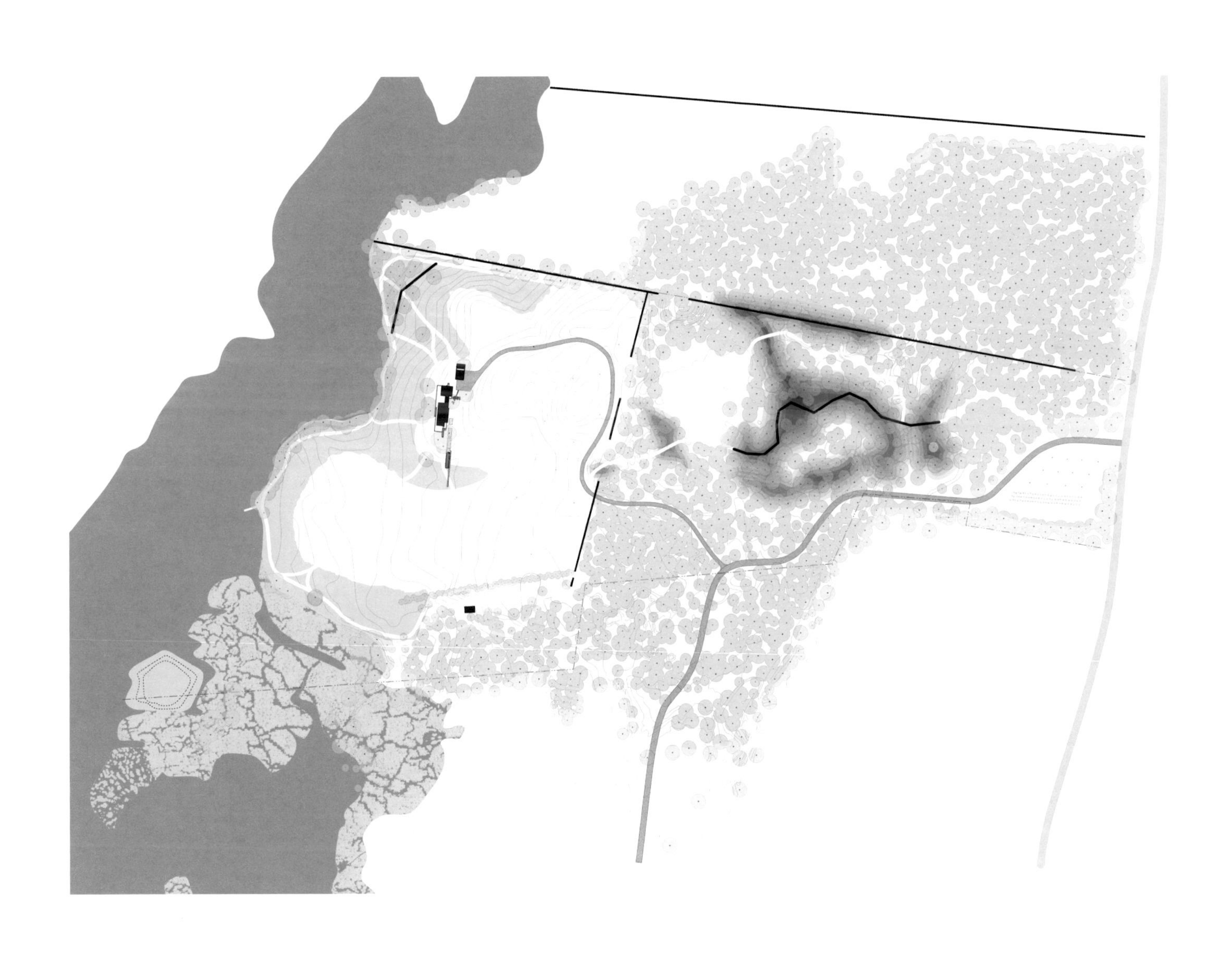

0 400

Rosserne Mount Desert Island, Maine

0 160

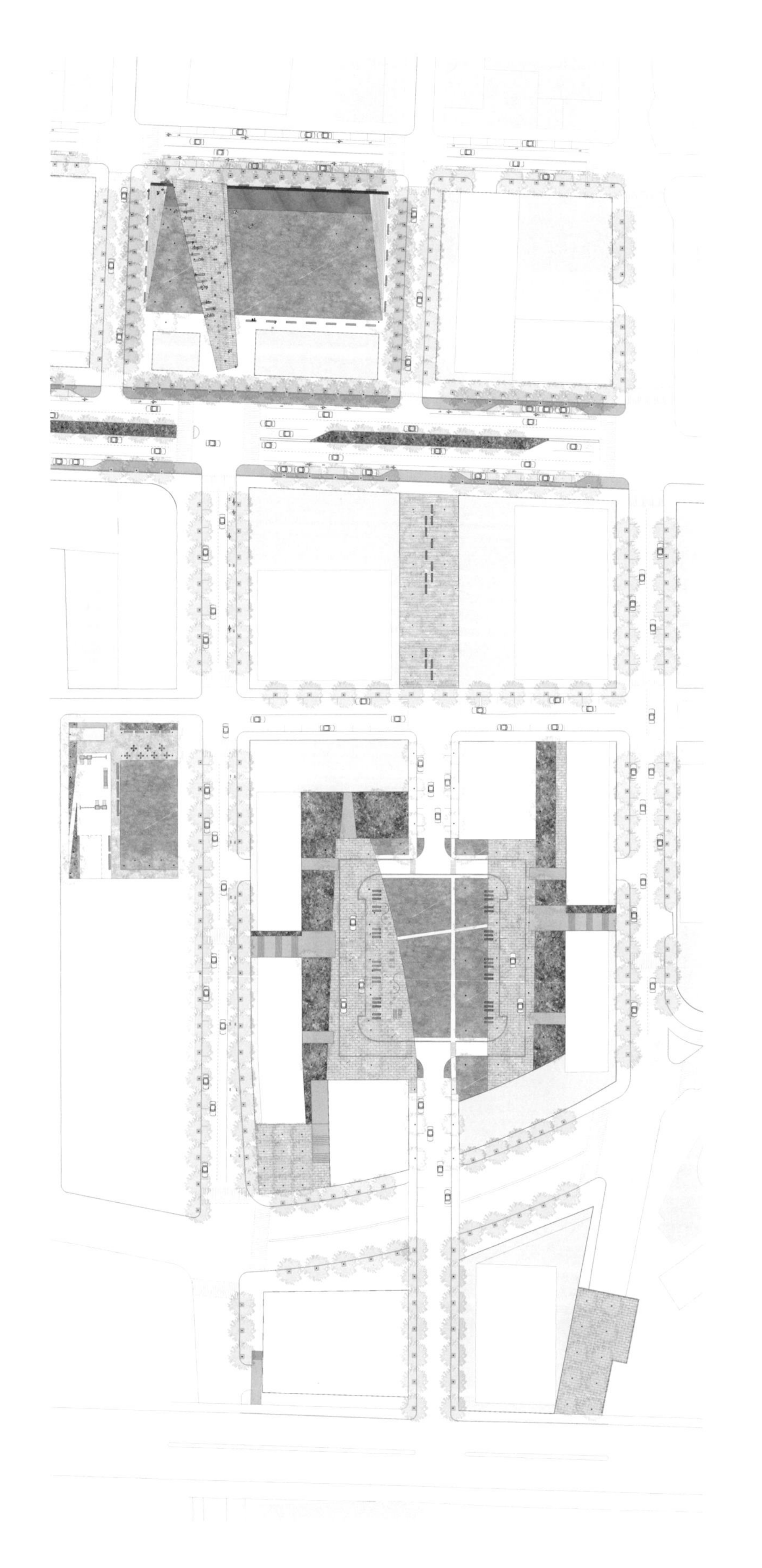

0 200

Boston, Massachusetts Seaport Square

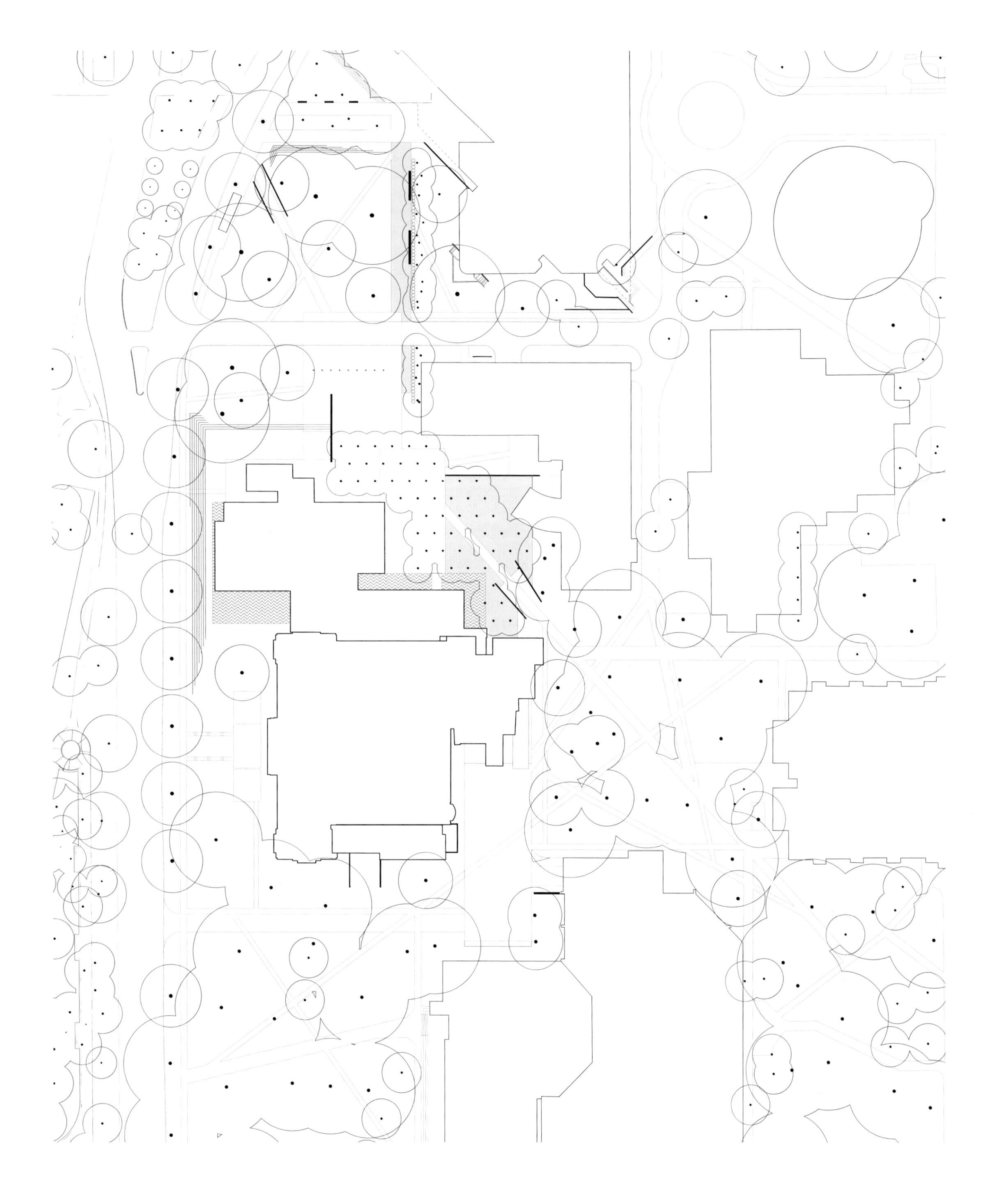

 Speed Art Museum Louisville, Kentucky

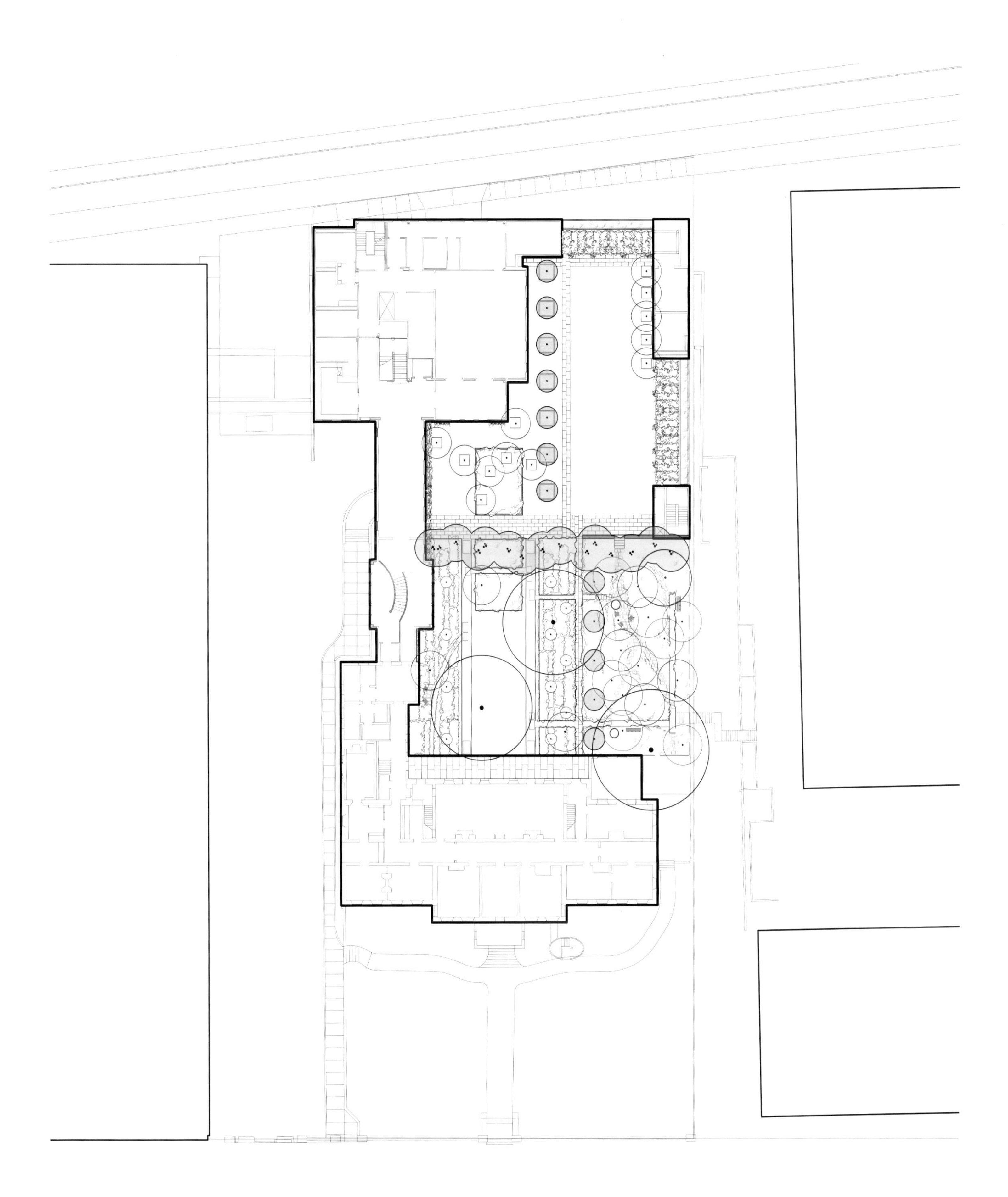

0 40

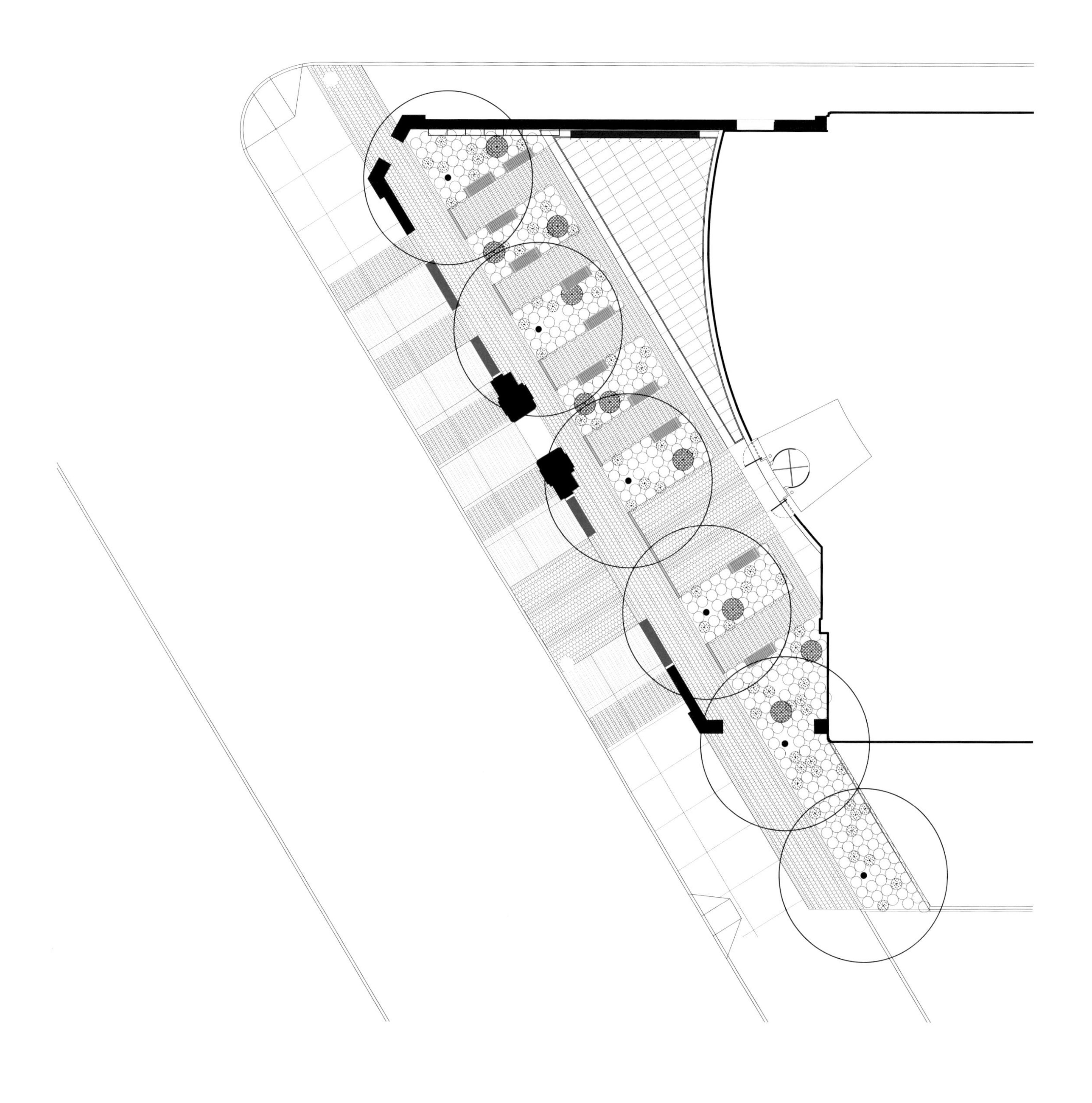

The First Church of Christ, Scientist Boston, Massachusetts

0
240

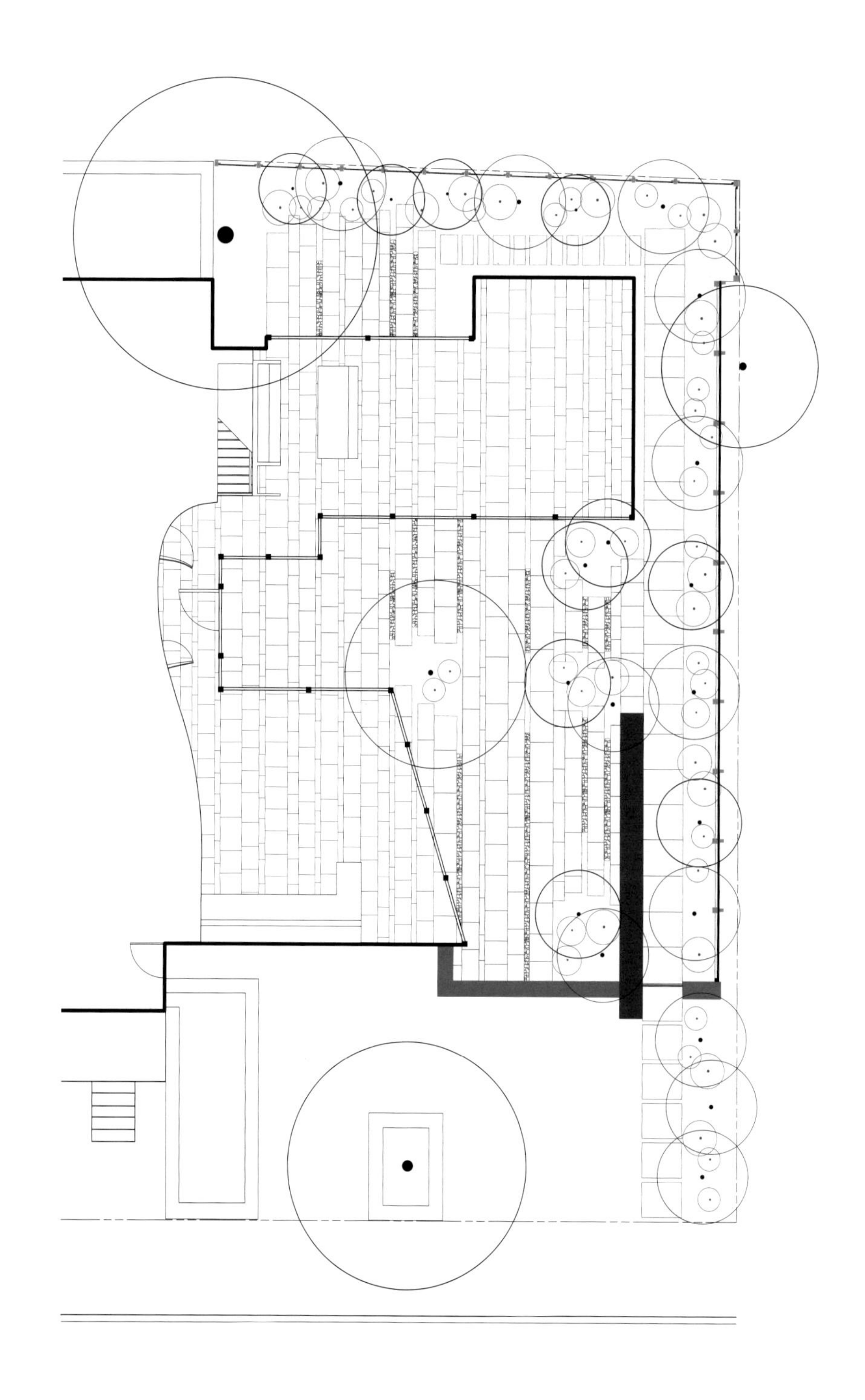

Upland Road Cambridge, Massachusetts

0 15

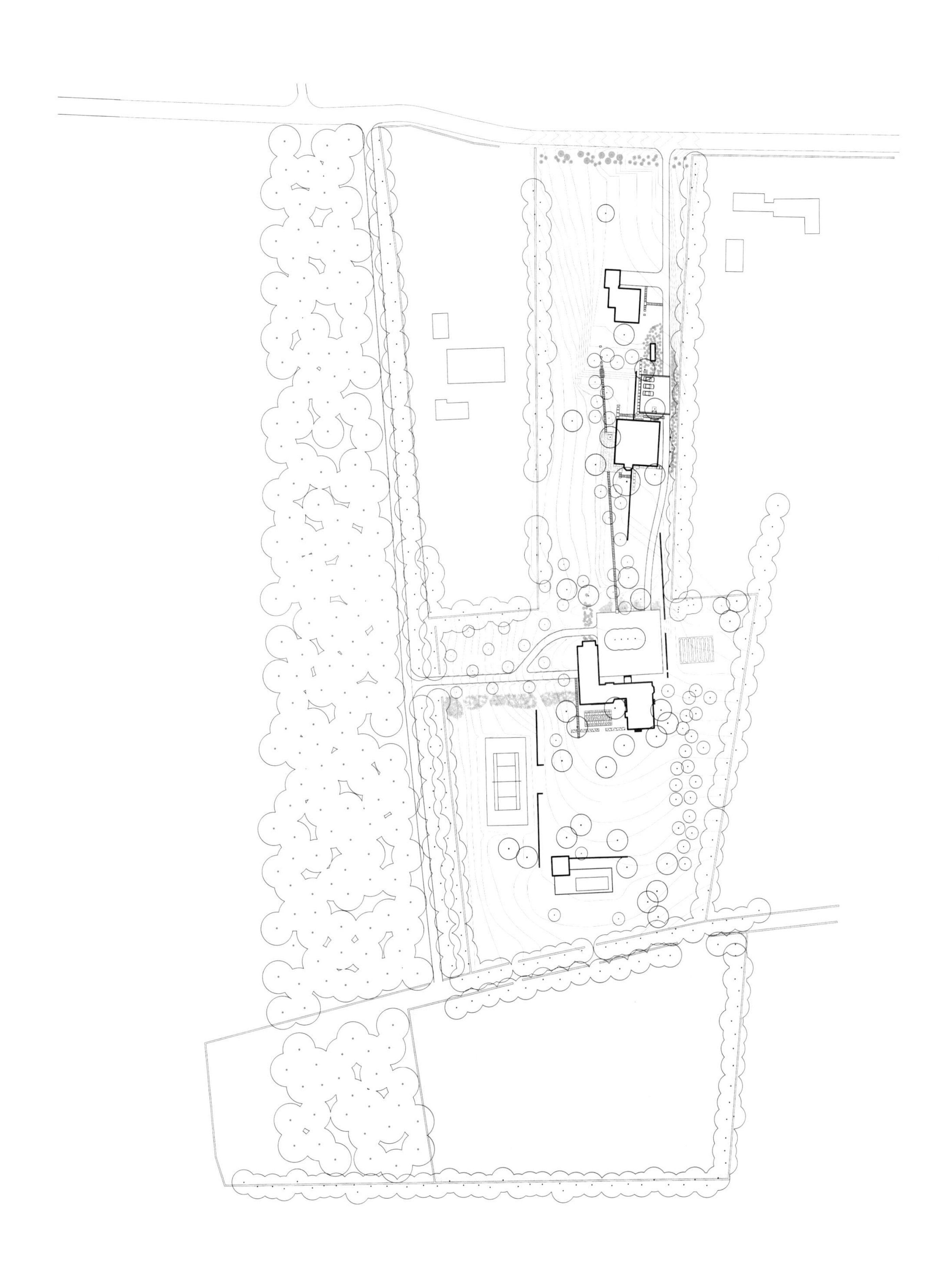

0 180

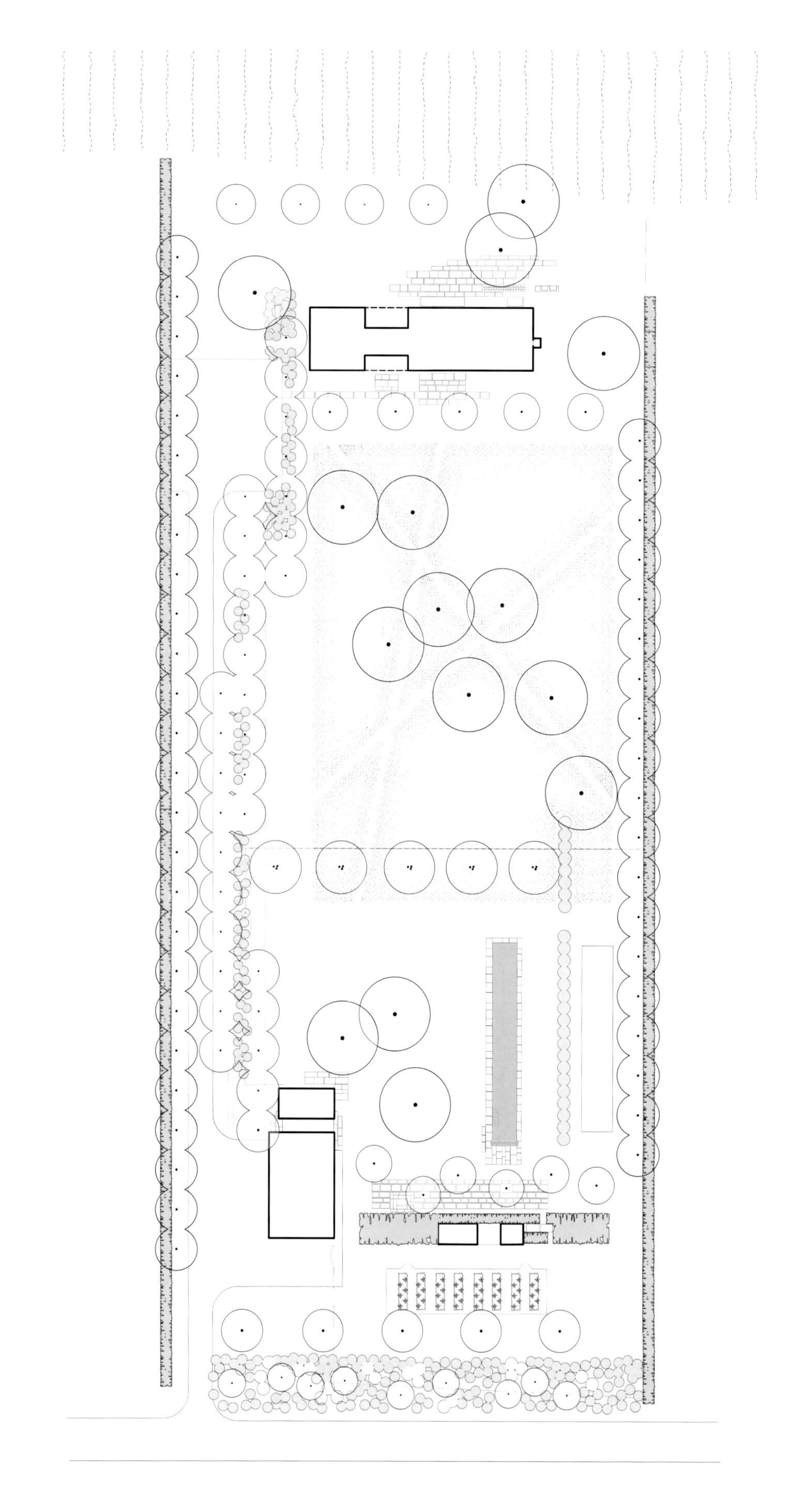

Wainscott Wainscott, New York

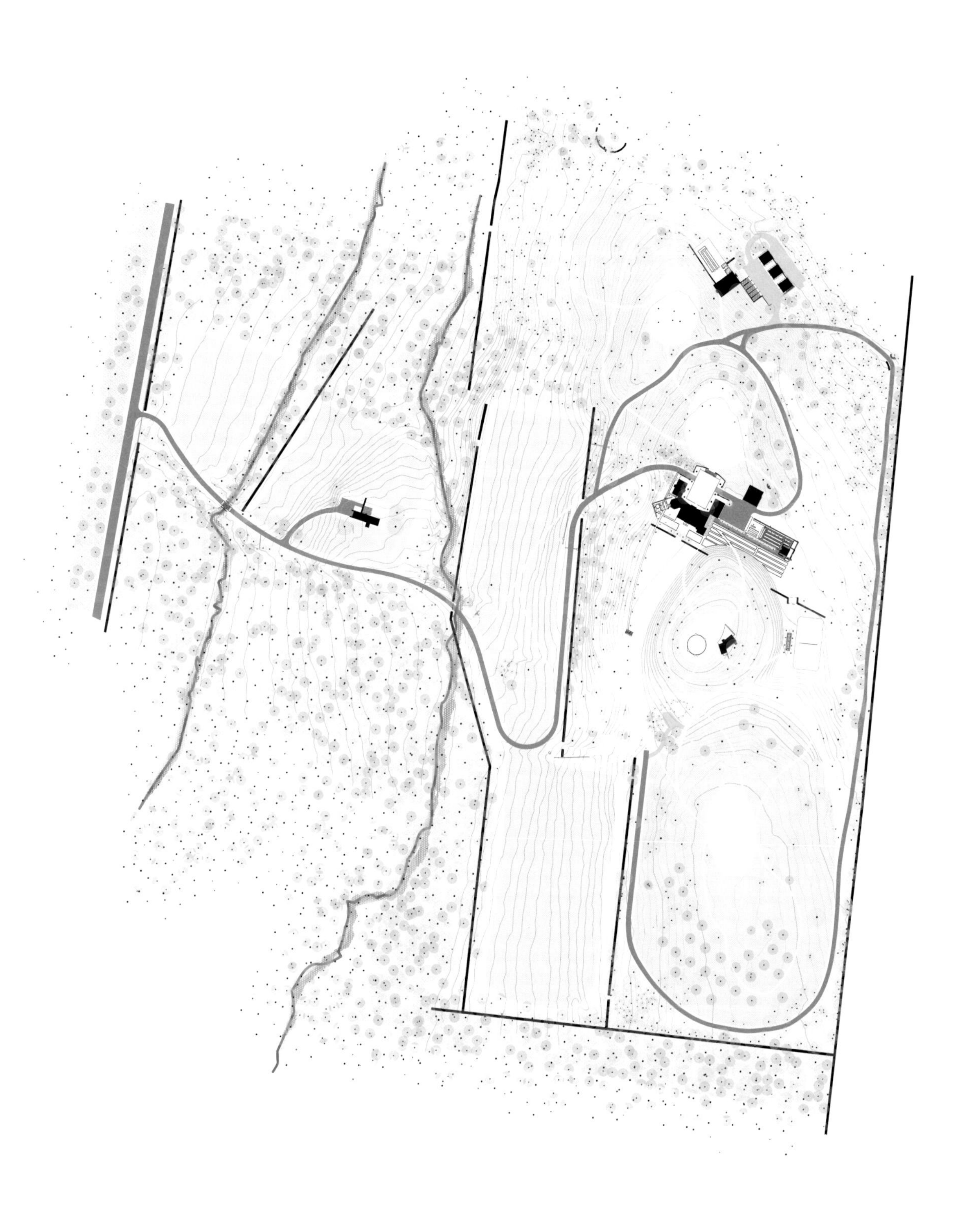

0 320

Acknowledgments

Our projects always involve digging and searching, reflecting and deliberating, unexpected disruptions and bursts of elation, tests of endurance, and, either immediately or at some distance, great satisfaction. They are always the work of many hands. Producing this book was no different—our colleague Sarah Vance has insisted all along that the process of making this book is similar to how we develop our landscapes. We need to acknowledge that we sometimes forget to acclaim the roles of collaborators and contributors on our projects; we hope to avoid committing the same sins of omission in giving credit where it's due for work on this publication.

Foremost, we thank our clients. We are always aware that our efforts reside somewhere along a spectrum between a design business helping clients turn aspirations into realities through specific commissions, and an artistic practice that works and reworks problems of a similar nature within a certain sphere of approaches and techniques. The work is perpetually built on relationships, and nowhere from service to art could we build anything well without ambitious, inquisitive, and patient clients. We cite a few in this volume, but many others who've entrusted some portion of their worldly domains to us do not appear here. Collectively, our clients share with us a certain worldview; we connect over a common passion for reshaping some of the characteristics of a place with an eye toward greater functionality and lasting beauty. We treasure these bonds, above all. We also derive enormous gratification from our relationships with fellow designers, contractors, artists and artisans, gardeners, and grounds managers who have dedicated their energies to building the projects and keeping them going. Some of this work landed with us through their invitation or referral. Again, only a few appear in the book, but we extend our sincere thanks to all our collaborators. Together with them we share the aim of making the best work we can, every time out.

We're proud to honor the labor and skill and intellectual drive of our colleagues in the firm, including our former employees and interns. We benefit from an uncommonly dedicated and supportive practice. Our fellow principals, especially—John Grove, John Kett, Eric Kramer, and Chris Moyles—have allowed us to carve out space for the demands of organizing the material and sweating endless details. Eric, in particular, gently prodded us for years to make this book, and he greatly influenced its production and outcome. For irrepressible dedication, intelligence, and true leadership in this effort, he deserves our sincerest thanks.

Sarah Vance prepared us well with her ever-sharp eye and with our many in-house publications, and then pushed us harder and farther than we wanted on this one, to great effect. Paul Weiner, Jeri Stedt, and Tamara Taylor endured countless studies, revisions, and recapitulations with absolute grace under pressure. Many of the staff served as readers and critics; and of course they have all helped shape every phase of the projects and the ways we think about them. We give special thanks to Ryan Gutierrez, Ruth Webb, and Phoebe White, who among others have helped us take our convictions about the relevance and the beauty of the plan—the map, the chart, the plot—to a higher place.

Connie Sullivan knows the book business well, and she steered hard and gave us access to the best production capabilities in view. She led us to Bethany Johns, Archie Hobson, and Meridian Press. Bethany deftly shaped this volume for a wily bunch of designers who were almost never around and who needed to see more alternatives and refinements than anyone would deem reasonable. We were constantly struck by the combination of authority and flexibility she brought to every design question throughout the project: timely, demanding, patient, and indispensable to every last breath of effort required to complete this remarkable production. Bravo, Bethany. Archie worked hard to save us from the perils of design lingo, passive voice, and other literary pitfalls; he may not have entirely succeeded, because we are stubborn. And we thank the brilliant production staff at Meridian; they make exceptionally beautiful printed matter and we were fortunate to land in their good hands.

We've had counsel from many friends, including Melissa Vaughn, who always conveys gracious wisdom, and Bill Saunders, who provided steady encouragement. Bill read everything near the end and reported back with the trusted combination of enthusiasm, alarm bells, and quizzical stares he has been providing to design writers for thirty years. We probably ignored at least a few of his most insightful words. To the writers, Bill included, big thanks for many rewarding conversations about the work, some long and enjoyable walks on sites, and innumerable exchanges—some annoying to them, no doubt, and others profoundly gratifying to us. The essays hold a special place for us. To the photographers, again, we extend our sincere gratitude. Their work brings us endless satisfaction and we are proud to share it in this book.

Finally to our spouses, Will and Pamela, whom we rarely honor the way they deserve: you have indulged us, endlessly. We so appreciate the wisdom and devotion you provide, without fail. Thank you. Thank you.
—Douglas Reed and Gary Hilderbrand

Contributors

Robert Pogue Harrison
Robert Pogue Harrison's published work is concerned with the cultural history of landscape, burial of the dead, and what he calls the "humic foundations" of Western civilization. He is the author of several books, among them *Forests: The Shadow of Civilization* (1992), *The Dominion of the Dead* (2003), and *Gardens: An Essay on the Human Condition* (2008). He was appointed Assistant Professor of Italian Literature at Stanford University, where he has held the Rosina Pierotti Professorship of Italian Literature since 2000.

Millicent Harvey
Award-winning photographer Millicent Harvey's work encompasses a variety of subjects, from natural landscapes and works of landscape architecture to the human form in its various stages of life. Her nationally recognized *Lives Well-Lived: Story Portraits* series reflects her ability to seamlessly merge emotional, spiritual, and physical components into images of great beauty. Millicent has created commanding editorial images for prestigious clientele, among them Fidelity Investments, WGBH, Random House, and Putnam Publishing. Millicent self-published a book titled *Inside Out* (2003), and she is currently working on a collection of photographs on smoke trees that grow in the desert washes near her home in Palm Springs, California.

Andrea Jones
Over the last twenty years Andrea Jones has built an international reputation photographing landscape architecture, gardens, and plants, the latter being the subject of her critically acclaimed book *Plantworlds* (2005). More recently, she traveled throughout the United States and Canada to illustrate *Great Gardens of America* (2009). Her latest solo book, *The Garden Source* (2012), depicts inspirational ideas for gardens and landscapes. Andrea studied art and photography and has been elected a fellow of the Royal Society of Arts.

Niall Kirkwood
Niall Kirkwood is Professor of Landscape Architecture and Technology at the Harvard Graduate School of Design, where he has been a faculty member since 1992. His publications include his award-winning book *The Art of Landscape Detail* (1999), *Weathering and Durability in Landscape Architecture* (2004), *Detroit Riverfront: Motor City Landscape* (2000), *Manufactured Sites: Rethinking the Post-Industrial Landscape* (2001), and *Principles of Brownfield Regeneration: Clean-up, Design, and Reuse of Derelict Land* (2010).

Charles Mayer
For over twenty years, Chuck has been photographing designed spaces for architects and artists. He works from a studio in Concord, Massachusetts, and travels throughout the Northeast, the United States, and Europe. His photographs are simply framed, direct compositions that lucidly and sensuously present the light, the look, and the story of being within the space.

William S. Saunders
William S. Saunders edited *Harvard Design Magazine* from 1997 to 2012 and worked at Harvard's Graduate School of Design for thirty years. He writes criticism of works of art and essays on theory, culture, and education. His Ph.D. is in literary criticism and modern British literature. He is author or editor of fourteen books, including *Modern Architecture: Photographs of Ezra Stoller* (1999) and, most recently, *Designed Ecologies: The Landscape Architecture of Kongjian Yu* (2012).

Suzanne Turner
Suzanne Turner is professor emerita of the Robert Reich School of Landscape Architecture at Louisiana State University, where she taught for almost twenty-five years. She holds a B.A. in the history of art from Emory University and an M.L.A. from the University of Georgia, and is principal of Suzanne Turner Associates, which specializes in analysis and design in historical and cultural landscapes. She is the author of *The Garden Diary of Martha Turnbull, Mistress of Rosedown Plantation* (2012); coauthor of *Houston's Silent Garden: Glenwood Cemetery, 1871–2009* (2010); and coauthor of *The Gardens of Louisiana: Places of Work and Wonder* (1997).

Alan Ward
Alan Ward has photographed the designed landscape for more than thirty years. His photographic work has appeared in more than forty periodicals and books, including *American Design Landscapes: A Photographic Interpretation* (2006). His exhibitions include *Dan Kiley: Classicist in the Modern Landscape* (1980), *Built Landscapes: Gardens of the Northeast* (1984, 1997), and *Beatrix Farrand's American Landscapes* (1985). Ward has lectured on photography at Harvard University, North Carolina State, and the University of Pennsylvania. Trained as an architect and landscape architect, Ward has taught university courses in both fields. He is currently a principal at Sasaki Associates in Watertown, Massachusetts.

Staff

Current

Jessica Brown
Leslie Carter
Jean-Paul Charboneau
Somkiet Chokvijitkul
Ariel Dungca
Adrian Fehrmann
Kristin Frederickson
Geoffrey Fritz
Kimberly Garza
John Grove
Diana Haynes
Gary Hilderbrand
Alison Hlivak
Ryan Ives
Joseph James
John Kett
Eric Kramer
Joseph Kubik
Cathy Langan
Matthew Langan
Heeyoung Lee
Elise Mazareas
Peter McGillicuddy
Brie Mendozza
Chris Moyles
Garrett Newton
Adrian Nial
Stephanie Pierce
Elizabeth Randall
Douglas Reed
Matthew Soule
Jeri Stedt
Alex Strader
Beka Sturges
Tamara Taylor
Sarah Vance
Ryan Wampler
Paul Weiner

Former

Trisha Bales
Charlotte Barrows
Jessica Bartenhagen
Scarlett Bartlett
Rita Basselah
Brenda Belanger
Paul Belanger
Leah Broder
Cristina Campa
Robin Carmichael
Naomi Cottrell
Michelle Crowley
Matthew Cunningham
Amy Cupples-Rubiano
Scheri Fultineer
Susan Funke
Nicole Gaenzler
Elizabeth Gilbert
Mary Glock
Megan Griscom
Ryan Gutierrez
Heather Hansen
Joseph Herda
Jessica Jia
Jason Kentner
Barry Kimmel
Keith Lane
Christopher Langlois
Hazel Marbury
Misty March
Karen M'Closkey
Jason Moreau
Lisa Morris
Erika Riddington
Haley Runne
Paul Russell
Adrian Smith
Joseph Sweeney
Josh Tompkins
Katie Towson
Jennifer Toy
Glen Valentine
Michael Wasser
Ruth Webb
Sissy Willis
Yan Wu

Interns

Claire Agre
Kunkook Bae
Morgan Barnicoat
Ashley Bastow
Steve Billings
Rachel Burnes
Sarah Carrier
Jerome Chou
Jenelle Clark
Ilana Cohen
Samantha Dabney
Maria Debye-Saxinger
Kristin First
Terence Fitzpatrick
Nathan Foley
Kenneth Francis
Michael Griffith
Laura Harmon
Joy Hu
Serena Jarvis
Bailey Kinkel
Conners Ladner
Luke Love
Michael Luegering
Scottie McDaniel
Heath Mizer
Gilberto Nieto
Blair Phillips
Izabela Riano
Cameron Ringness
Jason Shinoda
Ruth Siegel
Molly Steim
Cynthia Talley
Jessica Vanecek
Phoebe White
James Willeford

Project Credits

Arnold Arboretum Leventritt Garden, *Boston, Massachusetts, for Harvard University. Commenced 1990. 3.5 acres.* Maryann Thompson Architects; Vanasse Hangen Brustlin, Inc.; Craul Land Scientists; Haley & Aldrich, Inc.; ARUP; Irrigation Consulting Inc.; Lee Kennedy Co., Inc.; ValleyCrest Landscape Companies; M.F. Construction Corp.

Aurora, *Aurora, New York, for Pleasant Rowland Foundation and MacKenzie Childs Corporation. Commenced 2002. Six sites from 1000 square feet to 50 acres.* Holmes King Kallquist and Associates; RISE Group; EDR Companies; Northeast Construction; DDS Engineers and Contractors; Oakleaf Landscape Associates; RM Landscape Industries.

Austen Riggs Center, *Stockbridge, Massachusetts. Commenced 2006. 18 acres.* Kyu Sung Woo Architects; Webster Ingersoll.

Baltimore Hills, *Baltimore, Maryland. Commenced 2004. 7 acres.* Project-Space; Collaborative Lighting, LLC.; Winchester Construction; DMW Engineers; Chapel Valley Landscape Company.

Beck House, *Dallas, Texas. Commenced 2002. 11 acres.* Bodron+Fruit; Allan Schwartzman; Shade Masters, Inc.; American Civil Constructors; Dan Euser Waterarchitecture; Craig Roberts Associates; Sebastian Construction Group; O'Brien Engineering, Inc.; Walker Structural Engineering, Inc.; Pool Environments, Inc.; Arbor Associates.

Bennington College Master Plan, *Bennington, Vermont. Commenced 2003. 450 acres.* Landscape Master Plan: Kyu Sung Woo Architects. New Houses: Kyu Sung Woo Architects. Student Center: Taylor & Burns Architects. Center for the Advancement of Public Action: Tod Williams Billie Tsien Architects; Daniel O'Connell's Sons, Inc. Visual and Performing Arts: Daniel O'Connell's Sons, Inc. Signage Plan: Roll, Barresi & Associates. Joan Goodrich Courtyard at Crossett Library: Pembroke Landscape

Boston Harbor Islands Pavilion, *Boston, Massachusetts, for Boston Harbor Island Alliance and the National Park Service. Commenced 2005. 0.5 acres.* Utile, Inc. Architecture + Planning; Simpson Gumpertz & Heger; Vanasse Hangen Brustlin, Inc.; Pine and Swallow Environmental; Turner Special Projects Division; ValleyCrest Landscape Companies.

Brandeis University, *Waltham, Massachusetts. Commenced 2001. 120 acres.* Village Residence Hall: Kyu Sung Woo Architects; Vanasse Hangen Brustlin, Inc.; Berry Construction, D. Schumacher Landscaping; ValleyCrest Landscape Companies. Schneider Addition to the Heller School for Social Policy and Management: Kyu Sung Woo Architects; Leggatt McCall Properties; Nitsch Engineering; Bond Brothers Construction; D. Schumacher Landscaping. New Ridgewood Residence Halls: William Rawn Associates; Leggatt McCall Properties; Nitsch Engineering; John Moriarty & Associates; D. Schumacher Landscaping. Carl and Ruth Shapiro Admissions Center: Charles Rose Architect; Leggatt McCall Properties; Nitsch Engineering; John Moriarty & Associates; D. Schumacher Landscaping. Mandel Center for the Humanities and North Academic Quadrangle: Kallmann McKinnell and Wood Architects; Leggatt McCall Property; Nitsch Engineering; John Moriarty & Associates; ValleyCrest Landscape Companies.

Carisbrooke, *Wellesley, Massachusetts. Commenced 2002. 4 acres.* The Office of Peter Rose; F.H. Perry Builders; Sanford Ecological Services, Inc.; McPhail Associates; RSE Associates, Inc.; Robert Hanss, Inc.; Hartney Greymont; Custom Quality Pools; Ecological Landscape Management; Joseph E. Miner Associates.

Central Wharf Plaza, *Boston, Massachusetts, for Frog Pond Foundation. Commenced 2004. 0.5 acres.* Chan Krieger NBBJ, ARUP, Vanasse Hangen Brustlin Inc.; Lam Partners; Pine and Swallow Environmental; Turner Special Projects Division; ValleyCrest Landscape Companies; Bartlett Tree Experts; Ecological Landscape Management.

Charles River Pier, *Boston, Massachusetts, for Partners HealthCare. Commenced 1998. 1 acre.* Anmahian Winton Architects; Childs Engineering Corporation; Walsh Brothers Construction; DeAngelis Iron Works; ValleyCrest Landscape Companies.

Chazen Museum of Art, *Madison, Wisconsin, for University of Wisconsin-Madison. Commenced 2007. 4 city blocks.* Machado and Silvetti Associates; Continuum Architects + Planners, S.C.; Graef, Anhalt, Schloemer; Lam Partners; Steve Keller & Associates; Bloom Companies, LLC.; J.H. Findorff & Son, Inc.

The Clark, *Williamstown, Massachusetts, for the Sterling & Francine Clark Art Institute. Commenced 2001. 140 acres.* Stone Hill Center: Tadao Ando Architects & Associates; Gensler; Altieri Sebor Wieber; Buro Happold Consulting Engineers, P.C.; Pine and Swallow Environmental; Fisher Marantz Stone; RISE Group; Zubatkin Owner Representation; Barr & Barr, Inc.; JH Maxymillian, Inc.; Countryside Landscape Services.

Clyfford Still Museum, *Denver, Colorado, for Dean Sobel. Commenced 2008. 1 acre.* Allied Works Architecture; Romani Group; Studio InSite; V3 Companies; ARUP; Hydro Systems, Inc.; Saunders Construction; Landtech Contractors.

Crystal Bridges Museum of American Art, *Bentonville, Arkansas. Commenced 2006. 120 acres.* Safdie Architects; Buro Happold Consulting Engineers P.C.; CEI Engineering; Lam Partners; Pine and Swallow Environmental, Linbeck Nabholz Construction.

Dallas Museum of Art, *Dallas, Texas. Commenced 2006. 0.5 acres.* Richard Fleischner; Jeffrey L. Bruce & Company; Collaborative Lighting; Datum Engineers; Blum Consulting Engineers; Southern Botanical.

Deer Path, *East Hampton, New York. Commenced 1995. 5 acres.* Thad Hayes, Inc.; Whitmores Landscape Services; Seven Sons Masonry, Inc.

Duke University Campus Drive, *Durham, North Carolina. Commenced 2009. 80 acres.* Pelli Clarke Pelli Architects; William Rawn Associates, Architects, Inc.; Vanasse Hangen Brustlin, Inc.; Faithful + Gould; Nitsch Engineering; EcoEngineering.

Edward Leathers Community Park, *Somerville, Massachusetts, for the City of Somerville. Commenced 2005. 1 acre.* D&D Enterprises.

Family Retreat, *New Hampshire. Commenced 1995. 400 acres.* Janet Hurwitz; Emanual Engineering; Dan Euser Waterarchitecture, Inc.

Greenlee House, *Dallas, Texas. Commenced 2006. 4 acres.* Bodron + Fruit; Walker Structural Engineering; Craig Roberts Associates; Southern Botanical.

Groton School, *Groton, Massachusetts. Commenced 1995. 450 acres.* Shepley Bulfinch; CSL Consulting, LLC; Collaborative Lighting; Roll, Barresi & Associates; Samiotes Consultants, Inc.; RSE Associates, Inc.; Harrison Associates; Pinard Landscaping.

Half-Mile Line, *West Stockbridge, Massachusetts. Commenced 2003. 50 acres.* Foresight Land Services; Bayside Environmental Consultants; RSE Associates, Inc.; Webster Ingersoll.

Harvard Business School, *Boston, Massachusetts, for Harvard University. Commenced 2010. 65 acres.* Ecological Landscape Management; Bartlett Tree Experts; Nitsch Engineering; William Rawn Architects; Vanasse Hangen Brustlin, Inc.; Haley & Aldrich; Atelier Ten.

Harvard Naito/Bauer Laboratories, *Cambridge, Massachusetts, for Harvard University. Commenced 2000. 1 acre.* Ellenzweig; LeMessurier Consultants; Bryant Associates; Haley & Aldrich; Lam Partners; Daniel O'Connell's Sons, Inc.; ValleyCrest Landscape Companies.

Hilltop Arboretum, *Baton Rouge, Louisiana, for Louisiana State University. Commenced 2006. 11 acres.* ABMB Engineers; Newton Landscape Group.

Hither Lane, *East Hampton, New York. Commenced 2007. 11 acres.* B Five Studio LLP, Bulgin & Associates; Whitmores Landscape Services.

Hobart Urban Nature Preserve, *Troy, Ohio, for Miami County Park District. Commenced 2002. 85 acres.* Human Nature, Inc.; Elizabeth Benson.

Institute for Child and Adolescent Development, *Wellesley, Massachusetts. Commenced 1995. 1 acre.* Robert Hanss, Inc.

Kauffman Center for the Performing Arts, *Kansas City, Missouri. Commenced 2006. 9 acres.* Safdie Architects; BNIM; Jeffrey L. Bruce & Company; Lam Partners; J. E. Dunn Construction.

Liberty Wharf, *Boston, Massachusetts, for Cresset Development. Commenced 2007. 0.5 acres.* Elkus Manfredi Architects; Fort Point Associates; Childs Engineering Corporation; Craul Land Scientists; H W Moore, Associates, Inc.; RSE Associates, Inc.; Irrigation Consulting, Inc.; John Moriarty & Associates, Inc.; ValleyCrest Landscape Companies.

Long Dock Beacon, *Beacon, New York, for Scenic Hudson. Commenced 2004. 23 acres.* Architecture Research Office; Handel Architects LLP; Levin & Company, Inc.; Matthew D. Rudikoff, Inc.; Divney Tung Schwalbe LLP; Ecosystems Strategies, Inc.; McLaren Engineering Group; Robert Silman Associates; Viridian Energy & Environmental, LLC; VJ Associates; Craul Land Scientists; RSE Associates, Inc.; Kirchhoff-Consigli Construction Management; Harrison Park Associates; Greenscape Land Design, Inc.

Lowell Street, *Cambridge, Massachusetts. Commenced 2001. 2 acres.* Gund Partnership; RSE Associates, Inc.; Robert Hanss, Inc.

Manatuck, *Stonington, Connecticut. Commenced 2004. 200 acres.* Maryann Thompson Architects.

Marsh Court, *Stockbridge, United Kingdom. Commenced 2011. 120 acres.* Peter Inskip + Peter Jenkins; Leroy Street Studio; Mann Williams Consulting Engineers; Owlsworth OIJP; Scandor Landscape Construction; Hampton Tree Service; Tree Parts.

McBride House, *Boston, Massachusetts, for the Catholic Archdiocese of Boston. Commenced 2002. 0.25 acres.* Samiotes Consultants; Peabody Construction; D. Schumacher Landscaping; ValleyCrest Landscape Companies.

MIT North Court and Main Street, *Cambridge, Massachusetts, for Massachusetts Institute of Technology. Commenced 2007. 5 acres.* Ellenzweig; Vanasse Hangen Brustlin, Inc.; Nitsch Engineering; Pine and Swallow Environmental; Ecological Landscape Management; William A. Berry & Son; ValleyCrest Landscape Companies.

Monte Vista, *San Antonio, Texas. Commenced 1999. 2.5 acres.* Lake|Flato; Gregorian Engineers; Raymond Danysh; Kelly Francis Illumination; Kurt Voss; W. M. Greer Construction Company; Millberger Landscaping & Nursery; San Jacinto Materials; Bran Sharp Pools, LLC.

Mount Auburn Cemetery, *Cambridge, Massachusetts. Commenced 1998. 3.5 acres.* New England Environmental; Aquatic Engineering; Capizzi Landscape; Robert Hanss, Inc.

Nerman Museum of Contemporary Art, *Overland Park, Kansas, for Johnson County Community College. Commenced 2004. 20 acres.* Kyu Sung Woo Architects; Gould Evans Associates; J.E. Dunn Construction; Audrie Seeley & Co. LLC, Landscaping.

The Ohio State University, *Columbus, Ohio, for the Ohio State University. Commenced 2010.* Human Nature, Inc.; Korda/Nemeth Engineering Inc.; EMH & T; Jeffrey L. Bruce & Company; Lam Partners; Davey Resource Group; Brownstone Design.

Old Quarry, *Guilford, Connecticut. Commenced 2004. 1.5 acres.* Pirie Turlington Architects; Ocean and Coastal Consultants; Craul Land Scientists; Heller and Johnsen; David Christiensen.

Old Whitewood, *The Plains, Virginia. Commenced 1999. 100 acres.* Versaci Neumann & Partners; Mark Buchanan; Joseph Krewatch Construction Management.

Parrish Art Museum, *Water Mill, New York, for the Parrish Art Museum. Commenced 2006. 14 acres.* Herzog & de Meuron; Douglas Moyer Architect; Irrigation Consulting; Pine and Swallow Environmental; Nelson, Pope & Voorhis; Ben Krupinski Builder and Associates; Whitmores Landscape Services.

Phoenix Art Museum, *Phoenix, Arizona. Commenced 2004. 1 acre.* Tod Williams Billie Tsien Architects; Collaborative Lighting; Fleet-Fisher Engineering; RSE Associates, Inc.; Spectrum Irrigation Consulting; Pine and Swallow Environmental; Dan Euser Waterarchitecture; Kitchell Construction; Atwood Project Management.

Plan Baton Rouge, *Baton Rouge, Louisiana, for the Downtown Development District. Commenced 2009. 35 acres.* Chan Krieger NBBJ; HRA Advisors; Center for Planning Excellence; Glatting Jackson Kercher Anglin; Washer Hill Lipscomb Cabaniss Architecture.

Poetry Foundation, *Chicago, Illinois. Commenced 2008. 0.1 acres.* U.S. Equities Realty, LLC; John Ronan Architects; Terra Engineering; Rico Associates; Irrigation Consulting, Inc.; Craul Land Scientists; RSE Associates, Inc.; Norcon Inc.; Bent Oak Landscaping & Design, Inc.

Polly Park, *Rye, New York. Commenced 2003. 8 acres.* Collaborative Lighting, LLC.; Rico Associates; Prutting and Company Custom Builders; Rosedale Nurseries; Peter A. Navarra; Kuppino Landscaping & Masonry.

President's Park South Design Competition, *Washington, D.C., for the National Capital Planning Commission. Commenced 2011. 52 acres.* Architectural Research Office; Vanasse Hangen Brustlin, Inc.; Weidlinger Associates; Jeffrey L. Bruce & Company; Ecological Landscape Management; Domingo Bonzalez Associates; The Cultural Landscape Foundation.

Repentance Park, *Baton Rouge, Louisiana, for the Department of Public Works. Commenced 2011. 2 acres.* Reich Associates; Trahan Architects; Suzanne Turner Associates; Lam Partners; Dan Euser Waterarchitecture; Jeffrey L. Bruce & Company; ABMB Engineers; Assaf Simoneaux Tauzin and Associates; Arrighi Construction; Kusser FountainWorks; Bart Keller Co.; Francise Horticulture.

Richardson Olmsted Complex, *Buffalo, New York, for the Richardson Center Corporation. Commenced 2007. 95 acres.* Chan Krieger NBBJ; City Visions; Bero Architecture; Clarion Associates; Urban Design Project; Parsons Brinckerhoff.

River House, *Westport, Massachusetts. Commenced 2002. 43 acres.* Maryann Thompson Architects; Thad Hayes, Inc.; Kendrick Snyder Builder; D.P. Landscape Contractors.

Rosserne, *Mount Desert Island, Maine. Commenced 2002. 6 acres.* Atlantic Landscaping & Construction; Collaborative Lighting; Fresh Water Stone.

Seaport Square, *Boston, Massachusetts, for Boston Global Investors and Morgan Stanley. Commenced 2007. 23 acres.* Kohn Pedersen Fox Associates; Hacin + Associates; ADD Inc.; CBT Architects; Epsilon; Howard/Stein-Hudson Associates; Haley & Aldrich; Tetra Tech Rizzo; Vanasse Hangen Brustlin, Inc.; Nitsch Engineering.

Speed Art Museum, *Louisville, Kentucky. Commenced 2009. 6 acres.* wHY Architecture; K. Norman Berry Architects; RISE Group; Sabak, Wilson & Lingo, Inc.; Robert Pass + Associates.

Taft Museum of Art, *Cincinnati, Ohio. Commenced 1998. 2 acres.* Ann Beha Architects; KZF Design; Elizabeth Hope Cushing; Turner Construction; Viox Landscape Services.

The First Church of Christ, Scientist, *Boston, Massachusetts. Commenced 1998. 9 acres.* Ann Beha Architects; Vanasse Hangen Brustlin, Inc.; Shawmut Design and Construction; ValleyCrest Landscape Companies.

United States National Arboretum, *Washington, D.C., for Friends of the National Arboretum. Commenced 2008. 30 acres.*

Upland Road, *Cambridge, Massachusetts. Commenced 1998. 0.10 acres.* David Mullen Architect; Peter Forbes Associates; Anmahian Winton Associates; Cowen Associates; Robert Hanns, Inc.; Langione Brothers, Inc.

Waccabuc, *Waccabuc, New York. Commenced 1995. 15 acres.* Cooper Robertson & Partners; Thad Hayes, Inc.

Wainscott, *Wainscott, New York. Commenced 2002. 2 acres.* Leroy Street Studio; Lettieri Construction; Tom Johann Construction; Whitmores Landscape Services; Loebs + Gordon Poolcraft; Cape Cod Fabricators.

Westchester Estate, *Westchester County, New York, Commenced 2002. 65 acres.* B Five Studio; Dan Euser Waterarchitecture, Inc.; Hage Engineering; Haley & Aldrich, Inc.; S.B.E. Co. Inc.; RSE Associates, Inc.; Rico Associates; Freebar Construction; House of Fins; Alfredo LDC Landscaping; RK Irrigation; Edwin Sosa Masonry; Cape Cod Fabricators.

Projects

Parks, Plazas, and Public Spaces

Arnold Arboretum of Harvard University
Leventritt Shrub and Vine Garden
Perimeter Study
Weld Hill
Boston, Massachusetts

Aurora
Aurora, New York

Boston Harbor Islands Pavilion
Boston, Massachusetts

Central Wharf Plaza
Boston, Massachusetts

Charles River Pier
Boston, Massachusetts

D.W. Field Park
Brockton, Massachusetts

Edward Leathers Community Park
Somerville, Massachusetts

The Elms
Newport, Rhode Island

Greening of City Hall Plaza
Boston, Massachusetts

Hobart Urban Nature Preserve
Troy, Ohio

Kauffman Center for the Performing Arts
Kansas City, Missouri

Liberty Wharf
Boston, Massachusetts

Long Dock Beacon
Beacon, New York

Long Island Avenue Linear Park
Sag Harbor, New York

Louisiana's Old State Capitol
Baton Rouge, Louisiana

Martha's Vineyard Airport
Vineyard Haven, Massachusetts

Massachusetts Historical Society
Boston, Massachusetts

McBride House
Boston, Massachusetts

Mount Auburn Cemetery
Maple Avenue Interment Sites
Mary Baker Eddy Memorial and Halcyon Lake Environs
Meadow Extension
Cambridge, Massachusetts

Normans Kill Valley Park System
Guilderland, New York

Plan Baton Rouge
Baton Rouge, Louisiana

Poetry Foundation
Chicago, Illinois

Repentance Park
Baton Rouge, Louisiana

Richardson Olmsted Complex
Buffalo, New York

Rose Fitzgerald Kennedy Greenway
Carousel
Boston, Massachusetts

Seaport Square
Boston Innovation Center
Master Plan and Public Realm Plan
Parcel A-Hotel
Parcel B&C-Retail & Residential
Parcel Q-Park
Seaport Square Green
Boston, Massachusetts

Serenbe Town Center
Palmetto, Georgia

Stan Hywet Hall & Gardens
Estate of F.A. Seiberling, Esq.
Akron, Ohio

Tawasentha Park and Woodland Arboretum
Guilderland, New York

The First Church of Christ, Scientist
Christian Science Plaza Master Plan
Mary Baker Eddy Library Entry Garden
Seasonal Plantings
Boston, Massachusetts

United States National Arboretum
Ellipse Meadow and Flowering Tree Walk
Washington Youth Garden
Washington, D.C.

Campuses and Museums

Austen Riggs Center
Stockbridge, Massachusetts

Bard College at Simon's Rock
Daniel Arts Center
Landscape Master Plan
Great Barrington, Massachusetts

Baton Rouge International School
Baton Rouge, Louisiana

Bennington College
Center for the Advancement of Public Action
Crossett Library Extension
Deane Carriage Barn Music Hall
Joan Goodrich Garden
Landscape Master Plan
New College Houses
Student Center
Visual and Performing Arts Center North
Bennington, Vermont

Brandeis University
Carl and Ruth Shapiro Admissions Center
Chapels Field
Mandel Center for Humanities and the Mandel Humanities Quadrangle
Ridgewood Residence Halls
The Irving Schneider and Family Building
Village Residence Hall
Waltham, Massachusetts

Cambridge Friends School
Cambridge, Massachusetts

Chazen Museum of Art
University of Wisconsin–Madison
Madison, Wisconsin

The Clark
Landscape Master Plan
Stone Hill Center
Visitor Exhibition and Conference Center
Williamstown, Massachusetts

Clyfford Still Museum
Denver, Colorado

Colby College
Colby Green
Landscape Master Plan
Waterville, Maine

Colgate University
Case Library Information Technology Center
Hamilton, New York

Corning Museum of Glass
Corning, New York

Crystal Bridges Museum of American Art
Bentonville, Arkansas

Dallas Museum of Art
Interior Courts
Fleischner Court
Dallas, Texas

Duke University
Campus Drive Relocation
East Campus Landscape Master Plan
Events Pavilion
Keohane Quadrangle and Edens Connector
New Campus Plan
Perkins Library
Sustaining West Quad
West Union
Durham, North Carolina

Fairfield University
Fairfield Jesuit Community Center
Fairfield, Connecticut

Fuller Museum of Art
Brockton, Massachusetts

Groton School
Brooks House Improvements
Campbell Center Improvements
Campus Lighting and Signing
Campus Master Plan
Hundred House
Schoolhouse Expansion
Groton, Massachusetts

Hamilton College
Wellin Museum of Art
Theatre and Studio Arts Building
Hamilton, New York

The Hampton Library
Bridgehampton, New York

Harvard Business School
Campus Master Plan
Canopy Preservation Study
East Drive Improvements
Residence Courtyards
Tata Hall Executive Education Precinct
Boston, Massachusetts

Harvard Naito/Bauer Laboratories
Naito/Bauer Courtyards
Cambridge, Massachusetts

Hill-Stead Museum
Farmington, Connecticut

Institute for Child and Adolescent Development
Children's Therapeutic Garden
Wellesley, Massachusetts

MacDowell Colony
Savidge Library Expansion and Meadow
Peterborough, New Hampshire

MacKenzie-Childs, Ltd.
Aurora, New York

Massachusetts Institute of Technology North Court and Main Street
Eastman and McDermott Courts Study
Koch Center for Integrative Cancer Research
North Court
Cambridge, Massachusetts

Nerman Museum of Contemporary Art
Overland Park, Kansas

The Ohio State University
17th Avenue Rebuild
Academic Core North Landscape District Plan
Chemical and Biomolecular Engineering and Chemistry Building
Tuttle Park Place Rebuild
Woodruff Avenue Rebuild
Columbus, Ohio

Orange/France Telecom
Cambridge, Massachusetts

Parrish Art Museum
Water Mill, New York

Phoenix Art Museum
Jacquie and Bennett Dorrance Sculpture Garden
Phoenix, Arizona

Royalston Elementary School
Royalston, Massachusetts

Silver Hill Hospital
New Canaan, Connecticut

Speed Art Museum
Louisville, Kentucky

Syracuse University
New Residence Hall
Syracuse, New York

Taft Museum of Art
Cincinnati, Ohio

Tyler Museum of Art
Tyler, Texas

University of Virginia
Cocke Hall Restoration
Charlottesville, Virginia

Yale University
Institute of Social Policy and Study
New Haven, Connecticut

Residences

Connecticut
Alpine Road
Bermuda Road
Byram Shore Road
Calhoun Drive
Cross Ridge Road
Dogwood Farm
Lincoln Road
Lincoln Street
Manatuck
The Mill
North Main Street
Old Lyme
Old Quarry

Maine
Cushings Island
North Haven
Rosserne

Maryland
Baltimore Hills

Massachusetts
Back Bay
Barnstable
Berkeley Street
Brattle Street
Carisbrooke
Channing Place
Gloucester
Half-Mile Line
Heath Street
Ide Road
Lowell Street
Newton Center
Oyster Watcha
Page Farm
River House
Siasconset House
Sweet P Farm
Upland Road
Westfield Road
Westwood
York Street

Minnesota
Old Crystal Bay Road
Wayzata Bay

New Hampshire
Bearhill Road
Family Retreat
Ledge Road

New Jersey
Navesink River Road
North Murray
Stone Hill Farm

New York
Bank Street
Central Park West Roof Terrace
Croton
Deer Path
Duell Hollow
Fargo Lane
Fifth Avenue Roof Terrace
Georgica Pond
Hither Lane
Katonah
Meadow Lane
North Creek
Polly Park
Riverside Drive Penthouse
Sag Harbor Garden
Taghkanic
Town Line Road
Waccabuc
Wainscott
Washington Street
Westchester Estate
West Ninth Street

Ohio
Hunting Valley

Pennsylvania
Glenn Road
Point Pleasant

Rhode Island
Beacon Hill Road
Blockhouse Lane
Indian Avenue

South Carolina
Starglass Drive

Texas
Beck House
Greenlee House
Monte Vista
River Place
Wenonah Drive

Vermont
Putney House
Stowe

Virginia
Old Whitewood

Wisconsin
Cedarburg Farm

United Kingdom
Marsh Court
Sheffield Terrace

Recognition

2012

Duke University
Campus Drive
Durham, North Carolina
Excellence in Landscape Architecture
Society for College and University Planning

Old Quarry
Guilford, Connecticut
ASLA Award for Design

Old Quarry
Guilford, Connecticut
Suburbia Transformed International Design Competition

Poetry Foundation
Chicago, Illinois
AIA Award for Architecture

2011

Boston Harbor Islands Pavilion
Boston, Massachusetts
BSA Award for Design

Central Wharf Plaza
Boston, Massachusetts
ASLA Award for Design

Beck House
Dallas, Texas
ASLA Award for Design

Half-Mile Line
Stockbridge, Massachusetts
ASLA Award for Design

Edward Leathers Community Park
Somerville, Massachusetts
BSLA Award for Design

The Clark
Stone Hill Center
Williamstown, Massachusetts
BSLA Award for Design

Old Quarry
Guilford, Connecticut
BSLA Award for Design

2010

Family Retreat
New Hampshire
BSLA Award for Design

Beck House
Dallas, Texas
BSLA Award for Design

2009

Westchester Estate
Westchester County, New York
Green Award
Garden Design Magazine

Half-Mile Line
Stockbridge, Massachusetts
BSLA Award for Design

Rosserne
Mount Desert Island, Maine
BSLA Award for Design

Aurora
Aurora, New York
BSLA Award for Design

2008

Phoenix Art Museum
Phoenix, Arizona
BSLA Award of Excellence

Bennington College
Landscape Master Plan
Bennington, Vermont
Excellence in Planning
Society for College and University Planning

Central Wharf Plaza
Boston, Massachusetts
BSLA Award for Design

2007

Arnold Arboretum Leventritt Garden
Boston, Massachusetts
ASLA Award of Excellence

River House
Westport, Massachusetts
BSA Award for Design

Lowell Street
Cambridge, Massachusetts
BSLA Award for Design

Polly Park
Rye, New York
BSLA Award for Design

2006

Colby College
Landscape Master Plan
Waterville, Maine
BSLA Award for Landscape Analysis and Planning

Bucks County Residence
Bucks County, Pennsylvania
BSLA Award for Design

Bennington College
Landscape Master Plan
Bennington, Vermont
BSLA Award for Landscape Analysis and Planning

2005

The Architectural League of New York
Emerging Voices Award

Bard College at Simon's Rock
Great Barrington, Massachusetts
BSA Award for Design

2004

Brandeis University
Village Residence Hall
Waltham, Massachusetts
BSA Award for Design

McBride House
Boston, Massachusetts
BSLA Award for Design

The First Church of Christ, Scientist
The Mary Baker Eddy Library Entry Courtyard
Boston, Massachusetts
BSLA Award for Design

Charles River Pier
Boston, Massachusetts
BSLA Award for Design

Six Moon Hill
Lexington, Massachusetts
BSLA Award for Design

Upland Road
Cambridge, Massachusetts
BSLA Award for Design

2003

Hither Lane
East Hampton, New York
ASLA Award for Design

The First Church of Christ, Scientist
Boston, Massachusetts
ASLA Award for Design

Mount Auburn Cemetery
Cambridge, Massachusetts
ASLA Award for Design

2001

Mount Auburn Cemetery
Cambridge, Massachusetts
BSLA Award for Design

2000

Mount Auburn Cemetery
Mary Baker Eddy Monument and Halcyon Lake Environs
Cambridge, Massachusetts
Preservation Award
Cambridge Historical Commission

1999

Hobart Urban Nature Preserve
Troy, Ohio
ASLA Award for Design

Hither Lane
East Hampton, New York
BSLA Award for Design

Ridgewood
Ridgewood, New Jersey
BSLA Award for Design

1998

Coolidge Hill
Cambridge, Massachusetts
ASLA Award for Design

Arnold Arboretum Leventritt Garden
Boston, Massachusetts
BSLA Award for Design

Rifton
Rifton, New York
BSLA Award for Design

1997

Institute for Child and Adolescent Development
Wellesley, Massachusetts
ASLA President's Award

Waccabuc
Waccabuc, New York
ASLA Award for Design
BSLA Award for Design

Deer Path
East Hampton, New York
BSLA Award for Design

Oakmount
Lexington, Massachusetts
BSLA Award for Design

Stan Hywet Hall Foundation
Estate of F.A. Seiberling, Esq.
Akron, Ohio
National Trust for Historic Preservation Trustees Emeritus Award for Excellence in the Stewardship of Historic Sites

1996

Beth Israel Deaconess Medical Center
Carl J. Shapiro Clinical Center
Boston, Massachusetts
BSLA Award for Design

The Belvedere (North Cove Link)
Battery Park City
New York, New York
AIA Award for Urban Design

1995

Institute for Child and Adolescent Development
Wellesley, Massachusetts
BSLA Award for Design

1993

Shared Garden
Jamaica Plain, Massachusetts
BSLA Award for Design

Ayreheade
East Haddam, Connecticut
BSLA Award for Design

Select Bibliography

Bennett, Paul. "A Place in the City." *Landscape Architecture Magazine*, October 1999, 42–47.

Brake, Alan G. "Amazing Trace." *Landscape Architecture Magazine*, August 2012, 99–109.

Clendaniel, William. "A Tale of Two Lakes." *Public Garden*, June 2000, Vol. 15, 31–36.

Collins, Stephen. "Reshaping the Hill." *Colby Alumni Magazine*, Summer 2003, Vol. 92.

Crandell, Gina. "Perennial Abstraction." *Landscape Architecture Magazine*, May 2004, 108–115.

Dean Oppenheimer, Andrea. "Small Wonder." *Landscape Architecture Magazine*, September 1997, 28–31.

Dillon, David. "Bennington College Dorms." *Architectural Record*, February 2002, 94–99.

Fisher, Tom. "American Villa." *Gardens Illustrated*, April 2005, 80–85.

Freeman, Allen. "The Silent Edge." *Landscape Architecture Magazine*, June 2004, 96–101.

Freeman, Allen. "Engaging Estate." *Landscape Architecture Magazine*, February 2004, 100–107.

Gourley, Elizabeth. "Making Space." *Landscape Architecture Magazine*, December 2001, 26–27.

Griswold, Mac. "Romancing the Stone." *House & Garden*, March 2003, 126–138.

Griswold, Mac. "Pathfinder." *Garden Design Magazine*, February/March 1999, 54–59.

Griswold, Mac. "The Therapeutic Garden." *Landscape Architecture Magazine*, October 1994, 66–67.

Hammatt, Heather. "A Distinct Destination." *Landscape Architecture Magazine*, July 2000, 20.

Hammerslough, Jane. "The Children's Hour." *Garden Design*, June/July 1997, 50.

Hilderbrand, Gary R. "Reciprocal Acts." *Topos*, 2012, Vol. 78, 74–81.

Hilderbrand, Gary R. " Landscape Architecture Practice Now." *Harvard Design Magazine*, Fall/Winter 2010–2011, 6–21.

Hilderbrand, Gary R. "Torqued Parterre." *Topos*, 2008, Vol. 62, 27–31.

Hilderbrand, Gary R. "Inner Strengths." *Landscape Architecture Magazine*, September 2005, 114–115.

Hilderbrand, Gary R. "New England Pastoral." *Clark Art Institute Journal*, 2003, Vol. 4, 25–33.

Hilderbrand, Gary R. "Spirit of Place." *Architecture Boston*, November 2003, 8–17.

Hilderbrand, Gary R. "Project for 200 Interment Sites, Mount Auburn Cemetery." *Harvard Design Magazine*, Fall/Winter 2001.

Hilderbrand, Gary R. "Dan Kiley's Miller Garden: Coming to Light." in *Daniel Urban Kiley: The Early Gardens*, edited by William Saunders, New York: Princeton Architectural Press, 1999. 65–77.

Hilderbrand, Gary R. "Hither Lane, East Hampton, New York." *Land Forum*, 1999, Vol. 1, 47–50.

Hiss, Tony. "At Land's Edge, A Contentment of Light and Shape." *The New York Times*, October 19, 1990. C1 and C18.

Horowitz, Jeff. "Winning Big." *Landscape Architecture Magazine*, November 1997, 42–49.

Jones, Mary Margaret. "A Country Place." *Landscape Architecture Magazine*, November 1997, 58.

Jost, Daniel. "Oaks on Granite." *Landscape Architecture Magazine*, August 2012, 91–97.

Karson, Robin. "Massachusetts, A Room with a View." *Garden Design*, Fall 1989, 32–35.

Karson, Robin. "Battery Park City, South Cove." *Landscape Architecture Magazine*, May/June 1986, 48–53.

Lamster, Mark. "Soul Transplant." *Landscape Architecture Magazine*, August 2012, 111–121.

Landecker, Heidi. "New Public Spaces." *Architecture Magazine*, August 1995, 55–61.

Levinson, Nancy. "Reconstructed Grandeur." *Landscape Architecture Magazine*, June 1991, 64–65.

Linden–Ward, Blanche. "Stan Hywet." *Landscape Architecture Magazine*, May/June 1986, 66–70.

Reed, Christopher. "Sampler of Shrub and Vines Planned by Arboretum." *Harvard Design Magazine*, April 1999, 70–71.

Reed, Douglas P. "The Therapeutic Garden." *Art New England*, August/September 1995, 21.

Reed, Douglas P. "Der Park als Ort des Wandels." *Garten + Landschaft*, March 1995, 9–15.

Reed, Douglas P., and Gary R. Hilderbrand. "Ordering and Terracing in the Leventritt Garden." *Arnoldia*, 2003, Vol. 62, 17–19.

Saunders, William S. "The Inventions of Reed Hilderbrand." *Landscape Architecture Magazine*, August 2012, 81–89.

Snoonian, Deborah P. E. "Reed Hilderbrand and Maryann Thompson Join Forces for the New Leventritt Shrub and Vine Garden in Boston." *Architectural Record*, October 2005, 124–127.

Stocker, Carol. "The Healing Landscape." *The Boston Globe*, October 15, 1998. F1 and F8.

Tapert, Annette. "American Pastoral, Reinterpreting A Classic Country Aesthetic for Today's Living." *Architectural Digest*, June 1998, 168–177.

Thompson, William J. "Is Historic Preservation Design?" *Landscape Architecture Magazine*, December 1998, 56–69.

"Troy Residence." *Landscape Architecture Magazine*, November 1991, 57.

Vanderbilt, Thomas. "Borderlands." *Landscape Architecture Magazine*, August 1998, 62–69, 90–91.

Viladas, Pilar. "Arch Sophisticate." *The New York Times Style Magazine*, Spring 2010, 78–83.

Viladas, Pilar. "Garden Pavilion." *The New York Times Magazine*, August 9, 1998, 42–47.

Viladas, Pilar. "Clean Rustic Spaces." *Architectural Digest*, May 1997, 145–153.

Wilson, Karen. "Plenty of Merit." *San Diego Union Tribune*, November 1997.

Credits

Visible | Invisible:
Landscape Works of Reed Hilderbrand
is © 2012 Reed Hilderbrand.
Published in 2012 by Metropolis Books.

All rights reserved. This book may not be reproduced in whole or in part, in any form (beyond copying permitted by Sections 107 and 108 of the United States Copyright Law, and except by reviewers for the public press), without written permission from Metropolis Books, ARTBOOK | D.A.P., 155 Sixth Avenue, 2nd floor, New York, NY 10013, tel 212 627 1999, fax 212 627 9484.

Library of Congress Cataloging-in-Publication Data is available upon request.
ISBN 978-1-938922-13-8

Metropolis Books
ARTBOOK | D.A.P.
155 Sixth Avenue, 2nd floor
New York, NY 10013
tel 212 627 1999
fax 212 627 9484
www.artbook.com

Printed in the U.S.A.

Photography:
Chuck Choi: 172 (bottom), 174–175, 232 (bottom), 233 (bottom), 271 (bottom)
Peggy G. Davis: 126 (left)
Steve Dunwell: 216 (top), 217
James Ewing: 226, 227 (top)
Scott Frances: 128 (right), 270, 271 (top), 272–273, 275
Anton Grassl: 171 (top), 188–189
Steve Hall: 6–7, 264–266
Millicent Harvey: front cover, 2–5, 8–14, 19, 24 (bottom), 27–97, 99, 105 (left), 136–137, 139, 142–143, 149, 172 (top), 173, 177, 196–197, 219–225, 254–255, 257 (bottom), 267, 288–289, back cover
Timothy Hursley: 218
Andrea Jones: 150–152, 158–159, 179, 207 (right), 208–209, 210 (right), 214–215, 260, 263, 282–283
Alex MacLean: 112, 190, 206
Charles Mayer: 21, 153, 170, 171 (bottom), 176, 178, 180–183, 191 (bottom right), 202–204, 205 (bottom), 240, 241 (bottom), 256, 257 (top), 262, 276–277
Glen McClure: 258–259
Michael Moran: 169
Reed Hilderbrand: 105 (bottom right), 109, 110 (right), 111 (left), 121 (bottom), 128 (bottom), 131 (top), 134, 168, 180 (left), 216 (bottom), 227 (both bottom), 228–229, 238–239, 241 (top), 242
David M. Smith: 207 (left column)
Andreas Stavropoulos: 274
Bill Timmerman: 261
Paul Warchol: 290–291
Alan Ward: 104, 116, 140, 154–157, 160–167, 184–187, 191 (top, bottom left), 192–195, 198–201, 205 (top), 210 (left), 211–213, 230–231, 232–233 (top), 234–237, 243–253, 268–269, 278–281, 284–287, 292–295

Visible | Invisible: Landscape Works of Reed Hilderbrand
was organized and produced by Constance Sullivan
in coordination with Douglas Reed and Gary Hilderbrand.

The book was designed and typeset by Bethany Johns in Warnock,
designed by Robert Slimbach, and Bau, designed by Christian Schwartz.
She also worked on printing production with Daniel Frank
at Meridian Printing, East Greenwich, Rhode Island.

The book was printed in duotone and four-color process
on Phoenixmotion Xantur and Centura Dull papers
and bound by Riverside Bindery.

The text was copyedited by Archie Hobson.